"*Generation BULLIED 2.0* takes personal stories of our most vulnerable youth to illustrate what must be done from the federal level to the classroom. Bullying is not and has never been solely a school issue, and *Generation BULLIED 2.0* takes on the societal and cultural roots of bullying. This book will begin a conversation about what must be done to ensure *all* of our students are not only safe but also feel welcome in our nation's schools."

—Jamie Nabozny, Safe School Advocate

"*Generation BULLIED 2.0* is not only a powerful text, it is a necessary one. Despite the so-called 'new-openness' the society professes around notions of difference and diversity, school-aged children and youth are still battling to be accepted for who they are and who they are becoming. In far too many schools it is acceptable to bully and harass students based on their sexuality and gender identity. This has to stop and this volume says it loudly, cogently, and clearly."

—Gloria Ladson-Billings, Professor, Department of Curriculum & Instruction, Kellner Family Chair in Urban Education, Interim Assistant Vice Provost & Director, Chancellors & Powers Knapp Scholars Program, University of Wisconsin–Madison

generation
BULLIED 2.0

Gender **AND Sexualities** **IN Education**

Dennis Carlson and Elizabeth Meyer
General Editors

Vol. 1

The Gender and Sexualities in Education series is part of the Peter Lang Education list.
Every volume is peer reviewed and meets
the highest quality standards for content and production.

PETER LANG
New York • Washington, D.C./Baltimore • Bern
Frankfurt • Berlin • Brussels • Vienna • Oxford

generation
BULLIED 2.0

Prevention and Intervention Strategies for Our Most Vulnerable Students

sj Miller, Leslie David Burns, & Tara Star Johnson, EDITORS

PETER LANG
New York • Washington, D.C./Baltimore • Bern
Frankfurt • Berlin • Brussels • Vienna • Oxford

Library of Congress Cataloging-in-Publication Data

Generation bullied 2.0: prevention and intervention strategies for our most
vulnerable students / edited by sj Miller, Leslie David Burns, Tara Star Johnson.
pages cm. — (Gender and sexualities in education; vol. 1)
Includes bibliographical references and index.
1. Bullying in schools—United States—Prevention.
2. School discipline—United States. I. Miller, sj, editor of compilation.
LB3013.32.G46   371.5'8—dc23   2013005245
ISBN 978-1-4331-2072-5 (hardcover)
ISBN 978-1-4331-2071-8 (paperback)
ISBN 978-1-4539-1112-9 (e-book)
ISSN 2166-8507

Bibliographic information published by Die Deutsche Nationalbibliothek.
Die Deutsche Nationalbibliothek lists this publication in the "Deutsche
Nationalbibliografie"; detailed bibliographic data is available
on the Internet at http://dnb.d-nb.de/.

The paper in this book meets the guidelines for permanence and durability
of the Committee on Production Guidelines for Book Longevity
of the Council of Library Resources.

This book is dedicated to all students who have been bullied, those who are being bullied now, and those who have succumbed to bullycide.

How many more must suffer before we systematically stop such abuse?

"Our lives begin to end the day we become
silent about the things that matter."
—Martin Luther King

Contents

Foreword..ix
　Elizabeth J. Meyer

Preface..xiii
　Dianne Smith

Acknowledgments... xvii

Introduction: Bullied...1
　sj Miller

1　Where Are We Now? The Current State of Bullying in the United States........15
　sj Miller

2　The Distressing Realities About Queer-Related (LGBTQGV) Bullying........33
　sj Miller and James R. Gilligan

3　Bullies and Bodies: Addressing Weight Discrimination....................49
　Tara Star Johnson and Elana Cutter

4　Bullying and Students with Disabilities:
　The Bully, the Bullied, and the Misunderstood..........................61
　Joseph John Morgan and Deanna Adams

5　Black Ritual Insults: Causing Harm or Passing Time?....................75
　Tyrone Rivers and Dorothy Espelage

6　Bullying and Harassment Prevention in the Lives of Latina and Latino Students..85
　Rodrigo Joseph Rodríguez

7　Cyber-Digital Bullying.......................................99
　sj Miller and Stephanie Beyer

8　The Consequences of Bullying and Anti-Bullying Interventions for
　Individual and School Success...................................113
　Leslie David Burns

9　The Broader Contexts of Bullying:
　Disrupting Bullying Through Preventive and Interventionist Policy..........131
　sj Miller

10　Shifting the Tide of Bullying Through Teacher Education:
　Tools for the Classroom.......................................147
　sj Miller

Afterword...183
　Dennis Carlson

Contributors..189

Index..193

Foreword

Elizabeth J. Meyer

I was a first-year teacher in 1993 when the Massachusetts Governor's Commission on Gay and Lesbian Youth published its groundbreaking report titled "Making Schools Safe for Gay and Lesbian Youth." This report was important for me, as I was struggling to find ways to support one of my students at a rural school in New York who was suffering from persistent sexual and homophobic harassment. I attended a conference in Boston in the spring of 1994 organized by the Gay and Lesbian Independent School Teachers' Network (GLISTN, which later became the Gay, Lesbian & Straight Education Network, GLSEN) to learn more about what I could do for this student and my school. I learned about the report at this life-changing conference and learned valuable skills to begin addressing the problem of homophobia and diversity issues in general at my own school. The first recommendation listed in this report was "Schools are encouraged to develop policies protecting gay and lesbian students from harassment, violence, and discrimination" (The Governor's Commission on Gay and Lesbian Youth, 1993, p. 57). Twenty years later, I am honored to write the foreword to this book, which echoes and amplifies this call and adds to it in rich and meaningful ways. Since my first teaching experiences, I have been set on a path to better understand the complex issues of bullying and harassment in schools. I was frustrated by my own experiences in schools with the lack of awareness of and willingness to address the difficult issues of gender, sexuality, body size, race, ethnicity, and disability. These are exactly the issues that *Generation BULLIED 2.0* addresses in order to share cutting-edge research and practical advice for the education community.

My own early teaching experiences made me more sensitive to and aware of issues related to gender and sexuality in schools, and as I delved deeper, I learned about how issues of race, ethnicity, body size, and disability were also wrapped up in the complex notions of masculinity, femininity, and heteronormativity. Miller, Burns, and Johnson, along with their contributors, have put together a volume that adds critical voices to the public dialogue about bullying. In my early stages of doctoral research, I was disheartened to review the bullying literature and discover the dearth of studies that explicitly mentioned issues of race, gender, sexuality, and disability in their examinations of this phenomenon in schools (Meyer, 2007). I focus primarily on issues of gender and sexuality in my own research (Meyer, 2006, 2008, 2009; Meyer & Stader, 2009) and am grateful and encouraged to see more work emerging on issues of diversity and social difference in this area. I recently updated my literature review and am pleased to note that there was a turning point around 2007 when researchers began to consistently pay attention to these factors when researching and writing about bullying and harassment in schools (Meyer, in press). Unfortunately, this increased attention by scholars and researchers has not translated into widespread change in bullying intervention programs, state or federal policies, and everyday practice in most classrooms and school campuses.

The focus of this book is on the most vulnerable populations in our schools: students who are disproportionately targeted for the most frequent and severe forms of bullying and harassment, students who somehow find themselves outside the "norm" and can't find a place to fit in the social hierarchies of their schools. These students are the canaries in the coal mine. If school is a toxic environment for them, then everyone in that community is also being poisoned by being consistently exposed to those negative behaviors. These young people are sounding the alarm, and for whatever reason administrators, policymakers, teachers, and students alike are not responding to these warning signs. They continue focusing on other issues while ignoring the dangerous smog that is slowly squeezing the life, learning, and light out of so many of our children.

We continue to read about the tragic consequences of cyberbullying, sexual harassment, and homophobia in schools. The media have covered story after story of school-aged youth who have ended their lives as a result of the endless psychological violence they experienced in schools. Amanda Todd (14), Seth Walsh (13), Carl Hoover-Walker (11), and Phoebe Prince (15) are just a few of the lives we have lost due to the hostile climate in their schools and peer groups. I have worked with several parents who have lost their children to bullycide, and these parents all want to make some sense out of their loss and have become activists for educational change. They don't understand why the school didn't do more, why teachers are reluctant to intervene, why homophobic, fat-phobic, and misogynist cultures are tolerated and allowed to flourish in our schools. Unfortunately, this work won't bring back their children, but it can, it is hoped, prevent the loss of others. I don't just mean the loss of life, but the loss of light; many victims of bullying survive, but as this volume points out, they often live with the effects of Complex Post-Traumatic Stress Disorder or other negative health outcomes such as eating disorders, drug and alcohol abuse, depression, and self-harm. Our job as educators is to create safe and nurturing environments where children can learn and grow, where their lights will be protected and nourished, not diminished or extinguished.

I hope that as you read this book you will add your voice to the conversation and ensure that these perspectives are not forgotten or ignored in your school communities. It takes courage to speak out against the norms of any culture, but the research and evidence provided in this volume offer strong support for educators and advocates willing to take on this challenge. *Generation BULLIED 2.0* can help us turn a corner in our nation's conversation on bullying and violence in schools, and by taking its messages and applying them in your own classrooms and communities, you can be a part of creating safer and more inclusive schools for all.

References

The Governor's Commission on Gay and Lesbian Youth. (1993). *Making schools safe for gay and lesbian youth*. Boston: The Commonwealth of Massachusetts.

Meyer, E.J. (2006). Gendered harassment in North America: School-based interventions for reducing homophobia and heterosexism. In C. Mitchell & F. Leach (Eds.), *Combating gender violence in and around schools* (pp. 43–50). Stoke on Trent, UK: Trentham Books.

Meyer, E.J. (2007, April 9–13). *Bullying and harassment in secondary schools: A critical analysis of the gaps, overlaps, and implications from a decade of research*. Paper presented at the annual meeting of the American Educational Research Association, Chicago, IL.

Meyer, E.J. (2008). Gendered harassment in secondary schools: Understanding teachers' (non)interventions. *Gender & Education, 20*(6), 555–572.

Meyer, E.J. (2009). *Gender, bullying, and harassment: Strategies to end sexism and homophobia in schools*. New York: Teachers College Press.

Meyer, E.J. (in press). New solutions for bullying and harassment: A post-structural feminist approach. In R. Schott & D.M. Sondergard (Eds.), *School bullying: New theories in context*. Cambridge, UK: Cambridge University Press.

Meyer, E.J., & Stader, D. (2009). Queer youth and the culture wars: From the classroom to the courtroom in Australia, Canada, and the United States. *Journal of LGBT Youth, 6*(2), 135–154.

Preface

Dianne Smith

I was born in a small, segregated South Carolina town in 1953. I attended Black public schools until 10th grade, when the federal government finally decided to force the implementation of *Brown v. Board of Education*. (I offer the aforementioned historical piece for narrative context.) A popular conversation among my family is a story about Charlie (name changed) and me. Charlie was a menace to the elementary school society. He beat up kids, he stole hard-earned lunch money, and he enjoyed watching the fear illuminating the faces of boys and girls on a daily basis. I have to admit here that I was one of those girls who "dodged" Charlie on a regular basis. I surely did not want to be a target of his wrath.

However, one day, on our walk home from school, Charlie began his menacing, taunting behavior toward me. On this particular day, I was not in the mood to be "played with." I asked him to stop, but he continued to shower his wrath of verbal pain on me. I don't know what made me do it, but I hit him as hard as a little girl could. "Pow!" The next thing I know is that Charlie is hitting me hard, all over my body. My mind tells me that I need to get him on the ground and straddle him. What I remember is that I finally got him on the red clay dirt. My little fists were pounding Charlie in the face, chest, and head. What I know now is that I had become the menace, spewing my wrath on Charlie.

After the fight, my siblings, schoolmates, and I continued our walk home from school. My pretty school dress was stained with blood—Charlie's and mine. I was scared to return to school the next day, not knowing what was in store for me. My older sister and younger brothers were on vigil, too. To our surprise, Charlie spoke to me with a grin, and he never bothered me or my family and friends again. I relate this story in this preface because we did not use the word "bully" to define Charlie's menacing behavior. He was "just" being a misbehaving boy.

While I describe being bullied by Charlie, I have to confess to my own "bullying." I was raised and watched by Black women who were strong-willed, smart, and talked back (hooks, 1989), so for me it was normal for a Black girl to be strong-willed and smart. However, I did not know that I was bullying Essie and Tenar (both names changed) because they were not like me. In my child's mind, my intent was to make them normal: strong-willed and smart. (Maybe that was Charlie's intent—to make us like him. I will never know.) It was some years ago that my mother, Elizabeth, defined my menacing behavior toward Essie and Tenar as bullying. I am ashamed to admit it, but I must name it as it is—bullying. As a responsible adult, I have had an opportunity to talk with Essie and Tenar about my menacing acts toward them. I still do not know if they have forgiven me. Consequently, I work now to stop bullying and hatred in my school community and elsewhere.

When Miller, Burns, and Johnson asked me to write the preface for *Generation BULLIED 2.0*, I did not hesitate to join this important project. However, at the time of the invitation and my positive response, I did not think about my past in terms of being bullied and bullying. It was not until I read the manuscript for the book that it hit me: "I will have to 'come clean' and 'confess' my own harsh, mean, menacing behavior toward Essie and Tenar." This is another confession: I almost backed out of the project. Why? It is too revealing, and I feel nakedly vulnerable in public for having been a "bully."

However, the good news is this. In the "Introduction" to *Generation BULLIED 2.0*, Miller writes, "We begin with a narrative of hope...," and I concur with him. It is my hope that telling my story in this preface affords academics in teacher education, school counselors, and school leadership, school leaders, in-service teachers, teachers-in-waiting, parents, and community groups the opportunity to join us in this struggle to identify bullying as it occurs, to intervene when necessary, and to develop proactive curricula for change.

As I conclude, I leave readers with another brief narrative. As a Head Start teacher during the late 1970s and early 1980s, I watched 5- and 6-year-olds taunt each other about body size, skin color, hair texture, "smarts," nasty clothes, smelly bodies, boys playing with dolls, and living on the mill hill—the list continues. At the time, the school discourse around this language and behavior was: "Children are being children, playing with each other." I now know that the ideology embedded within "children are being children" is a regime of truth (Foucault, 1970) based upon power, normativity, and hate.

I implore you to join Miller, Burns, and Johnson, as well as the contributors, in this powerful work on social justice, activism, and the transformation of the ways in which we view, or do not view, *Generation BULLIED 2.0.*

References

Foucault, M. (1970). *Power and knowledge.* New York: Pantheon Books.

hooks, b. (1989). *Talking back: Thinking feminist, thinking Black.* Boston: South End Press.

Acknowledgments

This work would not be possible were it not for a group of compassionate educator-scholars who observed and even personally endured years of bullying in their classrooms and in school hallways. Together, unified by common concerns, we write this book first and foremost for every child who has ever been bullied or succumbed to bullycide.

We would like to thank our series editors Elizabeth Meyer and Dennis Carlson for their belief in this work and for contributing to the dialogue in both our foreword and afterword about supporting our collective efforts to try to reduce the incidence of bullying once and for all. We are grateful for their oversight of our project and for providing us guidance, reassurance, and continued hope. We thank Dianne Smith for her sensitivity, generosity, and compassion for providing our work with such a powerful and revealing preface. It takes a brave soul to admit to being a bully, and we can all find renewal and healing in her story by unveiling and unmasking the wounds we've unintentionally inflicted on others. We are grateful to our esteemed contributors, Deanna Adams, Stephanie Beyer, Elana Cutter, Dorothy Espelage, James R. Gilligan, Joseph Morgan, Tyrone Rivers, and Rodrigo Joseph Rodríguez, who have each provided unique and critical reflections about how to help stop bullying. We are grateful to Gloria Ladson-Billings, who has observed shifts in generational bullying during her lifetime, for believing in and endorsing our project. We are grateful to Kevin Kumashiro, whose commitment to anti-oppressive education and activism has served as a model for the change this book strives to incite. We are humbled by Jamie Nabozny's endorsement; his past trauma will forever remain as a neon sign for administrators and school personnel to DO something about bullying, especially queer bullying, in their schools. Jamie, we are sorry for what you've endured and hope that this book can be an agent for healing.

sj would like to personally thank his co-editors Les and Tara, who helped to conceive this project over three years ago while at AERA. Their unyielding friendships over the years have helped to buttress and sustain him against some of the institutional bullying he's endured. Les, I've learned from you that patience and calm are vital to growing a powerful work. Your care, thoughtfulness, attention to detail, and, above all, your ability to reframe pieces of my writing are mind-blowing and mind-bending. Tara, aka *superwoman*, I don't know how you balance family with professional life with such ease and yet write such powerful, provocative, mind-altering, and heartfelt pieces—you never cease to amaze me. I couldn't have asked for a better team of friends and editors with whom to work and grow. What's our next book, yo? I love you both! sj gives a shout out to his dear friends in KC, MO, Kevin Worley and Karen Gettlinger, or "Kevkar," whose unconditional love and support have helped ease the move from the Burgh to the Paris of the Plains. Your gentle spirits make me want to be a better person. sj also gives a shout out to his best friend, Tode Rubenstein, who over the years has showed seamless and consistent love, a shared passion for workouts (*just do it!*) and films, and has always been there for me whenever I needed to talk. Memaw, I miss you and love you—you are always here with me. Thanks go to the brilliant doctoral candidate Nicole Sieben of Adelphi University and her students in her *Adolescent Experience* class for their awesome and smart feedback on Table 1: The Manifestations of Bullying. You all rock! Last, thanks go to Sweet Pea and Whiz for keeping me grounded and making me laugh all of the time! If you see any odd typos, it was my cats—not Peter Lang.

Les would like to first thank sj and Tara—two people and scholars of such great power and character and passion that it is impossible to spend time with them and not grow and change for the better. I especially thank sj for recognizing that a White boy from Wisconsin can not only understand diversity, but be a part of that diversity—a person with a story worth telling, a person with a contribution to make, and a person who understands what it is like to be different even as he embodies so many of the things most people would call "normal." I grew up the "fat kid" and a boy named Leslie in a time and place where neither was very helpful. I was bullied mercilessly for both, and it may have been those experiences that helped me understand what others with far fewer advantages than I had must have endured. Thank you to Colleen Wolsky, the love of my life, for not just understanding but tolerating my pursuit of change for the better in this world. I know it can be hard to live with someone who is constantly crusading.

I came to this project at a time in my life when my best friend and closest colleague was bullied by colleagues so ruthlessly and systematically for her identity that she feels it led to her dismissal from our workplace. Because of her loss, I was forced more than ever to examine my own privileges as a White, male heterosexual in America. While I was attacked and threatened for fighting by her side, I did not pay the price she paid. But I paid, and I continue to suffer the effects as we complete this book. For you, my dear friend, I promise to fight and tell the truth forever. Finally, I dedicate this book to my parents, Robert and Patricia, who despite having a boy who felt it was necessary to beat up practically everybody he knew by the fifth grade, raised that boy to be a man who refuses to accept that the world can't be made a better place for *everyone*. Thanks, Mom and Dad.

Tara would like to thank sj for his patience and persistence in inviting me to participate in this project. As a Johnny-come-lately to the topic of bullying, I've felt a little out of my league in tackling the issue with any credibility, but I have nonetheless been borne along on the tide of sj's enthusiasm. He's a difficult man to say "no" to, and in this case I'm thankful for all I have learned as a result of working with him. I'd also like to thank my methods students for bearing with me as I struggle and experiment with ways to incorporate sizism into our dialogue effectively. Finally, I'd like to thank my dad, who recounts the story of overcoming a neighborhood bully with a satisfied gleam in his eye as if it were yesterday instead of nearly 70 years ago. He and another scrawny friend who had been repeatedly victimized banded together one sloppy winter day on the playground, jumped the bully, and rubbed an icy, gravelly mix into his face while a pair of nearby teachers, arms folded, looked off into the distance as if they were blithely unaware of the retribution being enacted before them. The bully never harassed either of them again. Although bullying wears a different face today, Dad's story is a testament to what can be accomplished when we work together in tandem with support, whether it be tacit like Dad's teachers or explicit as is the case with leaders of anti-bullying campaigns, from those in a position to facilitate change.

We invite you to respond with your thoughts.

—sj Miller, Les Burns, and Tara Star Johnson

Introduction: Bullied

sj Miller

We begin with a narrative of hope at the expense of the 2010 tragic bullycide of Phoebe Prince, a 15-year-old Irish girl who hanged herself because of an extreme case of gang bullying. We believe that there is much to be learned from the prosecution of the six teens who taunted her that can serve as a model for trying to lessen the life-changing impact bullying can have on today's youth. Unfortunately, in this day and age, it is rare that a bully is prosecuted for bullying behavior in the United States or that the victim is somehow provided any type of reparation. We understand bullying as a systemic issue that lives and thrives on the vulnerable in the social environment in which our pre-K–12 students are supposed to learn. Until laws are in place to protect our youth, we are all responsible for intervening, preventing, and redirecting bullying behavior when we are made aware of it. As teachers ourselves, we feel that all of us have a moral obligation as the benevolent custodians while students are at school (and when in-school bullying links to the outside) to intervene lest we be rendered morally culpable of inaction.

What Have We Learned about Bullying from Phoebe Prince's Bullycide?

Phoebe's parents, of British descent, moved to Northampton, Massachusetts, from Ireland so that their five children could have a better life in America, but mostly because Phoebe, who had emotional problems, struggled with self-mutilation and once tried to kill herself as a result of bullying. Phoebe was enrolled at

South Hadley High School. As a relative nobody, a freshman who had the dark misfortune of briefly dating a popular senior football player and then another male, she was vulnerable to bullying from the start. Perhaps her prior experience led her down this pathway to victimization when a group of popular female students at her school became jealous over the boys she was dating and began to stalk her and call her an "Irish slut." Over a period of 3 months she was inundated with an onslaught of bullying via texts, Facebook messages, and threats of physical harm at the school (CNN Wire Staff). Unable to disconnect from the taunts, she hanged herself on January 14, 2010, in the stairway leading to the family's second-story apartment. Even after her death, the bullies dedicated a Facebook page to celebrate her bullycide.

Although teachers and administrators admitted to knowing about the bullying, none of them has been held liable, nor will any of them face criminal charges. Six students, however—three males and three females—have been indicted on charges ranging from statutory rape to civil rights violations and stalking. Within 2 months of Phoebe's bullycide, stricter anti-bullying legislation in Massachusetts was enacted, and Phoebe's Law/Act, which covers all forms of bullying including verbal, physical, sexual, and cyber-harassment, has been proposed as federal anti-bullying legislation. Since the passing of Phoebe's Law in Massachusetts there has been a popcorn effect of anti-bullying state laws around the country.

To date, Massachusetts has one of the strictest and toughest anti-bullying laws in the country. It requires teachers and other school staff to report bullying to the principal or another administrator picked to handle reports when they see or become aware of it. It requires yearly training for teachers and staff on prevention and intervention related to all forms of bullying, and it calls for instruction on heading off bullying for students in every grade as part of the curriculum.

While it is quite painful to see beyond the immediate bullycide of a child, or one's student or friend, the bullycide of Phoebe Prince has generated a larger social awareness of the ubiquity of bullying and has inspired larger discussions of it in pre-K–12 education. Bullying has been foregrounded as a national epidemic and has turned some teachers, administrators, and parents into watchdogs for its nasty and pervasive effects in schools and at home.

Bullying in schools is an international problem, and it is of course neither a new problem nor one limited solely to schools. Bullying manifests across gender, ethnicity, age, social class, disability, ability, national origin, religion, sexual orientation, gender expression, color, height, weight, size, accent, and/or appearance. It occurs in schools, workplaces, and public spaces alike. This pandemic infiltrates nearly every aspect of daily life for both children and adults. Everywhere we turn, there is a sordid panorama of bullying and aggression that has, unfortunately, become accepted as normal—a common-sense part of life and even an expected rite of passage that is "just" part of growing up. Bullying has become accepted and normalized in the values, behaviors, and rhetoric of our country. We see examples of bullying among politicians in Washington, D.C. We see U.S. soldiers participate in egregious behavior against innocent civilians abroad, and we read stories and watch movies in which soldiers, athletes, and members of Greek letter and other extracurricular organizations "haze" pledges—bullying them as a way to make them "toughen up." We see examples across all media including film, radio, television, newspapers, and magazines, and in cyberspace. It is represented in books, magazines, adolescent literature, and graphic novels. We see it becoming part of the American social fabric in terms of how people treat one another. Whether it can be controlled in all aspects of public life or not, it certainly structures the lived realities of students in our public schools. But our public schools can be structured in ways that not only prevent it, but also educate children to both recognize the damage done by bullying and elect to behave civilly toward each other.

Even more troublesome, schools are microcosms of the nation and thus are hardly immune from the deleterious effects of bullying whether they are private or public, preschool, K–12, or college/university systems. Bullying may seem to many members of our society as "just the way it is," but scientific research has begun to show that when any individual or group faces a threat of any kind based on his or her identity, appearance, race, culture, language use, or even a stereotype, there are measurable and significantly negative effects (Steele, 2010). Students (indeed any people) who are bullied are literally unable to learn or perform as well as they would if they did not feel threatened. As such, when schools allow bullying (or when school officials, classmates, and parents ignore it), that permissive or dismissive attitude in fact predictably decreases academic success and miseducates students to behave in ways that really do have negative effects on their growth, productivity, happiness, and success in later life. Each day that passes without addressing bullying in schools, every time someone suffers because of it, we send a local, community, national, and global message about what we think about our youth and our lives: "If you are different or weaker, you are not entitled to basic human decency."

Our children, adolescents, younger adults, and even adults are bullying, being bullied, and taking their own lives on a daily basis because of it. Bullying doesn't stop when the school day is over or when the work week ends. Bullying does not stop when the lights go out at night, or when we wake up. No. It is happening 24 hours a day, 7 days a week. Bullying is as normalized as it is ubiquitous, and its monstrous face often begins taking shape for the first time at school—on the soccer field, in English class, in the locker room, on the bus, in the lunchroom, at the big game, on the walk home, in email, on Facebook, in text messages—and in our children's dreams.

Bullying negatively manifests in our children's thoughts, their feelings about their safety, their concern for their success in school, their desire for friendship and membership, their need for positive familial relationships, their belief in self-worth, their health, their eating habits, and sometimes even in their coffins. We are sorry. We do not yet have a panacea to cure what ails us all. Our hearts break for it. We bleed and bruise with the victims, we bleed and bruise for them, and we write and work for the children, adults, and families who suffer by the sides of loved ones whose lives and dreams have been poisoned and even ended because of bullying by others who felt they deserved it, asked for it, or were just easy targets for such a nasty sport. We want bullying to stop, and if you are still reading this, we suspect you want it to stop just as much as we do. We are here; we are trying to help.

For every story we share in this book, we know that thousands—strike that—millions will go untold, unreported, and maybe even barely recognized by the bullies and the bullied. We understand we cannot represent every story, let alone every group or even the intersectionalities within bodies that are being bullied. We do hope to shed new light on the issues involved through the narratives we share and to offer new perspectives that will contribute to projects that will make a difference. We write this book first and foremost for those whose lives have already been lost because of bullying, to let them and their loved ones know their lives were not lost in vain or without notice. We write for all who have been bullied, all who bully, and for all of us seeking a better way to live life together.

We specifically write to offer tools for secondary teachers, preservice teachers, and teacher educators that will support them in their stances against bullying and become allies to the bullied. While these constituents are our intended audience, the book may also be used in other disciplines. Of critical import, we address those who have legislative power in our country and exhort them to create a national anti-bullying policy that can be employed by every school and college in our country for the betterment of all. We write to you.

The contributors to this book are teacher educators and graduate students from around the country, each of whom has a different life experience and a different writing style. We build from those collective differences to share our research and, at times, even our own life experiences throughout each of our chapters. At times some of us will use the invented pronoun *per* and alternate it with s/he to authenticate students whose identities are gender non-conforming, gender variant, or transgender. While we recognize that there is a growing mass of pronouns such as "hir," "ze," and "they" that also refer to gender non-conforming, gender variant, or transgender people, using *per* in our book is an intentional stylistic decision. We feel that writing authentically is a critical example of how to make a dent in bullying.

That said, it will take a massive and collective effort for bullying to stop, and words alone are not enough. We must make a difference. Lives are at stake. Yet before this project even reaches its conclusion, we wonder how many more will suffer and die. Who will commit suicide because she is fat, and who will be killed because he is Black? Who will get a text that says "no one likes you" and despair because of that lie? Who will be mortified by the circulation of nude photos of themselves around their school? Who will be purposely left off a party invitation because *per* doesn't wear the right clothes or play sports? Who will cut herself because she thinks she is so unlovable she deserves the pain? Who will be beaten and called a "faggot," and who will be punched because she is a lesbian? Who will be shoved into a locker because he is in special education, and who will have food splattered on her chest because she is on the spectrum disorder? Too many to name.

Perhaps this book will offer some antidotes to all that pain. We need our youth to survive adolescence and far, far, beyond. We write this book in an attempt to help weather the storm of bullying that our nation has witnessed in recent years and which has scarred its victims and society itself. There is no one-size-fits-all solution, but respite and understanding can come from the tools and information we offer here that might impact secondary teachers, teacher educators, preservice teachers, parents, administrators, school counselors, school and district personnel, children, adolescents, young adults, bystanders, families, and legislators. Together we can stop bullying and change the way our society views such behavior so that it is anything but "normal."

These Stories about Bullying

We approach this critical work based on research that we've conducted on the normalization of bullying in our culture and because we want and desperately need comprehensive anti-bullying legislation. Unfortunately, searching for stories about bullying was not difficult. The stories we share with you are representative of the kind of bullying that transpires each and every day in schools across the country. Through our stories, we also hope to humanize the statistics that we foreground. We've searched the country to foreground selective stories that we hope will impact and alert you to the seriousness of these cases, as it did us. For that reason, we solicited "real-time" and "real-life stories" that offered us guidance about how to make sense of the phenomenon of bullying. We recognize that our work cannot foreground every story about bullying, let alone every type of bullying. We make every effort to be panoramic in scope about the topic, but we highlight the four target groups of bullying that generate the worst overall statistics: (1) secondary students who are either LGBTQ or gender variant/non-conforming, for example, those students whose behaviors, mannerisms, expressions, gender roles, or appearance—whether through clothing, make-up, height, size, or weight—is non-conventional; (2) students who regularly endure slights because of an actual or perceived physical, emotional, or intellectual disability—those with delicate organs and/or fragile parts (Siebers, 2010); (3) students of color; and (4) Latino/a students. We also decided to highlight cyber-bullying as its own chapter because of the growing number of casualties that are surfacing on a daily basis; it appears to be a new frontier for bullying with its own particularities that can exacerbate the experience. We hope that you will be able to draw hope from these compelling narratives as models for transformation in others.

We situate our work with those who are bullied rather than on the reasons or causality for the bullying, and provide the Olweus Cycle of Bullying as a temporal guide to help visualize where some fall in the cycle of bullying. We feel this is important, because prior work has focused more on the cycle of bullying and less on how people become agents of change after they have been bullied (Coloroso, 2004; Meyer, 2009). Much attention has already been paid to the bullies themselves. Prior research has shown that bullies are agitated and threatened when the ideology of the norm is challenged by the externalized non-normative representations in society and schools writ large (Miller, 2012), because they have come to identify "with a set of social narratives, myths, ideas, values and types of varying reliability, usefulness, and verifiability" (Siebers, 2010, p. 15). When these narratives are threatened, bullies go on the attack. Otherwise understood, the medical model has a biological orientation that focuses on the binary identifiers of sickness and mental health that are considered abnormal or unhealthy, or which require intervention or are in need of fixing, according to the *Diagnostic and Statistical Manual of Mental Disorders IV* (DSM IV). This model has widespread structural power, as it is reinforced throughout the dominant culture by generating and sanctioning normal/abnormal dichotomies. Bullies are attuned to these "deviations" and often feel vindicated because of the social acceptance of the norm by the medical model. This deeply frustrates us, because the medical model is part of the problem that has led us to this work. We feel that the stories about bullies that are shared vis-à-vis the media have led to copycatting, or even motivated other "haters." While we acknowledge that bullies are victims, too, their back-stories are beyond the scope of our work.

How Definitions of Bullying Manifest in School

The National School Safety Center identified different types of bullying, some of which involve direct action and indirect action. Direct action is bullying against the victim directly, while indirect action often—but not always—involves anonymity through "verbal, emotional, sexual, or passive-aggressive behaviors" (Ferrell-Smith, 2003, p. 2). Direct and indirect bullying can manifest through several domains of bullying: verbal, physical, material, relational, hate-motivated, and cyber-digital[1] bullying behavior (see Table 1). *Hate-motivated bullying* in some cases can legally constitute a hate crime when taunting is about race, national origin, ability, religion, sexual orientation, gender expression, and physical or mental abilities. *Cyber-digital bullying* is a relatively new phenomenon and is defined under H.R. 975[2] (House of Representatives) as conduct undertaken, in whole or in part, through use of technology or electronic communications (including electronic mail, internet communications, instant messages, or facsimile communications) to transmit images, text, sounds, or other data

and which causes deliberate or intentional social cruelty to victims by threatening, harming, humiliating, and engendering fear and helplessness in the victim (Strom & Strom, 2005) through any of these media. According to H.R. 975, cyber-digital bullying can also take the form of falsely identifying the self by

knowingly impersonating another person as the author of posted content or messages on the Internet in order to trick, tease, harass, or spread rumors about the other person.

Sexting is a specific form of cyber-digital bullying that includes transmitting a nude picture by means of any of the above-referenced methods.

In moving from these specific definitions, the actuality is that we see bullying taking place through verbal, physical, material, relational, and hate-motivated domains and through the most recent and emerging phenomenon of electronic and communication technologies.

Table 1: The Manifestations of Direct and Indirect Bullying through Verbal, Physical, Material, Relational, Hate-motivated, and Cyber-digital Bullying Behavior

	Direct Bullying	Indirect Bullying
Verbal Bullying Using verbal threats to intentionally inflict social cruelty on someone	•threats •insults •teasing/sarcasm •taunting •name-calling •snickering/whispering •laughing at someone out of cruelty	•rumors* •stereotypes •speaking in code •graffiti/bathroom tagging •hate mail via snail mail
Physical Bullying* Using physical force to intentionally inflict pain on another person	•hitting* •kicking •pushing •stealing •sexual misconduct* •killing someone •cutting	•physically moving away from someone as means to be hurtful •bringing harmful substances near someone (e.g., smoking near someone, trying to induce an allergic reaction—peanut allergies)
Material Bullying Taking away belongings to intentionally cause another person duress	•damage to belongings •extortion of money	•hiding belongings or pawning

	Direct Bullying	Indirect Bullying
Relational Bullying* Participating in behavior that intentionally positions the victim as the scapegoat	•back-stabbing •setting someone up to take blame •taking credit for someone else's accomplishments •blackmail	•social exclusion •breaking confidences •manipulating friendships •micro-aggressions •looks and stare-downs •slander •putting peers in unsafe situations
Hate-motivated Bullying Any manifestation of bullying that targets another because of race, national origin, ability, religion, sexual orientation, gender expression, and physical or mental abilities	Hate-motivated bullying could include any aspect of the different types of bullying in the chart and in some cases can legally constitute a hate crime when taunting is about race, national origin, ability, religion, sexual orientation, gender expression, and physical or mental disabilities	•burning a flag or cross •tagging a swastika •writing the "n" word on a wall or stall •graffiti or tagging •expressions of hostility toward any of these subjectivities •being out of compliance with the American Disabilities Act •tying a noose around a doll from one of these groups and hanging it
Cyber-digital bullying The intent is to inflict social cruelty on victims *repeatedly* by threatening, harming, humiliating, and engendering fear and helplessness in the victim through the use of electronic and communication technologies	•texts messages •emails •social networking sites •mobile phones •chat rooms •Blogs •facetime •emoji •IM •pictures •video clips •forwarding •writing confidential emails or messages	•sending lewd or nude images to others (*sexting*) •posting hurtful information on Blogs •spreading rumors online or via texts • "accidentally" hitting reply all that contains private or inappropriate information via email or text •hacking into an account and sending damaging messages •pretending to be someone else in order to hurt someone •portable gaming devices •3-D virtual, and social gaming sites •interactive sites such as Formspring and ChatRoulette

(*could be self-inflicted)

Note: Boys tend to engage in more physical bullying than girls, while girls tend to engage in more relational bullying than boys. This chart has been modified from the original in Miller (2012), p. 108. Thanks to Nicole Sieben's *Adolescent Experience* class at Adelphi University for additional suggestions with this chart.

Microaggressions:
Another Way of Understanding Bullying

By borrowing from the field of critical race theory, which focuses on how people of color experience unconscious and conscious slights and affronts throughout the course of daily interactions, acts of bullying can also be understood as microaggressions, which are described as "the everyday verbal, nonverbal, and environmental slights, snubs or insults, whether intentional or unintentional, that communicate hostile, derogatory, or negative messages to target persons based solely upon their marginalized group membership" (Sue, 2010, p. 3). The expression of microaggressions may invalidate and demean a group identity or the experiential reality of the targeted persons and may communicate that they are sub-human beings, suggest they do not belong with the majority group, threaten and intimidate them, or reduce them to inferior status and treatment. Targets in schools are often those students who are not part of the dominant ethnicity, whose gender expressions are non-conforming, who challenge gender norms, mannerisms, or behaviors, whose ability is perceived as lesser, whose accent sounds different from others, whose size and/or weight doesn't conform to the norms, who might be poor or working class, and/or whose sexual orientation is not perceived to be heterosexual. Microaggressions, when not identified as hurtful, can lead students to self-injurious behavior, and the work we do on bullying benefits when we broaden our understanding about what it constitutes.

Why Stopping Bullying Matters

Bullying takes its toll on its victims, the bystander (Hazler, 1996), and even the bully, impacting their cognitive, emotional, and psychological well-being (Beran, 2005; Rigby, 2000; Sharp, 1995; Sherer & Nickerson, 2010). Victims tend to skip school more often, have lower self-esteem and lowered academic performance, and experience depression at rates higher than non-bullied students (Harris & Isernhagen, 2003; Beran, 2005). Bystanders tend to feel helpless and vulnerable, and families tend to express deep sadness and anger about the child who is bullied. Siblings of those who are bullied experience a range of feelings related to the bullied sibling. For instance, some siblings may retaliate against the bully, some may feel that retaliation may turn them into victims, some feel socially marginalized and may experience fear and isolation, and some may be bullied by others who see an opportunity to exacerbate bullying against the family as a whole. We offer these concerns because they illuminate how bullying affects a student's ability to function emotionally, academically, and physically in school and how the consequences of bullying may provoke retaliatory violence, damage a school's reputation, and even instigate community conflict. It is highly ironic that the Safe and Drug-Free Schools and Communities Act that is part of the No

Child Left Behind Act provides federal support to promote school safety, but it fails to address bullying directly.

Our Chapters on Bullying

The chapters in *Generation BULLIED 2.0* have been organized strategically to move us from a historical overview of bullying to strategies teachers can immediately apply to their classroom practice. We conclude with the latter because the authors of this book work in the fields of English teacher preparation or teacher education and recognize that, as new teachers come into the field, they need salient tools for application to classroom practice. Elizabeth Meyer, in her compelling and heartfelt foreword, shared her expertise and a brief history of anti-bullying to prime our readership for the next set of chapters. Dianne Smith then shared her own story of how she was bullied and, as a result, became a bully without identifying herself that way. Her brutal honesty and vulnerability reminds us that the scars of bullying can last someone's lifetime unless we stand up to and heed the charge of making bullying a human rights issue. sj Miller in this introduction has provided a historical overview of the origins of anti-bullying legislation and broken down the current language proposed for federal anti-bullying laws so that it can frame the remaining chapters. The bullying chart (Table 1) shows the different types of bullying practiced most often among youth today so that the reader might use it as a touchstone to reflect on the bullying behavior that contemporary youth engage in.

Miller continues into Chapter 1, "Where Are We Now? The Current State of Bullying in the United States," and provides an overview of current state laws, how they were initially instantiated, and the bullying statistics for the most vulnerable populations. Citing Columbine as a pivotal moment in bullying's entry into the national discussion, he takes us back into its history as a way of understanding current anti-bullying legislative proposals and those who oppose them.

In Chapter 2, "The Distressing Realities about Queer-Related (LGBTQGV) Bullying," sj Miller and James R. Gilligan take us through harrowing statistics about the most vulnerable population to date for bullying and introduce us to a new way of understanding this as *queer bullying*. They provide historical causality, challenge the medical model and the "norm," and discuss the landmark case of *Nabozny v. Podlesny* (1996) and the Hate Crimes Prevention Act and its impact on LGBTQ and gender variant-related legislative policies in schools. They also draw us into a discussion on the microaggressions often aimed at LGBTQGV youth.

In Chapter 3, "Bullies and Bodies: Addressing Weight Discrimination," Tara Star Johnson and Elana Cutter discuss the issue of sizism, which contributes to the second most targeted population of students who are bullied because of aspects related to their physical appearance such as body weight. Johnson begins the chapter with an anecdote from her childhood and follows with information on weight-based bullying. She then describes the challenges and opportunities she has experienced in addressing sizism in her methods classes. The chapter concludes with Cutter, a student in one of those classes, providing insights from her action research project in which she investigated her students' awareness of and openness to the topic of sizism.

In Chapter 4, "Bullying and Students with Disabilities: The Bully, the Bullied, and the Misunderstood," Joseph John Morgan and Deanna Adams discuss disability from the perspective of the social model of disability and the framework of disability studies. These characterize disability as a difference from the norm, as compared to the biomedical model, which views disability as something that is inherently wrong within the individual that should be fixed or remediated. These perspectives lay the framework for a discussion on the impact of bullying on students with perceived differences/disabilities, as well as showcasing current research and statistics related to the bullying of students with disabilities. In addition, this chapter critically examines the issue of students with disabilities who are seen as perpetrators of bullying, whether in myth or reality, and interrogate the root of such understandings and misunderstandings.

From there we move to Chapter 5, "Black Ritual Insults: Causing Harm or Passing Time?" in which authors Tyrone Rivers and Dorothy Espelage introduce us to how students of color bully each other by trading insults, or *roastin'*. On the surface, such exchanges are normalized as funny, but they mask a deeper wounding that often structures and diminishes the lived realities of students of color, who then participate in a continuous cycle of bullying with one another. Rivers and Espelage share findings from two studies about the impact of roastin' (verbal aggression) on their lives and how it mitigates their feelings of belonging at school.

Rodrigo Joseph Rodríguez navigates us to the next vulnerable population in Chapter 6, "Bullying and Harassment Prevention in the Lives of Latina and Latino Students." Here he unpacks how institutionalized linguistic and racial prejudice facing Latinas and Latinos in education has become part of the normalization in a school's culture. He helps us see this by understanding how linguicism surreptitiously acts to maintain English for wider communication as the "correct" spoken form of English. He also reveals disheartening realities about how other students' perceptions of racial and ethnic stereotypes contribute as a dominant form of bullying toward Latina and Latino students. Rodriguez provides optimism toward the end of his work and models powerful and provocative strategies that can both support and protect Latina and Latino students and their peers in school, while also directing administrators to create more racially and linguistically equitable school environments.

Chapter 7, "Cyber-Digital Bullying," takes a slight turn as sj Miller and Stephanie Beyer take us into one of the more prevalent ways that students bully today. They begin with the story of Megan Meier and her bullycide and reflect on its impact on state and proposed federal cyber-bullying legislation. They explore different cyber-digital modalities used for bullying and how they have impaired students in and out of their schooling lives, and conclude with a rich discussion of how teachers and schools can offer concrete classroom and school-wide prevention strategies that educate students about the realities of cyber-digital bullying.

In Chapter 8, "The Consequences of Bullying and Anti-Bullying Interventions for Individual and School Success," Leslie David Burns demonstrates the ways in which bullying behavior, and the tolerance of such behaviors, has dramatic, measurable, negative consequences not only for the victims of bullying, but also for those who bully and those who bear witness to it. Using studies from social psychology, funds of knowledge research, culturally responsive pedagogies, Third-Space pedagogical theory, critical theories of education, and research on psychological motivation and engagement in school, Burns explores how projects designed to eliminate bullying are not merely moral projects intended to make adults and children feel good about themselves. While that is certainly important, in Chapter 8 we demonstrate how instituting anti-bullying policies and practices in public schools is not only morally and socially just, but also the key to optimizing success for *all* students and professionals in those schools.

Our work then shifts to Chapter 9, "The Broader Contexts of Bullying: Disrupting Bullying Through Preventive and Interventionist Policy," in which sj Miller takes us on a brief trip overseas and examines effective international models of anti-bullying reforms in Norway and the United Kingdom. He reflects on the efficacy these anti-bullying reforms could have on legislation in the United States and ends the chapter with specific recommendations to policymakers, health care providers, and schools about strategies for enacting bullying reforms.

We end the book with notes of optimism in Chapter 10, "Shifting the Tide of Bullying Through Teacher Education: Tools for the Classroom," in which all of the contributors to this work focus on how parents, teachers, school counselors, the larger school community, and the nation at large can interrupt the cycle of bullying. Together we offer suggestions for prevention and resources for creating safe spaces in schools and classrooms, including examples of successful anti-bullying campaigns and initiatives. Dennis Carlson then provides our readers with an afterword that addresses how the reinforcement and performance of hegemonic masculinities for both boys and girls generates deleterious consequences in the form of bullying for today's youth.

Bullying: Where's the Unifying Definition?

As we move into the chapters of the book, we provide an overview of the history of anti-bullying legislation. In 1999, Georgia was the first state to enact statewide anti-bullying legislation through the U.S. Supreme Court decision of *Davis vs. Monroe County Board of Education*, in which the Court held that a school board may be liable for damages for student-to-student harassment if the district receives federal funds and acts with indifference to known acts of bullying. (In this case, Title IX was applied because a student experienced pervasive and repeated sexual harassment, and school authorities failed to act.) The result was that schools could now be held liable for having knowledge of sexual harassment as a form of bullying but not taking action. In 2000, New Hampshire followed suit, and in the two years after Columbine, a cluster of states including Colorado[3] mandated that each school district must include a specific policy in the district conduct and discipline code concerning bullying prevention and education. Since then, a number of states have continued to develop, legislate, and mandate anti-bullying laws and have put pressure on the federal government to codify a federal anti-bullying law. However, our country has to yet arrive at a uniform definition of bullying. In retrospect, had there been a definition codified into policy, perhaps Columbine, Phoebe Prince, and other cases of bullying could have been prevented or interrupted.

In recognition of the ever-increasing bullycides around the country (though there is no single universal definition of bullying according to H.R 975), bullying is currently referenced as

> conduct, including conduct that is based on a student's actual or perceived identity with regard to race, color, national origin, gender identity, disability, sexual orientation, religion, or any other distinguishing characteristics that may be defined by a State or local educational agency that— (i) is directed at one or more students; (ii) substantially interferes with educational opportunities or educational programs of such students; and (iii) adversely affects the ability of a student to participate in or benefit from the school's educational programs or activities by placing a student in reasonable fear of physical harm.[4]

Continuing, H.R. 975 states that bullying may also be based on

> a student's association with another individual; and a characteristic of the other individual that is referred to [in the excerpt above].

To these definitions, Olweus (1993) adds that bullying is about an unequal distribution of power that occurs repeatedly in a relationship. And it is proactive (Espelage & Swearer, 2003), because bullies tend to target others without provocation on the victims' part.

We leave with this definition and these startling realities as we invite you to contemplate the current state of anti-bullying reform and the impact it has on students in the wake of its absence from federal law.

Notes

1   We refer to cyber-bullying as cyber-digital bullying, because the electronic means used to cyber-bully are digital forms of communication.

2   GovTrack.us. Retrieved May 8, 2011, from http://www.govtrack.us/congress/billtext.
    xpd?bill=h112-975
3   In 2001, Louisiana, Mississippi, Oregon, and West Virginia joined Colorado by passing state-
    wide anti-bullying policies.
4   GovTrack.us. Retrieved May 8, 2011, from http://www.govtrack.us/congress/billtext.
    xpd?bill=h112-975

References

American Psychiatric Association. (2000). *Diagnostic and statistical manual of mental disorders* (4th ed., text rev.). Washington, DC: Author.

Beran, T. (2005). A closer look at the relationship between bullying and behavior problems: A syndrome of misconduct. *Exceptionality Education Canada, 15*(3), 41–55.

CNN Wire Staff. (2010). *Prosecutor: 9 teens charged in bullying that led to girl's suicide.* Retrieved July 17, 2012, from http://cnn.com/2010/CRIME/03/29/massachusetts.bullying.suicide/index.html

Coloroso, B. (2004). *The bully, the bullied, and the bystander: From preschool to high school—How parents and teachers can help break the cycle of violence.* New York: Collins Living.

Espelage, D., & Swearer, S.M. (2003). Research on school bullying and victimization. What have we learned and where do we go from here? *School Psychology Review, 32,* 365–383.

Ferrell-Smith, F. (2003). *School violence: Tackling the schoolyard bully. Combining policy making with prevention.* Denver: National Conference of State Legislatures, Children and Families Program.

GovTrack.us. Retrieved May 8, 2011, from http://www.govtrack.us/congress/bill.xpd?bill=h108-4776&tab=summary

Harris, S., & Isernhagen, J. (2003, November). Keeping bullies at bay. *American School Board Journal, 43–45.*

Hazler, R.J. (1996). *Breaking the cycle of violence: Interventions for bullying and victimization.* Washington, DC: Accelerated Development.

Meyer, E. J. (2009). *Gender, bullying, and harassment: Strategies to end sexism and homophobia in schools.* New York, NY: Teachers College Press.

Miller, s. (2012). Mythology of the norm: Disrupting the culture of bullying in schools. *English Journal, 101*(6), 107–109.

Olweus, D. (1993). *Bullying at school: What we know and what we can do.* Mahwah, NJ: Blackwell.

Rigby, K. (2000). What it takes to stop bullying in schools: An examination of the rationale and effectiveness of school-based interventions. In M.F. Furlong, M.P. Bates, D.C. Smith, & P.M. Kingery (Eds.), *Appraisal and prediction of school violence: Methods, issues and contexts* (pp. 171–197). Hauppauge, NY: Nova Science.

Siebers, T. (2010). *Disability theory.* Ann Arbor: University of Michigan Press.

Sharp, S. (1995). How much does bullying hurt? The effects on the personal well-being and educational progress of secondary aged students. *Educational and Child Psychology, 12,* 81–88.

Sherer, Y.P., & Nickerson, A.B. (2010). Anti-bullying practices in American schools: Perspectives of school psychologists. *Psychology in the Schools, 47*(3), 217–229.

Steele, C. M. (2010). *Whistling Vivaldi and other clues how stereotypes affect us.* New York: W.W. Norton.

Strom, P.S., & Strom, R.D. (2005). When teens turn cyberbullies. *The Education Digest, 71*(4), 35–41.

Sue, D.W. (Ed.). (2010). *Microaggressions and marginality: Manifestation, dynamics, and impact.* Hoboken, NJ: Wiley.

CHAPTER ONE

Where Are We Now?

The Current State of Bullying in the United States

sj Miller

Columbine: A Moment That Changed Schooling Forever

If we go back in time 11 years before the bullycide of Phoebe Prince, we come to a pivotal moment when bullying was catapulted to national prominence as a major problem in schools. On April 20, 1999, seniors Eric Harris and Dylan Klebold walked unsuspected into their high school in Columbine, Colorado, and fired guns at their teachers and classmates in one of the most tragic events ever to unfold in an American school. The Columbine tragedy forever shifted public perspective on school safety. Dylan and Eric shot and killed 12 students and 1 teacher, wounded 21 students, and then committed suicide. Their acts sparked a national outcry based on evidence that the pair murdered their peers and teachers as revenge on those they felt had ridiculed them for their style, picked on them for being different, and made them feel like outcasts in a conformist society. The Columbine Massacre forced Americans to confront the reality that schools were becoming battlegrounds rather than safe places for children to learn. It forced Americans, for perhaps the first time, to think seriously about the nature and consequences of bullying in a national debate.

People often try to reconcile why bad things happen to good people, and media and community voices across the country were quick to place blame for Columbine. Rumors circulated as to why Eric and Dylan acted so unforgivably. One rumor purported that the school climate supported marginalization of the "goth-like" clique the boys were in, dubbed "The Trenchcoat Mafia."[1]

Other rumors fueled the belief that the boys' fanatical consumption of music and lyrics produced by pop musicians such as Marilyn Manson, KMFDM, and Rammstein motivated their hatred and violence. Some speculated that Harris was a "clinical psychopath" and Klebold was a "depressive," that the side effects of their various medications included aggressive behavior, sociopathic tendencies, depersonalization, and, especially, mania in Harris, the presumed mastermind. Some blamed the young men's love of violent video games such as *Doom* and *Wolfenstein 3D*[2] as something they sublimated into their hostilities about life in school. Dylan's and Eric's parents emphasized that when they restricted their children's access to such games, the boys actually began to unleash their pent-up anger in the real world.

Some media outlets blamed the boys' infatuation with Adolf Hitler, whose birthday, April 20th, served as the ideal date for their terroristic acts. Evidence, however, suggests that April 19th was the intended date, since it coincided with the anniversaries of the Oklahoma City bombing[3] and the killings of David Koresh's cult members in Waco, Texas, by the Federal Bureau of Alcohol, Tobacco, and Firearms.[4] The attribution that has most lingered in the public imagination, however, is that bullying combined with homophobia motivated the Columbine killings.[5] At Columbine High School, the climate purportedly privileged students who were jocks. Teachers were perceived as doing little to stop such students when they bullied others. As a consequence, those favored groups felt entitled to treat others badly. Evidence from the Columbine Tapes (Gibbs & Roche, 1999) shows that the school's more popular student cliques did not want boys like Harris and Klebold around. Evan Todd, a defensive lineman for the Columbine High School football team, was recorded saying, "If you want to get rid of someone, usually you tease them."

It was rumored that both Eric and Dylan endured homophobic taunts from the school's most popular students and had endured years of bullying because of presumed homosexuality. Based on years of pent-up trauma and resentment because of such taunting, some suspected the boys simply snapped and took their anger out on those who bullied them and those who turned a blind eye to it.

If there had been a working anti-bullying policy in place, could the Columbine Massacre have been averted? Would those who died be alive today if the school had recognized the bullying, identified the perpetrators, and both reprimanded and prevented their behavior? What *did* Columbine teach us? As a country, have we learned our lessons yet? Or have we continued to overlook or dismiss bullying victims like Phoebe Prince, Megan Meier, Tyler Clemente, Sladjana Vidovic, Hamed Nastoh, Aiden Rivera Schaeff, Jaheem Herrera,[6] and too many others to name who might otherwise convince us that bullying has attained the status of a legitimate crisis in our schools today?

The Students Behind Bullying Statistics

In spite of anti-bullying programs that now exist in 49 of 50 states, there is controversy over how research is used to show declines in anti-bullying behavior. Most current anti-bullying programs are "for profit" and have their own mission; some are funded by right-wing groups that do not support LGBTQ rights.[7] The Protect Kids Foundation, Focus on the Family, the Family Research Council, the American Family Association, Concerned Women for America, the Liberty Institute, and MassResistance (Big Bullies) are just some of the right-wing groups that believe anti-bullying programs that take on LGBTQ bullying include (and even emphasize) attempts to indoctrinate students into an LGBTQ lifestyle. These programs have great leverage to financially back government funding, thereby impacting comprehensive national anti-bullying reform and even the kinds of studies that are conducted by the Department of Justice to generate an ostensibly scientific body of knowledge about the problem.[8] Consequently, statistics about the effectiveness of anti-bullying programs framed by these explicitly partisan organizations tend to mislead the public by claiming there is a decline in bullying, when in fact most anti-bullying programs are too narrow in scope and focus only on certain kinds of bullying. They frequently ignore LGBTQ bullying altogether. When viewing the statistics, then, the public must be skeptical about what such programs eradicate, who sponsors such programs, and what claims such partisan anti-bullying programs make.

While some research reveals that there has been little decrease in the statistics showing the numbers of students who are bullied each year (Smith, Schneider, Smith, & Ananiadou, 2004; Vreeman & Carroll, 2007), the National Center for Educational Statistics (NCES) and the research conducted by Pediatrics and Adolescent Medicine (Crary, 2010) found that the percentage of children who reported being bullied through direct and indirect actions over the past year had declined from nearly 22% in 2003 to under 15% in 2008. The NCES also noted that in 2007–2008, 25% of public schools reported that bullying occurred among students on a daily basis; about 32% of 12- to 18-year-old students reported having been bullied at school during the school year, and 4% reported having been cyber-bullied. For those who were cyber-bullied, 73% said it had occurred once or twice during that period, 21% said it had occurred once or twice a month, and 5% said it had occurred once or twice a week. Five percent of female students reported being cyber-bullied, compared to 2% of male students.

Neither the findings from the NCES nor the reports from the Pediatrics and Adolescent Medicine Association included statistics for LGBTQ students or for those who were bullied based on their identification (perceived or real) with other social categories. The findings exclusively reported on bullying related to ethnicity, gender, and social class in grades 6–12 (National Center for Educational Statistics, 2011).[9] Such gross oversight belies the truth about bullying in our nation, limits the public understanding, leads districts and legislators in positions of power to believe that bullying is less pervasive in schools, and bolsters the view that the smaller-scale, for-profit programs already in place are working.

Why aren't anti-bullying programs making a larger dent in the reported statistics? Beyond the obvious—small-scale implementation—programs often lack follow-through, accountability, adequate training for all school members, and incentives. Where statistics reveal decreases in bullying, more research is required to understand how to sustain positive changes over time. Anti-bullying programs should be regularly evaluated and updated, and they should take into account the voices of all constituents. Until we have legislatively bound, comprehensive anti-bullying reform that assures accountability across all social categories, all grade levels, and in both the public and private sectors, small-scale programs cannot succeed.

Where Does School Bullying Begin?

While there are a handful of reports about bullying that begins in elementary schools (GLSEN & Harris Interactive, 2012; Jimerson, Swearer, & Espelage, 2010; Pepler, Craig, & Pardy, 2002; Ringrose & Renold, 2011), many of them tend to be lumped into statistics that include middle and high schools. This is problematic, because understanding how bullying could be interrupted early on could eliminate many problems before it peaks in junior high and then persists through senior high school (Harris & Isernhagen, 2003; Markow & Fein, 2005; Sherer & Nickerson, 2010). In elementary school, bullying tends to be less physical or violent. As students move into their middle and high school years, however, it becomes far more pervasive and aggressive (Markow & Fein, 2005; Sherer & Nickerson, 2010). Extensive documentation of bullying in elementary schools could draw increased attention to focused interventions and possibly decrease bullying in schools overall.

Across all three school levels, statistics in the United States reveal that three of every four students report that they have been bullied, while one of every three report that they are involved as the bully, victim, or both (Nansel, 2001). Each month over 250,000 students report being physically attacked. Ninety percent feel that being bullied caused social, emotional, or academic problems. Other studies (Harris & Isernhagen, 2003; Markow & Fein, 2005) show that *both* bullies and victims have problems later in life because of bullying. Even when victims stand up for themselves, they often face more taunting and social isolation, which can lead to depression, distress, anxiety, and (worst of all) *bullycide*—the act of taking one's life because of bullying.

In the 1999 U.S. Supreme Court decision *Davis vs. Monroe County Board of Education*, the Court held that, under Title IX, a school board may be liable for damages for student-to-student harassment if the district receives federal funds and acts with indifference to known acts of bullying. Schools can be sued for having knowledge of sexual harassment-related bullying but doing nothing about

Figure 1: Statewide School Bullying Laws and Policies in the United States, Especially as They Pertain to Sexual Orientation and Gender Identity

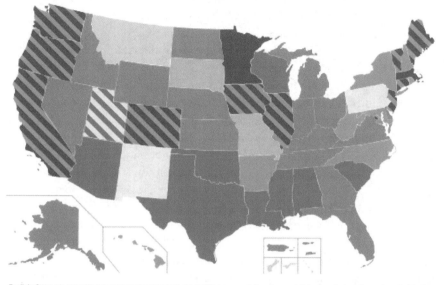

English: Statewide school bullying laws and policies in the United States, especially as they pertain to sexual orientation and gender identity

Law that prohibits discrimination against students based on sexual orientation and gender identity

Law that prohibits discrimination against students based on sexual orientation only

Law that prohibits bullying of students based on sexual orientation and gender identity

School regulation or ethical code for teachers that address discrimination and/or bullying of students based on sexual orientation and gender identity

School regulation or ethical code for teachers that address discrimination and/or bullying of students based on sexual orientation only

Law that forbids school-based instruction of LGBT issues in a positive manner

Law that forbids local school districts from having anti-bullying policies that enumerate protected classes of students

Law that prohibits bullying in school but lists no categories of protection

No statewide law that specifically prohibits bullying in schools

Note: from Wikipedia, retrieved July 18, 2012. Sources: Human Rights Campaign (anti-bullying laws and non-discrimination laws), Bully Police (which states/territories have anti-bullying laws), and the Gay, Lesbian & Straight Education Network ("no promo homo" laws and laws that prohibit enumeration).

it. Sadly, 69% of students believe schools respond poorly to reports of bullying.[10] Currently, the five states with the highest number of reported cases of bullying, according to surveys conducted by the Bully Police, are Connecticut, Maine, Washington, Montana, and New Hampshire. Based on student enrollment, the five states with the highest number of youth involved in bullying are Illinois, Florida, New York, Texas, and California. In response to the public outcry fueled by these statistics, 49 states have enacted anti-bullying laws; Montana remains the lone state without any such laws at this time.

The Most Vulnerable Populations of Students

The GLSEN data show that sexual orientation, gender expression, and body size are the three leading characteristics that incur harassment (Frisen, Jonsson, & Persson, 2007; Wallace, 2011). Data reveal that the victim was targeted because s/he/per was or was perceived as LGBTQGV (Lesbian/Gay/Bisexual/Transgender/Questioning/Gender Variant), that is, gender-non-conforming,[11] and bullies target individuals with defaming words such as "dyke," "faggot," "homo," or "queer," regardless of actual or perceived sexual orientation. We especially highlight and home in on their bullied statistics, because these students incur the highest incidence of violence and suicidalilty (Markow & Fein, 2005; Sherer & Nickerson, 2010). We refer to bullying against these populations as *queer* bullying. By queer, we mean breaking binaries that reinforce compulsory heteronormative norms for LGBTQ students and those whose gender expressions, mannerisms, roles, behaviors, and appearance are non-conforming, variant, or challenge the dominant narrative.

The next most cited characteristic that incurred bullying was that the victim had an "unconventional" appearance or was perceived as not being at a "conventional" weight (Kosciw et al., 2012). In these studies researchers found that boys tend to bully more often than girls, and that males engage in more physical and aggressive behaviors (fighting, shoving, hitting, and pushing). Girls tend to engage in more relational bullying (using rumors, slander, exclusion, and manipulation of friendships) than boys. Markow and Fein (2005), in their comprehensive study on school climates across the United States, found that girls are more likely to report feeling unsafe in schools for reasons related to personal appearance.

Following these statistics, and without taking into account the intersections of LGBTQGV bullying and ethnicity, the NCES (2011) study concludes that 82.2% of African Americans were bullied in grades 6–12, making them the largest group of students bullied overall (and based solely on ethnicity). In the same study it was reported that 74.8% of Latino/a students experience the third largest percentage of racially biased harassment (the second largest was White students). In a different study on students with disabilities, Rose, Espelage, Aragon, and Elliott (2011) indicated that students with disabilities (visible and non-visible) may be two to three times more likely than their "abler" peers to be targeted for bullying on public school campuses.

Understanding the egregious lack of research on LGBTQ bullying conducted by the Department of Justice, the Gay, Lesbian & Straight Educators Network (GLSEN) conducted three major national studies spanning 6 years related to the prevalence of LGBTQ-related bullying in schools. Statistics have been consistent throughout GLSEN's studies and reveal that for 9 of 10 LGBTQ students who experience bullying, 6 of 10 non-LGBTQ students experience bullying. This suggests that anti-bullying reforms related to LGBTQ youth are in great need. Markow and Fein's *From Teasing to Torment: School Climate in America* (2005), a study surveying 3,400 secondary students, reported that nearly two-thirds of non-LG-BTQ middle and high school students (65%) said they had been bullied in school in the past year, compared to nearly 9 of 10 LGBTQ students (86.4%) who said they had been harassed in the past year. The study also reported that LGBTQ students are three times more likely than non-LGBTQ students to say that they do not feel safe at school (22% vs. 7%), and 90% of LGBTQ students, in contrast to 62% of non-LGBTQ students, have been harassed or assaulted during the past year. This trend is consistent with findings reported in GLSEN's *2007 National School Climate Survey* of more than 6,000 LGBTQ students (Kosciw, Greytak, & Diaz, 2008), which revealed that 60.8% of LGBTQ students felt unsafe at school because of their sexual orientation, and that nearly one-third (32.7%) skipped at least one day of school in the past month to avoid bullying.

Similarly, the *2009 National School Climate Survey* of 7,261 LGBTQ students between the ages of 13 and 21 revealed that 90% of LGBTQ students reported victimization, compared to just 40% of non-LGBTQ students. A total of 61.1% of LGBTQ students felt unsafe at school because of their sexual orientation, and 39.9% felt unsafe because of how they expressed their gender (whether LGBTQ or heterosexual).[12] Most alarming, LGBTQ students are two to five times more likely (depending on location) to attempt suicide than heterosexual students. When we reflect on these disheartening statistics and their implications, to assert that bullying must stop in schools is a gross understatement.

Many of these statistics reflect a divided political reality backed by a strong religious right in American politics that purposely undercuts LGBTQ students' civil rights in schools. While schools with sexual orientation or gender expression written into their anti-harassment policies reported fewer problems with school safety, only 11 states currently have statutes protecting students in schools from discrimination on the basis of sexual orientation or gender expression (California, Georgia, Kansas, Maine, Michigan, New Jersey, New York, North Carolina, Texas, Virginia, and Washington) (Transgender Law and Policy Institute, n.d.). Seven states have legislation *prohibiting the positive portrayal of homosexuality* (Alabama, Arizona, Mississippi, Oklahoma, South Carolina, Texas, and Utah) (Kosciw & Diaz, 2006, p. 86). California Governor Jerry Brown became the first governor to sign a law (under SB48) mandating that K–12 public schools *must* teach materials that cover the contributions and roles of sexual minorities in social studies classes beginning in 2013. Across the country we are sending inconsistent messages to our youth about who is valued and valuable in our educational system—and therefore in our society.

GLSEN's 2005, 2007, and 2009[13] studies revealed other alarming statistics for secondary students. We feel it is important to be mindful of the following additional statistics.

- 65% of all teens had been verbally or physically harassed or assaulted during the past year because of perceived or actual differences in appearance, gender, sexual orientation, gender expression, race/ethnicity, disability, or religion.

- 39% of teens reported that students in their school were frequently harassed because of physical appearance.

- 52% frequently heard other students make homophobic remarks.

- 69% of teens heard students say "that's so gay" or "you're so gay"—expressions in which "gay" means something bad or devalued.

- 51% heard students make sexist remarks.

- Over 50% of African American/Black, Latino/a, Asian/Pacific Islander, and multiracial students reported verbal harassment in school based on their ethnicity.

- Native American students experienced particularly high levels of victimization because of their religions, with more than half reporting the highest levels of verbal harassment possible (54%), and a quarter experiencing physical violence (26%), although they were less likely than other students to report racially motivated verbal harassment.

- Less than 50% of students of color who had been bullied in school during the past year said that they reported the incident to school staff. For those students who did lodge formal complaints, fewer than half felt their school's response was effective.[14]

GLSEN's studies also found similarly alarming statistics for junior high school students. In fact, junior high school teachers were more likely to describe bullying and harassment as a serious problem at their schools compared to high school teachers (64% vs. 46%). Junior high school students were more likely to report harassment because of physical appearance or body size (48% vs. 39%), and were more likely to have rumors or lies spread about them. These statistics might suggest that more junior high school students are reporting bullying incidents because they feel safer coming forward than their older peers. Perhaps in the high school grades, the risks involved in reporting bullying are more numerous and more dangerous.

Why Bullies Bully

There are many theories about why bullies bully. Some suggest that bullies have low self-esteem, are deeply insecure, have psychological problems,[15] have problems at home, want to be perceived as cool, are jealous of the victim, lack respect for others, are annoyed by the victim, are also victims, are lonely and lack friends, or are under peer pressure to bully. Miller (2012) writes:

> Because of the social power of the norm, any deviation away from it might agitate social and relational aggression. When a person cannot be readily understood or identified, there may be a psychological need to minimize, hurt, or make the person disappear altogether. Bullies are attuned to these differences because of their own inadequacies, shortcomings, or personalized experiences. (p. 107)

Cyber-digital bullying[16] adds another dimension to why bullies bully, because it can allow for anonymity and an infinite audience to observe the bullying act (Shariff, 2005). Cyber-digital bullies are attuned to the fact that their victims are less likely to seek help because it heightens public humiliation. In such cases of cyber-digital bullying, sexual harassment tends to be more prevalent, because it enables students who are not comfortable enough to express their sexuality in healthier ways to hide behind technology. Cyber-digital bullies may be drawn to the thrill, release, or sensation of deviance for these reasons, and because of the immediate impact their bullying can have on a victim.

Perhaps a more systemic explanation for bullying is the tolerance of educational climates that, in fact, create and sanction inequities and that privilege and reinforce the binaries of normal/abnormal, inclusion/exclusion, superior/inferior, and desirable/undesirable in the minds of both adults and children. Such pairings are often reinforced top-down through administrative policies that are non-inclusive, and they polarize students (and even teachers) into oppositional identity groups. Bullying becomes acceptable and even predictable when the environment privileges exhibitions of heteronormativity, gender conformity, White-racialized discourses, and able-istic attitudes over parallel exhibitions of alternate identities by students who are LGBTQ, gender non-conforming, non-White, and non-able-bodied. Taking a closer look at the system that reproduces such inequities is vital to discouraging bullying behaviors. The system that reproduces such inequities, however, tends to create a dangerous cycle of bullying that manifests in schools.

Cycle of Bullying[17]

The Olweus Bullying Prevention Program suggests that most students participate in a cycle of bullying. *Students who bully* are those who bully, initiate bullying, and take the lead role in bullying acts. *Followers*, or *henchmen*, are those who support bullying and take an active part without planning or leading bullying acts. *Supporters*, or *passive bullies*, openly support bullying and may call attention to it. *Passive supporters*, or *possible bullies*, consider bullying but do not actively participate in it. Thinking bullying is none of their business, *disengaged onlookers* do not get involved or take a stand. *Possible defenders* dislike bullying and want to help but do not act, while *defenders* dislike bullying and come to the defense of the victim.

Figure 2: The Olweus Bullying Prevention Program

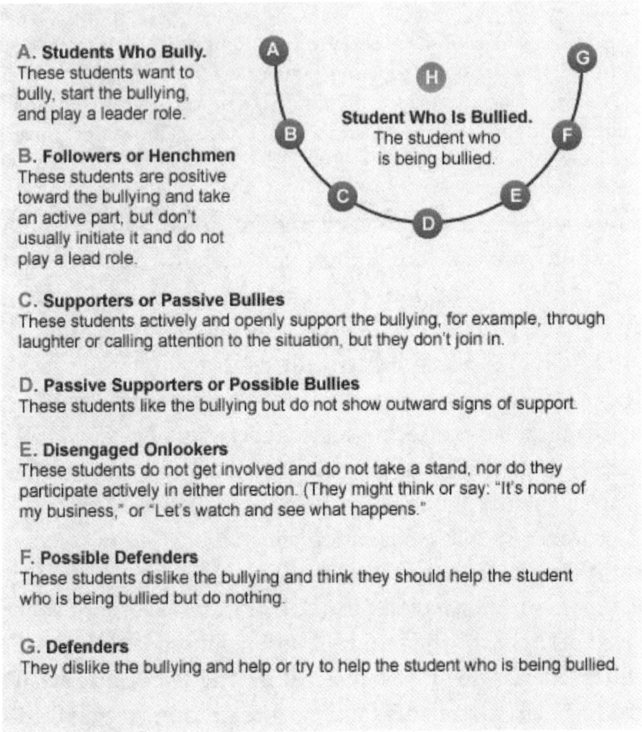

A. Students Who Bully.
These students want to bully, start the bullying, and play a leader role.

B. Followers or Henchmen
These students are positive toward the bullying and take an active part, but don't usually initiate it and do not play a lead role.

C. Supporters or Passive Bullies
These students actively and openly support the bullying, for example, through laughter or calling attention to the situation, but they don't join in.

D. Passive Supporters or Possible Bullies
These students like the bullying but do not show outward signs of support.

E. Disengaged Onlookers
These students do not get involved and do not take a stand, nor do they participate actively in either direction. (They might think or say: "It's none of my business," or "Let's watch and see what happens."

F. Possible Defenders
These students dislike the bullying and think they should help the student who is being bullied but do nothing.

G. Defenders
They dislike the bullying and help or try to help the student who is being bullied.

Student Who Is Bullied.
The student who is being bullied.

Note: The figure describes students involved in or witnessing a bullying situation as having roles in the Bullying Cycle.[18] One in five students in an average classroom is experiencing bullying in some way. The rest of the students, called bystanders, are also affected by the bullying. Source: Salmivalli, Lagerspetz, Bjorkqvist, Osterman, & Kaukianinen, 1996; adapted and reprinted with permission of The Guilford Press.

Understanding this cycle not only helps us to recognize how students may participate in it, but also serves as a tool to disrupt their own or others' participation in it. As you read the following chapters, consider the roles of the various individuals who are discussed, and how they did or didn't choose to intervene in bullying. Consider whether the bullying could have been prevented had a national anti-bullying policy been in place.

Shifting the Cycle and Domains of Bullying for Student Safety

No national legislation currently addresses harassment in any comprehensive way or prohibits bullying in schools. Taking this issue head-on, the National Safe Schools Partnership (NSSP), an informal coalition representing over 30 leading national education, health, civil rights, law enforcement, youth development, and other organizations committed to ensuring that America's schools are safe for all children, made a decision to push anti-bullying into the federal policy arena. It joined forces with GLSEN (the Gay, Lesbian & Straight Education Network), which had completed comprehensive studies on harassment of GLBTQ youth. Now on board with these political watchdog groups is the Office of Safe and Drug-Free Schools (OSDFS),[19] which administers, coordinates, and recommends policies for improving the quality of programs and activities that include violence prevention activities and promote the health and well being of students in elementary, secondary, and higher education school sites.[20] The OSDFS is trying to broaden the definition of bullying, because doing so would create a more inclusive frame and identify any type of peer-to-peer bullying and harassment as a form of violence. If the definition of violence in schools were to be codified to include bullying and harassment, such action could impact anti-bullying legislation for the improvement of schools.

While there have been attempts to include the prevention of bullying in schools, those attempts have frequently failed, languished, or died in legislative committee processes. As far back as the 108th Congress in 2003–2004, a proposed amendment to the Safe and Drug-Free Schools and Communities Act to include bullying and harassment prevention for all schools was first introduced to (1) include bullying and harassment under the definition of violence, and (2) provide for programs to address and prevent bullying and harassment.[21] The same act was introduced again but died in committee in the 109th, 110th, and 111th Congresses. It is currently being considered in the 112th Congress under H.R. 975, otherwise known as the Anti-Bullying and Harassment Act of 2011. While the act has yet to be codified, there has been some headway with Section 2: Bullying and Harassment Prevention Policies, Programs and Statistics of the act. On March 9, 2011, Section 2 was amended to include this definition of harassment:

> the term "harassment" means conduct, including conduct that is based on a student's actual or perceived identity with regard to race, color, national origin, gender, disability, sexual orientation, religion, or any other distinguishing characteristics that may be defined by a State or local educational agency, that…(a) is directed at one or more students; (b) substantially interferes with educational opportunities or educational programs of such students; and (c) adversely affects the ability of a student to participate in or benefit from the school's educational programs or activities because the conduct as reasonably perceived by the student is so severe, or pervasive.[22]

The bill would require states to collect and report information on the incidence of bullying and harassment, and to notify parents and students annually of conduct prohibited under their school discipline policies, including bullying and harassment. It would also establish formal procedures for students and parents to register complaints. Sadly, there is only a 2% expectation that the bill will pass (H.R. 975: Anti-Bullying and Harassment Act of 2011).

Concurrent to the introduction of this bill is the proposed amendment to H.R. 1648—the Safe Schools Improvement Act of 2011 to the Elementary and Secondary Education Act of 1965. The amendment would address and prevent bullying and harassment of students. These bills, however, are still in the early stages of the legislative process and face a long series of deliberations, investigations, revisions, and negotiations before they are even released by their relevant committees for broad debate and voting by our legislative representatives. The majority of bills and resolutions related to bullying and harassment often never make it out of committee. This can be attributed to the prominence of sexual orientation as a concern of activists from the religious right who view "the protection of gay and gay-perceived children as a component of the homosexual agenda" (Draper, 2010). Higdon (2010) admonishes that current anti-bullying legislation is problematic because it "focus[es] almost exclusively on how schools should respond to bullying without paying sufficient attention to how schools can help prevent bullying" (p. 47). Bloom (2007) contributes to this critique by adding that "school officials' failure to prevent harm to a student is not alone a violation of due process rights" (pp. 18–19); school personnel are only potentially accountable if and after they are notified and fail to stop the bullying. They are not responsible for preventing bullying in the first place.

There is obviously much work to be done to establish clear and comprehensive laws that prohibit bullying and ignorance of bullying. It will take much more than changing the minds of those who oppose even today's typically insufficient anti-bullying programs. Perhaps if enough citizens take up the cause and draw more attention to this national crisis, these bills will become law—next time.

Failure to Act Perpetuates Hate

While bullying may appear to impact only the targeted individual, that notion is a myth. Bullying can cause long-term, pervasive, and even life-altering trauma to the bullied, and a community of individuals incur the ripple effect of that incident. This community can include, but is not limited to, parents, siblings, friends, relatives, bystanders, teachers, and yes, even the bullies themselves. According to the DSM IV and the soon-to-be-released DSM V, the bullied (and in some cases the bystanders) experience lifelong *complex post-traumatic stress disorder* (C-PTSD) due to repeated exposure to traumatic life events that cause emotional, psychological, and even physical suffering.

C-PTSD, which can develop at any age, sometimes manifests immediately after exposure to bullying; for some, it may appear as long as 6 months later. Unfortunately, without treatment and therapy it can last a lifetime, and it may manifest in myriad ways. While the ultimate causes of C-PTSD are unknown, a person's psychological, genetic, physical, and social makeup contributes to his/her response to trauma. Exposure to stressful trauma can change the body's response to stress, and it can affect the hormones and chemicals that carry information between the nerves or the neurotransmitters.[23]

Victims of bullying may experience C-PTSD in several ways: (1) repeated reliving of the event(s), (2) avoidance, or (3) arousal. Victims may *relive bullying events* by having frightening dreams and nightmares; they may experience flashbacks or develop school-related anxiety or school-based phobia; or they may avoid places at school or specific locations where the bullying transpired. Victims also experience *avoidance* that manifests by numbing out at school, detaching socially, avoiding school-related activities, staying away from places, people, or objects that remind them of the bullying, and sensing that they have no future. *Arousal* manifests as difficulty concentrating at school, exaggerated responses to events that may startle a person, negative behavior in terms of excessive awareness of one's surroundings, irritability, outbursts of anger, and/or sleeping difficulties.

Bullying is not experienced as a fleeting moment in time or an isolated incident. Rather, its consequences are embedded in the victims' lived memories. They wait patiently, like mental tripwires to stumble across on the paths to maturity and adulthood, and they can have terrible and even deadly consequences once they are triggered. Even if their initial shock subsides, these traps can re-set and spring time and again in subtle and often unpredictable or uncontrollable ways. Bullying, even though it may happen to an individual just once, can cause lifelong trauma and leave ugly scars. It is simplistic and foolish to think or believe otherwise.

Looking Ahead to Bullying Reform

Where do we as society place blame for Columbine and other events involving bullying and bullycide? Do we fault the government or the state for lacking clear anti-bullying policies? Do we fault the school for not identifying bullies and condoning bullying behavior? Do we fault parents for failing to notice or to interrupt their children's behaviors or victimization? Regardless of the answers, the questions point to the systemic nature of the issue at hand. Bullying is a systems-level issue and must be approached broadly with all constituents in mind.

This is our vision. We believe that what we describe and recommend in this book is reasonable and attainable. We believe that any stance on bullying must be seamless and tied to law, education, and preventive health care. We offer some initial suggestions for your consideration as you read the following chapters. Bullying could be extinct, we speculate, if the following suggestions were implemented.

1. Legislatively preclude it by putting in place a systems-based anti-bullying program in every school in the country.

2. Implement an anti-bullying curriculum in which students take anti-bullying classes every year during their pre-K–16 preparation.

3. Have a federally appointed official serve as a "minister of anti-bullying" who studies and reviews successful models of anti-bullying programs for use in local systems (based on models such as those found in the United Kingdom[24] and Sweden[25]).

4. Fund anti-bullying programs at the federal level and reward states and schools that show reductions in bullying.

5. Tie anti-bullying to preventive mental health and health-care screenings so that prevention/intervention becomes a standard aspect of our citizenry's annual checkups.

We will return to these suggestions in Chapter 9.

Bullying is an issue of social justice. We believe all students should be free to study, learn, thrive, and grow in school environments that foster their intellectual, physical, emotional, mental, and spiritual health with regard to promoting respect across multiple social categories such as race, gender, gender expression, sexual orientation, ethnicity, language, national origin, spiritual belief, class, socioeconomic status, size, height and/or weight, disability, and ability (Conference on English Education Commission on Social Justice, 2009). We believe that every student deserves to be supported and should have enhanced (not limited) opportunities for life, liberty, and the pursuit of happiness. Schooling should be about learning, not survival. The fact that our current president added gender, sexual orientation, gender identity, and disability to the Federal Hate Crimes Bill on October 8, 2009, validates the idea that we *do* have the political ability to legislate anti-bullying policies. Now we just need the widespread political *will*. As you read this book, jot down your thoughts, reflect on your experiences, send us your feelings, and share your responses, suggestions, and support for this long-overdue change. We believe it is our duty as citizens of this country to take care of our students now and in the future. Our youth are not expendable.

Notes

1 Goth refers to a subculture that honors and celebrates nihilistic ideas and language, and assumes poses of purposeful depression, apathy, cynicism, and rebellion against "normal" ways of being. Many goths wear black clothes and inverted religious symbols.

2 *Doom* was a landmark video game that was invented in 1993. It popularized the first-person shooter genre, with 3D graphics, networked multiplayer gaming, and support for customized additions and modifications. The game was known for its graphic and interactive violence, as well as satanic imagery. *Wolfenstein 3D* also popularized the first-person shooter genre and focused on an American soldier who was held hostage by Nazis and had to shoot and fight his way out of captivity.

3 Up until the attacks of September 11, 2001, the Oklahoma City bombing was the most destructive act of terrorism ever on American soil. Timothy McVeigh's bombs took 168 lives, including 19 children under the age of 6, injured more than 680 people, and destroyed 324

buildings within a 16-block radius, destroyed or burned 86 cars, and shattered glass in 258 nearby buildings.

4 David Koresh preached polygamy, was sexually and physically abusing children, and was involved in illegal firearms distribution. During a 51-day standoff, deaths on the ranch occurred during the raids of the Bureau of Alcohol, Tobacco and Firearms and negotiations with the Federal Bureau of Investigation. David Koresh was responsible for a fire that killed 76 people, including more than 20 children, 2 pregnant women, and himself.

5 It is pure speculation that either killer was gay.

6 *Tyler Clemente* was an 18-year-old freshman male at Rutgers University who was illegally videotaped having sexual relations with another man by his roommate, who streamed the video live. He jumped from the George Washington Bridge and killed himself. *Sladjana Vidovic*, a 16-year-old female from Croatia, was bullied for her accent and taunted daily in her Cleveland, Ohio, high school. She hung herself by jumping out of her bedroom window. *Hamed Nastoh*, a 14-year-old Armenian living in British Columbia, was harassed daily for being gay. He killed himself by jumping from a bridge. *Aiden Rivera Shaeff* was a 17-year-old female-to-male living in Bethesda, Maryland, who took his life because he was taunted daily for being transgender. *Jaheem Herrera*, an 11-year-old, fifth-grade male from the Virgin Islands living in DeKalb County, Georgia, hung himself in his bedroom closet with his own belt because he could not face the bullies who taunted him daily at school over his ethnicity and perceived sexuality.

7 Here we use the acronym LGBTQ because it reflects the nomenclature used by right-wing groups.

8 For more information about which right-wing groups financially back government funding, see http://www.rightwingwatch.org/category/groups/citizenlink

9 To review the entire report, see *Student Reports of Bullying and Cyber-Bullying: Reports from the 2007 School Crime Supplement to the National Crime Victimization Study*, http://nces.ed.gov/pubs2011/2011316.pdf#page=1

10 Bully Police USA. Retrieved May 8, 2011, from http://www.bullypolice.org/

11 We recognize that intersexed students are left out of the continuum of statistics but that they are also bullied.

12 There is a clear absence of statistics from elementary schools relating to LGBT and non-LGBT issues. This could stem from the difficulties that arise from the Institutional Review Board or from districts that restrict access to elementary classroom research. GLSEN recently published a groundbreaking study of bias, bullying, and homophobia in grades K–6 (GLSEN & Harris Interactive, 2012).

13 GLSEN'S study also found that bullying or harassment varies by the type of school the students attend. Public school students are more likely than others to consider bullying or harassment to be a serious problem at their school (38% vs. 14%); public school students are less likely than private or parochial school students to feel very safe at their school (44% vs. 81%); and public school students are more likely than private or parochial school students to report that harassment based on sexual orientation frequently occurs (34% vs. 18%). However, private school students are much less likely to know a student in their school who identifies as LGBTQ (36% vs. 57%), to have a close friend who is LGBTQ (10% vs. 20%), or to identify as LGBTQ themselves (2% vs. 6%).

14 The underreporting of bullying by students of color is problematic, as is the lack of effectiveness over interventions. The lack of reporting might have to do with saving face in particular communities and may lead to taking matters into one's own hands. This area warrants further attention.

15 Some psychological problems that can lead to bullying include anxiety, depression, suicidal ideation, and antisocial personality disorder.

16 Although the official term is cyber-bullying, we will refer to this modality for bullying as cyber-digital because it provides for a range of technologically based bullying that can include new forms of technology as they emerge. We use the term cyber-bullying when it is referenced in the literature and cyber-digital when it is our work.

17 Retrieved July 5, 2011, from http://www.olweus.org/public/bullying

18 Olweus, D. (2001). Peer harassment: A critical analysis and some important issues. In J. Juvenon and S. Graham, *Peer Harassment in School* (pp. 3–20). New York: Guilford.

19 Kevin Jennings was the OSDFS Assistant Deputy Secretary from 2009 to 2011 and had risen to this position after a 10-year-plus tenure as GLSEN's founder and executive director.

20 Ed.Gov. Retrieved May 9, 2011, from http://www2.ed.gov/about/offices/list/osdfs/index.html

21 GovTrack.us. Retrieved May 8, 2011, from http://www.govtrack.us/congress/bill.xpd?bill=h108-4776&tab=summary

22 GovTrack.us. Retrieved May 8, 2011, from http://www.govtrack.us/congress/billtext.xpd?bill=h112-975

23 Public Med Health. *Post-traumatic stress disorder.* Retrieved May 18, 2011, from http://www.ncbi.nlm.nih.gov/pubmedhealth/PMH0001923/

24 Schools in England are legally required to have an anti-bullying policy, as stated in the Education and Inspections Act (EIA) of 2006 (Smith et al., 2008).

25 Schools in Sweden are required by law to have an anti-bullying policy (Frisen et al., 2007).

References

American Psychiatric Association. (2000). *Diagnostic and statistical manual of mental disorders* (4th ed., text rev.). Washington, DC: Author.

Bloom, L. (2007). School bullying in Connecticut: Can the statehouse and the courtroom fix the schoolhouse? An analysis of Connecticut's anti-bullying statute. *Public Interest Law Journal, 7*(1), 105–135.

Conference on English Education Commission on Social Justice. (2009). *CEE position statement: Beliefs about social justice in English education. First Biennial CEE Conference.* Chicago: CEE.

Crary, D. (2010, March 3). Columbine school shooting spawned effective anti-bullying programs. *Huffington Post.* Retrieved January 17, 2013, from http://www.huffingtonpost.com/2010/03/03/columbine-school-shooting_n_484700.html

Draper, E. (2010, August 29). Focus points to bully pulpit. *Denver Post,* p. B-01.

Frisen, A., Jonsson, A.-K., & Persson, C. (2007). Adolescents' perceptions of bullying: Who is the victim? Who is the bully? What can be done to stop bullying? *Adolescence, 42*(168), 749–761.

Gibbs, N., & Roche, T. (1999, December). The Columbine tapes. *Time,* pp. 40–51.

GLSEN & Harris Interactive (2012). *Playgrounds and prejudice: Elementary school climate in the United States. A survey of students and teachers.* New York: GLSEN.

Greytak, E., Kosciw, J., & Diaz, E. (2009). *Harsh realities: The experiences of transgender youth in our schools.* New York: GLSEN.

Harris, S., & Isernhagen, J. (2003, November). Keeping bullies at bay. *American School Board Journal,* pp. 43–45.

Higdon, M.J. (2010). To lynch a child: Bullying and gender non-conformity in our nation's schools. University of Tennessee Legal Studies Research Paper No. 102. Available at SSRN: http://ssrn.com/abstract=1558135

H.R. 975: Anti-Bullying and Harassment Act of 2011. (2011). Retrieved November 8, 2012, from http://www.govtrack.us/congress/bills/112/hr975

Jimerson, S.R., Swearer, S.M., & Espelage, D.L. (Eds.). (2010). *The international handbook of school bullying.* Mahwah, NJ: Lawrence Erlbaum.

Kosciw, J., & Diaz, E. (2006). *The 2005 national school climate survey: The experiences of lesbian, gay, bisexual and transgender youth in our nation's schools.* New York: GLSEN.

Kosciw, J., Greytak, E., & Diaz, E. (2008). *The 2007 national school climate survey: The experiences of lesbian, gay, bisexual and transgender youth in our nation's schools.* New York: GLSEN.

Kosciw, J., Greytak, E., Diaz, E., & Bartkiewicz, M. (2010). *The 2009 National School Climate Survey: The experiences of lesbian, gay, bisexual and transgender youth in our nation's schools.* New York: GLSEN.

Kosciw, J.G., Greytak, E.A., Bartkiewicz, M.J., Boesen, M.J., & Palmer, N.A. (2012). *The 2011 national school climate survey: The experiences of lesbian, gay, bisexual and transgender youth in our nation's schools.* New York: GLSEN.

Markow, D., & Fein, J. (2005). *From teasing to torment: School climate in America. A survey of students and teachers* (commissioned by the Gay, Lesbian & Straight Educational Network). New York: Harris Interactive.

Nansel, T.R., et al. (2001). Bullying behaviors among US youth: Prevalence and association with psychological adjustment. *Journal of the American Medical Association, 285*, 2094–2100.

National Center for Educational Statistics (2010). *Indicators of school crime and safety: 2010.* Retrieved August 11, 2011, from http://nces.ed.gov/programs/crimeindicators/crimeindicators2010/key.asp

National Center for Educational Statistics (2011). *Student reports of bullying and cyber-bullying: Reports from the 2007 school crime supplement to the national crime victimization study.* Retrieved August 11, 2011, from http://nces.ed.gov/pubs2011/2011316.pdf#page=1

Olweus, D. (1993). *Bullying at school: What we know and what we can do.* Mahwah, NJ: Blackwell.

Olweus, D. (2001). Peer harassment: A critical analysis and some important issues. In J. Juvenon & S. Graham (Eds.), *Peer harassment in school* (pp. 3–20). New York: Guilford Press.

Pepler, D., Craig, W., & Pardy, R. (2002). Understanding the development of children's and adolescents' aggression. Review paper submitted to Nestles Canada.

Public Med Health. *Post-traumatic stress disorder.* Retrieved May 18, 2011, from http://www.ncbi.nlm.nih.gov/pubmedhealth/PMH0001923/

Ringrose, J., & Renold, E. (2011). Boys, girls and normative violence in schools: A gendered critique of bully discourses. In C. Barter & D. Berridge (Eds.), *Children behaving badly? Peer violence between children and young people* (pp. 181–195). Chichester, UK: Wiley and Sons.

Rose, C.A., Espelage, D.L., Aragon, S.R., & Elliott, J. (2011). Bullying and victimization among students in special education and general education curricula. *Exceptionality Education International, 21*(3), 2–14.

Salmivalli, C., Lagerspetz, K., Bjorkqvist, K., Osterman, K., & Kaukianinen, A. (1996). Bullying as a group process: Participant roles and their relations to social status within the group. *Aggressive Behavior, 22*, 1–15.

Shariff, S. (2005). Cyber-dilemmas in the new millennium: School obligations to provide student safety in virtual school environment. *McGill Journal of Education, 40*(3), 457–477.

Sherer, Y.P., & Nickerson, A.B. (2010). Anti-bullying practices in American schools: Perspectives of school psychologists. *Psychology in the Schools, 47*(3), 217–229.

Smith, J.D., Schneider, B.H., Smith, P.K., & Ananiadou, K. (2004). The effectiveness of whole-school anti-bullying programs: A synthesis of evaluation research. *School Psychology Review, 33*, 548–561.

Smith, P.K., Smith, C., Osborn, R., & Samara, M. (2008). A content analysis of school anti-bullying policies: Progress and limitations. *Educational Psychology in Practice, 24*(1), 1–12.

Transgender Law and Policy Institute. (n.d.). *Transgender and gender non-conforming youth: Recommendations for schools.* Retrieved December 20, 2009, from http://www.transgenderlaw.org/resources/tlcschools.htm

U.S. Department of Education. Office for Civil Rights. (1999). *Protecting students from harassment and hate crime*. Jointly issued by the National School Boards Association, Washington, DC, and the National Association of Attorneys General.

Vreeman, R.C., & Carroll, A.E. (2007). A systematic review of school-based interventions to prevent bullying. *Archives of Pediatric and Adolescent Medicine, 161*, 78–88.

Wallace, J.A. (2011). Bullycide in American schools: Forging a comprehensive legislative solution. *Indiana Law Journal, 86*(735), 735–761.

CHAPTER TWO

The Distressing Realities About Queer-Related (LGBTQGV) Bullying

sj Miller and James R. Gilligan

Jamie Nabozny, a gay public high school student in Ashland, Wisconsin, was subjected to relentless anti-gay verbal and physical abuse by fellow classmates. They urinated on him, feigned raping him, and—when they discovered him alone—kicked him in the stomach so brutally that he required surgery. When school authorities were notified of the taunts and injuries, officials said that Nabozny should have expected it simply by virtue of being homosexual. Nabozny internalized his suffering and attempted suicide many times, dropped out of school, and ultimately ran away. His family later sued the school, but a trial court dismissed the lawsuit.

In 1996, Lambda Legal, an LGBT legal advocacy group, took the case, *Nabozny v. Podlesny*, to a federal appeals court, which—for the first time in U.S. history—ruled that public schools can be held accountable for ignoring, tolerating, and/or failing to prevent or stop the abuse of homosexuals. While the case marked the first time Title IX was applied to support an openly gay student, the ruling was decided on facts related to sex-stereotyping and differential treatment of male and female students (the mock rape in particular) and not protections based on sexual orientation. When the case went to trial, a jury found school officials liable for the harm they caused Nabozny. The case was settled for close to $1 million and resulted in mandates that public schools, administrators, counselors, and teachers report anti-gay abuse or face liability for not doing so.

We live in a country that is as divided politically as it is geographically, racially, economically, religiously, culturally, and linguistically, and changes in policy do not guarantee compliance, nor do they generally change people's minds. The Nabozny case highlights solutions our society can pursue to enforce protections and create real cultural changes: for example, the laws enacted by the federal government under its new hate crimes legislation. Yet we still face the challenge of helping that change to trickle down into classrooms. The Nabozny ruling and other legal cases like it can only go so far.[1]

Although the Nabozny ruling was a landmark victory and the first successful legal challenge to anti-gay violence in public schools, it did not guarantee that bullying behavior would stop, even when reported directly to a teacher or administrator. In the absence of a federal anti-bullying policy, some people still believe that they can get away with bullying behavior or with ignoring such behavior and even expecting it as a matter of course. In addition, because of the polarizing representations of LGBTQGV issues in the media, some students often feel that they deserve to be vilified by bullies (Wallace, 2011, p. 754). A comprehensive anti-bullying policy at the state and/or national level could hold schools, teachers, administrators, parents, and students accountable, regardless of their beliefs about homosexuality. Such legislation could require them to intervene when an LGBTQGV student is bullied, even in cases where the intervening authority does not agree with homosexuality as a socially acceptable identity.

We need zero tolerance for bullying against *all* students and a comprehensive federal anti-bullying policy that identifies bullying based on sexual orientation and gender identity. Bullied students often take their own lives, and the longer we wait to implement such a policy, the more lives we will lose. What would our country look like if LGBTQGV students were protected by federal law? What would our country look like if this generation of youth came to believe that their mental, social, and emotional well-being mattered for *everyone*? While *Nabozny v. Podlesny* (1996) does provide a legal precedent for protecting LGBTQGV students from harassment in schools, a law or an act does not guarantee compliance, nor does it have the power or outright ability to fully change people's minds…or to stop them from bullying.

Possible Origins of Queer (LGBTQGV) Bullying

Throughout history, homosexuality has often been considered deviant by different societies and cultures at different times. Although homosexual acts were sometimes tolerated or ignored by society, in the second half of the 12th century hostility toward homosexuality began to develop throughout European religious and secular institutions. Homosexual behavior (and other non-procreative sexual behavior) was viewed as "unnatural" and—in some cases—was even punishable by death. Contemporary homophobia is affirmed by military groups, religious institutions, state and federal laws, psychiatry, and physical medical practices.[2] We might, then, deduce that these beliefs were supported as the dominant narratives activating heteronormative and masculine images within our nation's hegemonic culture—a conceptualization of heterosexuality as "common sense" that is supported by the recent history of heightened queer bullying.

In the late 19th century, medical and psychiatric discourses on homosexuality shifted from the domain of religious sin to legal crime to psychological and medical pathology (see, for example, Chauncey, 1982/1983; D'Emilio & Freedman, 1988; Duberman, Vicinus, & Chauncey, 1989). In 1952, homosexuality was officially pathologized in the first edition of the *Diagnostic and Statistical Manual of Mental Disorders* (DSM I). Fortunately, in the early 20th century, Sigmund Freud and Havelock Ellis adopted tolerant stances toward homosexuality, which resulted in significant strides toward de-pathologizing it as a mental illness. Ellis (1901) argued that homosexuality was inborn and therefore not immoral, asserted that it was not a disease, and demonstrated that many homosexuals made outstanding positive contributions to society. Freud believed that all human beings were innately bisexual and only became heterosexual or homosexual as a result of their experiences with parents and others through nurturing and environmental conditions. While their claims were contested by other psychoanalysts over the next several decades, the work of Alfred Kinsey and his colleagues in the 1950s ultimately supported the hypothesis that homosexuality, same-gender sexual behavior, and same-sex fantasy were far more prominent in society than many people otherwise wished to believe, and Evelyn Hooker's research during the same period suggested that homosexuality was not associated with psychopathology. Estelle Freedman's research with lesbians in the early 1970s corroborated Kinsey's and Hooker's findings. Because of the overwhelming empirical evidence and changing social opinions about homosexuality that emerged over the course of the 20th century, psychiatrists and psychologists have radically altered their views. In 1973, their research led to the removal of homosexuality from the DSM II,[3] which meant that it was no longer considered a mental illness.

In 1980, transgender people who had undertaken genital reassignment surgery, otherwise known as transsexuals, were first pathologized as mentally ill in the DSM III.[4] Those who were transsexual were considered to have "Gender Identity Disorder" (GID), which is described in the DSM III. In 1994, the DSM IV entry for people who identified as transgender changed officially from "Transsexualism" to "Gender Identity Disorder," thus assigning a set of pathologies to those who did not identify with their biological sex.

Since 2006, the debate about depathologizing GID as a mental illness altogether has continued. Some transgender people benefit from the diagnosis because it qualifies them for some mental health care benefits. Allowing GID to remain in the DSM IV, however, is damaging because it perpetuates the stigma that transgender people are mentally ill. A decision is still pending, and the new manual is due out in May 2013.[5] The history of LGBTQGV people and their institutionalization as mentally deviant and even "sick" can be easily linked to the bullying of such people in schools and society even today.

Gender Norms and Bullying

Other ways of understanding queer bullying are discussed in Young and Sweeting's (2004) research. Their findings suggest "an association between masculinity or 'maleness' and bullying behavior" (p. 527), and they argue that "boys are subject to stronger 'gender policing' than girls are" (p. 534). In addition, they reason, "the presumed association between gender-atypical behavior and sexual orientation may be particularly sensitive at a developmental stage when boys are keen to reinforce their masculinity and likely to shun less masculine peers for fear of being stigmatized themselves" (p. 527). Pascoe (2007) found that "heterosexist and homophobic discourses about masculinity permeated the educational process" at the high school where she conducted research (p. 39) and asserted that "homophobia is indeed a central mechanism in the making of contemporary American adolescent masculinity" (p. 53).

> A boy could get called a fag for exhibiting any sort of behavior defined as unmasculine…being stupid or incompetent, dancing, caring too much about clothing, being too emotional, or expressing interest (sexual or platonic) in other guys…. These nonsexual meanings didn't replace sexual meanings but rather existed alongside them. (Pascoe, 2007, p. 55)

Therefore, for some adolescents, the concept of *fag* or *queer* (in pejorative terms) becomes conflated with a lack of masculinity—or gender nonconformity. Queer bullying, then, constitutes a form of adolescent enforcement of heteronormativity fueled by heterosexism, "a systematic process of privileging heterosexuality relative to homosexuality, based on the assumption that heterosexuality and heterosexual power and privilege are normal and ideal" (Chesir-Teran & Hughes, 2009, p. 964).

Swearer and colleagues (2008) theorize that "attitudes toward gender nonconformity, particularly for boys, becomes a foundation for bullying and, ultimately in some tragic cases, for lethal school violence" (p. 162). They also identify consent implied by adult inaction or adult silence as factors that encourage such behavior.

> The lack of adult sanctions for homophobic name-calling may serve to support and maintain these behaviors. This tacit support on the part of adults may be an important factor in the development of attitudes that children have toward the acceptability of bullying behaviors. (pp. 162–163)

Swearer and her fellow researchers (2008) characterize queer bullying as "a culturally proscribed socialization process of restrictive masculinity" (p. 170). Similarly,

Tharinger (2008) links the cultural power of hegemonic masculinity to homophobia: "Homophobia works to make sure that both heterosexual and homosexual boys who do not conform to the requirements of hegemonic masculinity always have the potential to be subordinated within the social organization of masculinity" (p. 225).

The social climate in schools today is hardly free of the cultural power exerted by hegemonic notions of masculinity and its concomitant gender policing. As Graham (2011) explains, when bullying occurs in school settings, it is usually a communal event.

> Bullying incidents are often public events that have eyewitnesses. Studies…have found that in most bullying incidents, at least four other peers were present as either bystanders, assistants to bullies, reinforcers, or defenders of victims. Assistants take part in ridiculing or intimidating a schoolmate, and reinforcers encourage the bully by showing their approval. (Graham, 2011, p. 15)

Media as Mirror and Window to Queer Bullying

Birkett and Espelage (2009) consider the identity development of Lesbian/Gay/Bisexual/Transgender/Questioning/Gender Variant (in other words, gender-non-conforming)[6] (LGBTQGV) students as a factor that exacerbates or magnifies the effects of a non-supportive school environment.

> The stress of having to come to terms with their own sexuality in early adolescence while simultaneously negotiating their school environment's heterosexism and homophobia may place many LGB and questioning students at-risk for depression, suicidality, drug use, and school problems. (pp. 989–990)

Anti-gay comments and compulsory, heteronormative, and hegemonic discourses and expectations are (consciously and unconsciously) ubiquitously reinforced, woven into the fabric of society, and disseminated by multiple media forms. Television, film, video games, the Internet, music lyrics, sermons, political speeches, and classroom environments continue to exacerbate negative attitudes against LGBTQGV people and an impressionable younger generation who are vulnerable to internalizing discriminatory messages. When negative and inhumane attitudes toward LGBTQGV people are not challenged or are condoned by non-LGBTQGV adults, such messages suggest that queer bullying against these populations is not just tolerated—it's normalized.

The media, however, also help re-frame, represent, and disseminate positive strides made on behalf of the LGBTQGV community and those who identify themselves as members. Examples include an increased attention to same-sex marriage and domestic partnerships, President Barack Obama's 2012 endorsement of marriage equality, political races that are won by openly LBGTQ candidates, TV and movies positively depicting non-stereotypical LGBTQGV characters, and a growing number of out actors, musicians, athletes, and politicians. All of these help to provide positive images and an increasing acceptance and recognition of LGBTQGV people as a highly diverse group. Such "outness" provides positive examples of LGBTQGV individuals as normal people living productive lives in ways our society has never been given the chance to see or consider before. It also increases the likelihood that children in the next generation will experience such positive LGBTQGV representations as a normal part of their own worlds as they reach maturity and become leaders in our society.

Why turn to the media to examine the proliferation of bullying against LGBTQGV students? Consider a typical adolescent tuning in to multiple media outlets and experiencing a popular culture that offers nothing but heteronormatively prejudicial beliefs that are validated in those media by celebrities, public officials, and other people in powerful positions. Now consider the impact those ubiquitous representations can have on a young person, how they might play out in an LGBTQGV child's life in school, and how that child's apparent violation of accepted norms is likely to be met with discomfort, fear, confusion, and even (too often) hatred, anger, and resentment.

LGBTQGV people are mostly forced to operate in a social context wherein they may often see/hear/experience nothing but heteronormative messages about who they ought to be, how they should look, act, feel, think, talk, move, and so forth. That alone leads members of this group to operate out of fear to protect their feelings and identities. But at the same time we are seeing a shift (at least a slight one, but in many ways a dramatic one, given the 2012 elections, for example) wherein media outlets are representing LGBTQGV people in new ways—often very positive ways, and even in ways that make their identity a secondary, tertiary, or even non-existent issue. But because gender typing and heteronormativity are still dominant, members of this group face huge threats to their ways of thinking, feeling, and being in the world while non-members, who do not access the positive media representations (or who reject—and are taught to reject—those representations), are going to school with them. That leaves LGBTQGV students extremely vulnerable and likely to feel under siege much of the time, and it also leaves the door open for others to bully them because they are different. This ever-present and pervasive media split between representations of heteronormativity and positive portrayals of LGBTQGV people leaves no doubt about why we lack consensus regarding federal anti-LGBTQGV legislation that censures bullying.

The Distressing Realities About Queer (LGBTQGV)-Related Bullying

Although queer bullying is one of the more prevalent sources of distress for LGBTQGV youth, "bullying with content based on gender nonconformity is not exclusively targeted at youth who are gay, lesbian, bisexual, or transgender[ed]"

(Swearer et al., 2008, p. 162). Many victims of bullying are often targeted because of "non-normative gender behavior" (Conoley, 2008, p. 217).

While most non-LGBTQ students experience some type of bullying, it is often less persistent, invasive, and damaging compared to the daily bullying endured by LGBTQGV/gender non-conforming youth. We use the terms *gender-variant* and *gender non-conforming* to refer to students who express their gender in ways that may appear incongruous with the general style/dress, attitudes, social mores, and expected norms often associated with the traditional binary of male/female.

Findings from the Gay, Lesbian & Straight Educators Network (GLSEN) highlight the most comprehensive statistics related to LGBTQGV bullying. Viewed together, *Shared Differences: The Experiences of Lesbian, Gay, Bisexual, and Transgender Students of Color in Our Nation's Schools* (2007), *Harsh Realities: The Experiences of Transgender Youth in Our Schools* (2009), and *The 2009 National School Climate Survey* reveal that LGBTQGV students are two to five times more likely to attempt suicide than heterosexual students. In addition, a spate of recent research studies—all quantitative—has identified numerous factors that contribute to the elevated risk of violence and suicide for LGBTQ youth.

> GLBT youth are nearly three times as likely as their heterosexual peers to have been assaulted or involved in at least one physical fight in school, are three times as likely to have been threatened or injured with a weapon at school, and are nearly four times as likely to have skipped school because they felt unsafe. (Swearer et al., 2008, p. 161)

Hatzenbuehler (2011) characterized research aimed at preventing the incidence of suicide among queer youth as "a critical area for public health" (p. 897) and found that "living in environments that are less supportive of gays and lesbians is associated with greater suicide attempts among LGB youth" (p. 900). Citing recent research conducted in Austria, Plöderl and Fartacek (2009) mention that "all measures of previous suicidality (suicide ideation, serious suicide ideation, aborted suicide attempts, suicide attempts) were elevated for LGB compared to heterosexual participants. The same applied for current suicide ideation and a summary measure of current suicidality" (p. 408). Chesir-Teran and Hughes (2009) found that for many students "personal experiences of victimization were related to the perceived prevalence and tolerance of anti-LGBQ harassment in schools" (p. 971). They also noted that the culture of the school, as measured by the "perceived inclusiveness of programs (but not perceptions of non-discrimination and harassment policies) influenced victimization rates both indirectly (via perceived harassment) and directly (even after controlling for perceived harassment)" (p. 971). As Hatzenbuehler did, Russell and colleagues (2011) contextualize their research on school bullying as "a widespread public health problem" (p. 227). They acknowledge that "school victimization of LGBT students and those who are perceived to be gay or gender nonconforming has been reported for decades"

(p. 227), and they conclude that "students who identify or are perceived to be LGB are at dramatically higher risk for a wide range of health and mental health concerns, including sexual health risk, substance abuse, and suicide, compared with their heterosexual peers" (p. 228).

Statistics also show that nearly nine out of ten LGBTQGV students experience harassment during school. According to Kosciw and his fellow researchers (2010), 84.6% of LGBGV students reported being verbally harassed, 40.1% reported being physically harassed, and 18.8% reported being physically assaulted at school in 2009 because of their sexual orientation. Transgender students specifically reported an even higher rate of verbal harassment than did LGBGV students, with almost 100% experiencing harassment. Over 50% reported being physically harassed, while 25% reported being physically assaulted in the same period because of their sexual orientation or gender expression. Transgender students absorbed more bullying than any other population of students overall.

Relational bullying statistics from the same study show that 88.2% of LGBGV students felt deliberately excluded or "left out" by other students at least sometimes because of their identities, and 46.0% experienced such exclusion often or frequently. A total of 84% had their reputations smeared through rumors or lies told about them during school, and 40.3% experienced this often or frequently (Kosciw et al., 2010). Consonant with the findings that transgender students experience higher percentages of both physical and verbal levels of harassment, it has been documented that they also experienced higher percentages of relational bullying. Nine in ten transgender students experienced some sort of relational aggression, 89% reported being the target of rumors or lies, and 92% felt deliberately excluded or "left out" by other students. Transgender students also experienced a higher degree of material bullying, with 67% reporting that their property (such as cars, clothing, or books) was stolen or deliberately damaged at school, compared to 49.7% of LGBGV students. Sixty-two percent of transgender students reported that they experienced some sort of cyber-digital bullying, compared to 52.9% of LGBGV, who reported experiencing a form of cyber-digital bullying (Kosciw et al., 2010).

When we examine the lived experiences specifically of transgender students in school, the statistics are equally alarming. Sixty-nine percent of transgender students, or roughly seven in ten, felt unsafe in school because of their sexual orientation, and 65% felt unsafe because of how they expressed their gender. Fifty-four percent of transgender students who were victimized in school did not report the events to school authorities. Among those who did, few students (33%) believed that staff addressed the situation effectively. Sixty-one percent reported feeling unsafe at school because of their sexual orientation and reported avoiding places like school bathrooms and locker rooms because they felt unsafe or uncomfortable in those spaces (Kosciw et al., 2010). Across all ethnic groups, sexual orientation and gender expression were the most common reasons LGBTGV students of color reported feeling unsafe in school.

For both groups, school safety was directly related to high rates of absenteeism and lower grade point averages (GPAs) among them, and was found to affect their plans to attend college or continue their education beyond high school. For transgender students, almost half (47%) reported skipping a class at least once in the previous month, and 46% reported missing at least one day because they felt threatened. Transgender students who experienced high levels of harassment were more likely than other transgender students to miss school for safety reasons (Kosciw et al., 2010). For LGB students, 29.1% reported missing a class at least once, and 30.0% missed at least one day of school in the previous month because of safety concerns. Transgender students who missed school because of harassment had significantly lower GPAs than those who experienced lower levels of harassment. Students who experienced verbal harassment based on sexual orientation earned GPAs at an average of 0.8 lower than their non-bullied peers (nearly a full letter grade), while those harassed for gender expression averaged a loss of 0.5 (or half a letter grade). The reported GPAs of students who were more frequently harassed dropped when they reported severe or frequent harassment based on sexual orientation and/or race/ethnicity. Students experiencing severe or frequent harassment also reported missing school more often.

Teachers' responses to bullying—whether active ignorance, complicity, tolerance, or active participation—significantly contributed to LBGTQGV students' sense of school safety. Fifty-nine percent of transgender students heard teachers or other staff make negative comments about a student's gender expression, and 33% heard school staff make homophobic, sexist, or otherwise negative remarks about someone's gender expression either sometimes, often, or frequently in the previous year. In fact, less than a fifth (16%) of transgender students said that school staff intervened either most of the time or always after witnessing criticism of a student's gender expression (Kosciw et al., 2010). Sadly, 47% of the time teachers and other school staff did not intervene at all. Among other student identity groups, 60.4% reported hearing homophobic remarks from teachers or other school staff, and 41.4% of the time teachers and staff did not intervene when witnessing bullying of students based on sexuality or gender presentation.

GLSEN's studies also reported that public school students are more likely than private or parochial school students to report frequent harassment based on sexual orientation (34% vs. 18%). However, private school students are much less likely to know a student in their school who identifies as LGBTQGV (36 % vs. 57%). Private and parochial school students were also less likely to have a close friend who is LGBTQGV (10% vs. 20%) or to identify as LGBTQGV themselves (2% vs. 6%) (Kosciw et al., 2010). It is possible that these differences are related to the open-admissions nature of public schools in contrast to the more restrictive, selective, or exclusive admissions criteria used by private schools.

Microaggressions as Bullying

Many microaggressions relating to LGBTQGV students stem from the structural environment that surrounds and supports a heteronormative and cisgendered[7] school climate (Miller, 2012). As discussed in the introduction to this book, microaggressions are "the everyday verbal, nonverbal, and environmental slights, snubs or insults, whether intentional or unintentional, that communicate hostile, derogatory, or negative messages to target persons based solely upon their marginalized group membership" (Sue, 2010, p. 3). These microaggressions are symptomatic of how the patterned absences or gaps in information expressed via school policies, curriculum, discourse, and lack of social services for LGBTQGV students occur as a normative aspect of the social fabric and social processes that comprise school environments. In fact, these unnamed and/or unidentified or unrecognized norms constitute a hidden curriculum that teaches and positions both students and professionals to behave in ways that at least implicitly enable bullying. Such norms and policies that neglect inclusivity enable microaggressions to sustain homophobic and heteronormative practices.

LGBTQGV students who enter normalized school environments where they are automatically marked as abnormal are forced into a learned detachment and toleration of microaggressions specific to their lived experiences. Here we distinguish the T and GV from the LGB, because some microaggressions apply to only one of the two groups. LGB microaggessions include:

- Being called derogatory names such as "gay," fag," "dyke," or "queer," whether for conscious or non-conscious reasons

- Being harassed, mocked, or publicly humiliated for holding hands or showing affection with a same-sex partner at school

- Hearing "that's so gay" in a classroom or on school grounds without intervention by authority figures, even when authority figures have clearly witnessed and recognized the behavior

- Exclusion of stories about or written by LGB people from classroom curricula, and/or failure to discuss LGB people in positive ways (or only in negative ways, and in some cases not at all)

- Absence of informational displays, resources, and representations related to LGB people and identities, or an imbalanced abundance of such materials about heterosexual people and identities

- Asking an LGB student to speak on behalf of all LGB students or people

- Absence of a gay-straight alliance organization in the school
- Self-advocacy as the only viable option for LGB students to gain support, safety, equality, or recourse
- Lack of systematically inclusive discourses about student identities in all school-level materials and communications
- Explicit statements against LGB identities and lifestyles, and/or sanctions for students who exhibit such identities and behaviors

Microaggressions specifically experienced by transgender and gender-variant youth include:

- Being stared at
- Being asked intrusive questions about their identities, behaviors, and/or practices
- Being referred to using inappropriate pronouns or names
- Lack of gender-neutral facilities such as bathrooms and locker rooms
- Being medicalized or pathologized by school personnel and/or other students
- Being sexually objectified by peers
- Being treated as strange, marginal, or awkward by peers and school personnel
- Being singled out based on physical characteristics
- Being treated as "invisible" or aberrant by peers and personnel who divert their eyes
- Failure to discuss transgender people in positive ways as part of school curricula (or only in negative ways, and in some cases not at all)
- Absence of informational displays, resources, and representations related to transgender people and identities, or an imbalanced abundance of such materials about cisgendered people
- Deployment of outdated information, misuse of pronouns, or dissemination of inaccurate information about transgender people by school personnel, whether intentional or not
- Self-advocacy as the only viable option for transgender students to gain support, safety, equality, or recourse
- Lack of peer understanding or knowledge about what to call transgender students

- Being asked to speak on behalf of all transgender students or people during school

- Lack of systematically inclusive discourses about student identities in all school-level materials and communications

Because of microaggressions such as those noted above, LGBTQGV students are far more likely than their peers to struggle emotionally (Hochschild, 1983; Nadal, River, & Corpus, 2010; Nordmarken, 2012) or placate others by representing themselves in incomplete or false ways that they believe will be seen as socially acceptable and simply allow them to survive a school day. Such false fronts or defensive strategies are emotionally and cognitively exhausting and difficult. The emotional labor required to sustain learned or detached tolerance and buffer one's self against the countless microaggressions experienced throughout a typical school day imprints students with emotional and sometimes physical scars that can last a lifetime. A school climate that supports and privileges the normalization of heterosexist and cisgendered beliefs—even unconsciously—forces students who fall outside of those dominant identifiers to focus on simple survival rather than success and fulfillment in school.

LGBTQGV Bullying and School Environments

School environments may well breed, enable, perpetuate, or even encourage bullying behaviors targeted at LGBTQGV students, because they are historically and institutionally designed to socialize and normalize children for life in what is assumed to be a universal society in which all citizens share common identities, goals, beliefs, values, and so on. However, the statistics on LGBTQGV school experiences belie the assumption that those identities, goals, beliefs, and values are in fact universal. In fact, those statistics highlight the fact that when students deviate from presumed norms during school, they face serious psychological and sometimes physical consequences that include bullying, harassment, assault, rumor-mongering, slander, exclusion, and the withdrawal of support from school authorities. Consequently, those students are much more likely to feel disconnected and alienated from school life, to avoid attending school, and to achieve at lower levels. Further, they become more likely to exhibit low self-esteem, higher rates of anxiety and depression, increased risk of suicide, and avoidance of plans to continue their educations beyond minimum legal requirements. These implications are staggering for LGBTQGV children and would likely create a firestorm of action if they were associated with nearly any other identity group.

Queer bullying must be stopped. Teachers, staff, and school personnel must be made aware of and trained to intervene when they witness or identify bullying behaviors, and held accountable when they do not, regardless of their personal beliefs. The protection and support of *all* children is among their professional duties and is often explicitly stated as such in state-level teacher ethics codes.

One of the saving graces for LGBTQGV students is that being "out" in school may have some positive consequences—96% of students who were open about their identities and orientations also enjoyed higher levels of psychological well-being (Kosciw et al., 2010). This latter finding suggests that if administrators, teachers, students, and even support staff are equipped with anti-bullying strategies and trained to support LGBTQGV students in their pursuit of school success and social equality, then perhaps bullying would occur less frequently, if not disappear entirely.

Because of repeated exposure to traumatic life events that have caused emotional, psychological, and even physical suffering, bullying can manifest as C-PTSD (complex post-traumatic stress disorder) for the rest of an individual's life. Symptoms of post-traumatic bullying can be triggered by entering locales of past abuse, seeing other individuals bullied, or reliving the trauma through nightmares, flashbacks, or grief and sadness during unanticipated or even random moments. If untreated, the quality of life for victims of bullying can be dramatically diminished. Until we have a comprehensive federal anti-bullying policy, professional educators—as the moral custodians for all students in their classrooms—must prevent bullying in any form. Despite an array of other curricular and professional responsibilities, teachers must work against queer bullying at all times.

One reminder (perhaps the most troubling one of all) that queer bullying is a problem of huge proportions: when bullying is treated as normal, tolerable, or just an unavoidable fact of life, people—including children—become desensitized to bullying as they grow older. Conoley (2008) found that students tend to tolerate and even become more approving of bullying as they progress from elementary school to high school. This increased tolerance and its strengthening over time implies that "both the behaviors associated with bullying and the effects of being bullied on young people are not merely the products of individual histories"; they are also the result of cultural heteronormative enforcement within educational institutions (p. 218).

Because of the ruling in *Nabozny v. Podlesny* (1996), which has made a significant impact on the treatment and inclusion of LGBTQGV students' issues in schools and possibly influenced President Obama's endorsement on October 28, 2009, of the federal Hate Crimes Law, the general public has learned what all lesbian, gay, bisexual, transgender, and queer persons have known all their lives: growing up in the United States as an LGBTQGV child/adolescent is often an inhumane and unnecessarily horrifying experience, fraught with the synergistic terrors of self-doubt, peer bullying, and adult indifference. The trauma of growing up queer can lead to grave—and sometimes fatal—consequences.

Notes

1   The full story is told in *Bullied: A Student, a School and a Case that Made History*. See http:// www.tolerance.org/kit/bullied-student-school-and-case-made-history

2   While President Barack Obama successfully repealed "Don't Ask, Don't Tell," and many people agreed with this decision, serving as an "out" homosexual in the military has been a long-standing divisive issue for our country.

3   The DSM II was published in 1968.

4   Not all transgender people have sexual reassignment surgery. Those who opt to are both transgender and transsexual.

5   For more information see http://gidreform.org/

6   We recognize that intersexed students, those who have a variation in sex characteristics including chromosomes, gonads, and/or genitalia that do not allow individuals to be distinctly identified within the female/male binary, are left out of the continuum of statistics but that they are also bullied.

7   *Cisgender* refers to people whose biological sex is in accordance with their assigned gender, their bodies, and their personal identity. It is a signifier that marks the unmarked or unnamed category that emerged out of transgender theories (Schilt & Westbrook, 2009).

References

Birkett, M., & Espelage, D.L. (2009). LGB and questioning students in schools: The moderating effects of homophobic bullying and school climate on negative outcomes. *Journal of Youth and Adolescence, 38*, 989–1000.

Chauncey, G., Jr. (1982/1983). From sexual inversion to homosexuality: Medicine and the changing conceptualization of female deviance. *Salmagundi, 58–59*, 114–146.

Chesir-Teran, D., & Hughes, D. (2009). Heterosexism in high school and victimization among lesbian, gay, bisexual, and questioning students. *Journal of Youth and Adolescence, 38*, 963–975.

Conoley, J.C. (2008). Sticks and stones can break my bones and words can really hurt me. *School Psychology Review, 37*(2), 217–220.

D'Emilio, J., & Freedman, E.B. (1988). *Intimate matters: A history of sexuality in America*. New York: Harper & Row.

Diaz, E., & Kosciw, J. (2009). *Shared Differences: The experiences of lesbian, gay, bisexual, and transgender students of color in our nation's schools*. New York: GLSEN.

Duberman, M.B., Vicinus, M., & Chauncey, G., Jr. (1989). *Hidden from history: Reclaiming the gay and lesbian past*. New York: New American Library.

Ellis, H. (1901). *Studies in the psychology of sex. Volume 2: Sexual inversion*. Philadelphia: Davis.

Freedman, M. (1971). *Homosexuality and psychological functioning*. Belmont, CA: Brooks/Cole.

Freud, S. (1905). Three essays on the theory of sexuality. In J. Strachey (Ed. & Trans.), *The standard edition of the complete psychological works of Sigmund Freud* (vol. 7, pp. 123–245). London: Hogarth Press.

Graham, S. (2011). What educators need to know about bullying. *Educational Horizons, 89*(2), 12–15.

Greytak, E., Kosciw, J.G., & Diaz, E. (2005). *Harsh realities finds transgender youth face extreme harassment in school*. New York: GLSEN.

Greytak, E., Kosciw, J., & Diaz, E. (2009). *Harsh realities: The experiences of transgender youth in our schools*. New York: GLSEN.

Hatzenbuehler, M.L. (2011). The social environment and suicide attempts in lesbian, gay, and bisexual youth. *Pediatrics, 127*(5), 895–903.

Hochschild, A. (1983). *The managed heart: The commercialization of human feeling.* Berkeley: University of California Press.

Kosciw, J., & Diaz, E. (2006). *The 2005 national school climate survey: The experiences of lesbian, gay, bisexual and transgender youth in our nation's schools.* New York: GLSEN.

Kosciw, J., Greytak, E., & Diaz, E (2008). *The 2007 National School Climate Survey: The experiences of lesbian, gay, bisexual and transgender youth in our nation's schools.* New York: GLSEN.

Kosciw, J., Greytak, E., Diaz, E., & Bartkiewicz, M. (2010). *The 2009 National School Climate Survey: The experiences of lesbian, gay, bisexual and transgender youth in our nation's schools.* New York: GLSEN.

Lambda Legal. Retrieved December 15, 2009, from http://www.lambdalegal.org/in-court/cases/nabozny-v-podlesny.html

Markow, D., & Fein, J. (2005). *From teasing to torment: School climate in America. A survey of students and teachers* (commissioned by the Gay, Lesbian & Straight Educational Network). New York: Harris Interactive.

Miller, s. (2012). Mythology of the norm: Disrupting the culture of bullying in schools. *English Journal, 101*(6), 107–109.

Nadal, K.L., River, D.P., & Corpus, M.J.H. (2010). Sexual orientation, and transgender microaggressions: Implications for mental health and counseling. In D.W. Sue (Ed.), *Microaggressions and marginality: Manifestation, dynamics, and impact* (pp. 217-240). Hoboken, NJ: Wiley.

Nordmarken, S. (2012). *Everyday transgender emotional inequality: Microaggressions, micropolitics, and minority emotional work.* Unpublished paper presented at The American Sociological Association Annual Meeting, Denver, CO.

Pascoe, C.J. (2007). *Dude, you're a fag.* Berkeley: University of California Press.

Plöderl, M., & Fartacek, R. (2009). Childhood gender nonconformity and harassment as predictors of suicidality among gay, lesbian, bisexual, and heterosexual Austrians. *Archives of Sexual Behavior, 38,* 400–410.

Russell, S.T., Ryan, C., Toomey, R.B., Diaz, R.M., & Sanchez, J. (2011). Lesbian, gay, bisexual, and transgender adolescent school victimization: Implications for young adult health and adjustment. *Journal of School Health, 81*(5), 223–230.

Schilt, K., & Westbrook, L. (2009). Doing gender, doing heteronormativity: "Gender normals," transgender people, and the social maintenance of heterosexuality. *Gender & Society, 23*(4), 440–464.

Swearer, S.M., Turner, R.K., Givens, J.E., & Pollack, W.S. (2008). "You're so gay!": Do different forms of bullying matter for adolescent males? *School Psychology Review, 37*(2), 160–173.

Tharinger, D.J. (2008). Maintaining the hegemonic masculinity through selective attachment, homophobia, and gay-baiting in schools: Challenges to interventions. *School Psychology Review, 37*(2), 221–227.

Wallace, J.A. (2011). Bullycide in American schools: Forging a comprehensive legislative solution. *Indiana Law Journal, 86*(735), 735–761.

Young, R., & Sweeting, H. (2004). Adolescent bullying, relationships, psychological well-being, and gender-atypical behavior: A gender diagnosticity approach. *Sex Roles, 50*(7/8), 525–537.

CHAPTER THREE

Bullies and Bodies

Addressing Weight Discrimination

Tara Star Johnson & Elana Cutter

A s a former high school English teacher and current teacher educator, I—Tara—have made a conscious effort to incorporate in my classes the intersecting issues of race, class, gender, and sexual orientation as they pertain to literacy and pedagogy. Lately, though, I've come to realize that body type is an identity category that can transcend or in some cases supercede the four I have focused on in my teaching.In this chapter I share a personal anecdote, information on weight-based bullying, and the challenges and opportunities I've experienced in addressing sizism in my methods classes.Following this,Elana, a student in one of those classes, will join the dialogue with conclusions from her action research project.We use the term *sizism* synonymously with *fatism* and *weight-based discrimination* to refer to the discriminatory practices, prejudices, and bullying that people experience as a result of their non-normative body type, though we focus on people of size more so than thin people, since the former are targeted more frequently for bullying (Fox, 1997; Taylor, 2011).

My Story

"Earthquake, earthquake, Butch makes the earth shake!" a straggly gaggle of girls (there was safety in numbers) would call out with bravado from the farmhouse where I grew up when we saw my neighbor, nicknamed Butch, from a far-enough distance that we would have time to run away if he showed signs of retaliating. "Butch is a big, fat tub-o-lard!"

I didn't know what a tub of lard actually was at age 6 or 7, but I knew it was bad, and therefore fitting, for my childhood nemesis, who routinely tortured my tween-aged sister and me and any other young girls who had the ill fortune to be in his vicinity. He was around a lot because he was friends-by-propinquity with my brother Lance; I'd like to think it was convenience rather than compatibility that motivated their companionship. At any rate, Butch's bullying peaked (along with his weight) when he was in high school, and I was 10 years his junior and rail-thin, so I was easy prey.

I credit Butch, who returned to his given name of Don during a life-altering stint with the Marines, with my immunity to tickling. One of his favorite activities was to hold us down and tickle us until we screamed for mercy or peed our pants, and so I schooled myself not to react when he got me. But I didn't have the wherewithal to defend myself against another fetish of his, which he apparently reserved solely for me, the runt of the litter. If he caught me alone in the house (a common enough occurrence on the farm), he'd herd me upstairs to my older sister's bedroom and make me strip and put on her underwear. I vividly remember the mortification I felt, the sick dread that would come over me when I realized he had me cornered. This went on for a while before I summoned the courage to tell someone. I remember this moment, too; it's one of the few still images I have ingrained in my mind from my childhood. We are in the car, a metallic-green Dodge Coronet. Mom is driving, I am in the backseat, and there's a vague, shadowy passenger who I think was my brother. I awkwardly confessed what had been happening to me, which was somehow easier to do when I was looking at the back of Mom's head. She turned to Lance and asked whether he knew—this was negative—and then she was ominously silent. That was the end of it. Nothing more was said, and the bullying stopped. I've often wondered what happened behind the scenes, especially now that I am a parent to a skinny little mini-me who could also be a potential target for a neighborhood bully. I want to equip my daughter with the confidence and courage to speak out against tormentors and ask for help without shame, not only for herself but for all children.

Weight-Based Bullying

I see Don differently now, through the lens of adulthood. Even as a teenager, when I interacted with him while babysitting his children, he bore little trace of who he'd been, quite literally in that he had to lose about 100 pounds in order to make weight for the military. Undoubtedly Butch was a bully, but chances are good that he was bullied, too. I doubt we girls were the only ones who taunted him for being fat, and through the foggy perspective of history I can't say whether we were retaliating or instigating.

Studies show a strong correlation between obesity and bullying, particularly the relational and overt varieties. Overweight and obese kids are much more likely to be victimized than average-weight children (Janssen, Craig, & Boyce, 2004; Kosciw et al., 2012; Lumeng et al., 2010), though there's a gendered difference in the perpetrators: bullies are more often obese boys and underweight girls, according to a U.K. study (Griffiths, Wolke, Page, & Horwood, 2006).

As sj Miller notes in the first chapter of this book, students who are perceived to be LGBTQGV are the number one target of bullying, but in second place are students who are bullied because of aspects related to their physical appearance such as body weight (Kosciw et al., 2012).Because obesity is often attributed to a personal failing (Puhl & Heuer, 2010), weight-based bullying can have more damaging emotional effects than characteristics such as race that are perceived to be outside a person's control. Greenleaf et al. (2006) noted in their study of Hispanic and White middle school students that their participants stigmatized peers who were presented as fat regardless of race or gender, claiming that "the stigma of fatness overrides race-related differences in attitudes toward weight" (p. 550). As Weinstock and Krehbiel (2009) have observed, "[The] view of weight as controllable leads many to blame those who are fat for being fat, and thus to treat fatness as a character flaw. Negative treatment is then viewed as deserved, making it very easy for those who bully fat people to 'blame the victim'" (p. 123).

I can attest to this problematic perception of what can and can't be controlled from my own miserable middle school experience, when Butch's bullying was supplanted by that of peers. Though I was very late to mature and was teased for wearing glasses and braces, I didn't feel personally responsible for my nearsightedness and overbite or my waiflike physique; they were part of my genetic makeup and thus my parents' fault, not mine. I clung to the belief that contacts and orthodontia and eventual maturity would make me less of a target. I have a vivid memory of a sixth-grade conversation with my BFF Rebecca, during which I told her, "We may be ugly ducklings now, but one day we'll be swans." Apparently not having the self-esteem issues I had, she was furious at my assimilation of her into an ugly identity. When I see my insecure younger self manifested in my daughter, who is beyond beautiful, I'm mindful that it's not mirrors or peers who measure us so much as ourselves. Whether or not we can control our weight may not be as important to our emotional health as whether we can control how people make us feel about it. Perhaps if bully-Butch and others of his ilk hadn't felt the need to compensate for their weight-based insecurities by controlling people more vulnerable than them, childhoods like mine wouldn't be tainted.

There is evidence to support a linkage between weight-based bullying and eating disorders (Puhl & Heuer, 2010), though most psychologists feel that bullying exacerbates a pre-existing condition rather than causes it. Regardless, legal precedent is being set to hold school authorities accountable for body type bullying that occurs within their doors. In 2009 a Pittsburgh parent was awarded $55,000 from her daughter's school district for failing to protect her against the bullying that she claimed triggered her anorexia—several boys routinely called her "fat" while she was in middle school, and the administrators' response was that the boys must have liked her if they were teasing her (James, 2009).

In an apparent paradox, we are living in a sociological moment during which eating disorders such as anorexia and bulimia coexist with epidemic obesity among our nation's youth. Both ends of the spectrum have serious consequences for health. According to the Renfrew Center, a residential eating disorder facility, "the mortality rate associated with anorexia nervosa is 12 times higher than the death rate of *all* causes of death for females 15–24 years old," and obesity is now second to smoking as the leading cause of death in the United States. The Centers for Disease Control and Prevention show an alarming trend in the past 20 years. In 1990, less than 15% of the people in all states were obese; by 2010, all states had more than 20% obese people, with a significant concentration in Southern states at more than 30% (CDC).Young people are especially at risk; obesity has tripled over the past 2 decades among 6- to 19-year-olds, according to the National Health and Nutrition Survey (Bryner, 2010). While obesity is strongly correlated with poverty, and eating disorders are more prevalent among middle- and upper-middle-class White females, racial and class distinctions are blurring for both obesity and eating disorders, which can be attributed in part to changing demographics and the pervasive influence of the media. As people of color are increasingly joining the ranks of the middle class, they are subjected to White, middle-class values, including the unattainable standard of beauty—thin, light-skinned, straight-haired—perpetuated by the entertainment and advertising industries (Wolf, 1990).

While both ends of the body type spectrum have serious and potentially mortal physical consequences, the psychological ramifications of living outside "normal" body-type parameters are also significant. Taylor (2011) cites several studies suggesting that overweight youth who are teased by peers are at greater risk for developing negative body images and low self-esteem that lasts into adulthood. Weight-based teasing is also correlated with depression and suicide attempts. Though overweight females are subjected to weight-based discrimination more than males (Fox, 1997), boys are certainly not immune (including skinny boys who, unlike skinny girls, are also targeted for bullying).The book and movie *The Fat Boy Chronicles*, based on a true story about an obese eighth grader subjected to bullying, vividly and sensitively demonstrates that the humiliation and self-loathing experienced by the main character as a result of his peers' cruelty is not the sole domain of girls.

Addressing Sizism in Teacher Education

With massive anti-bullying efforts and initiatives such as Michelle Obama's "Let's Move" campaign gathering momentum in both the public and private sectors, now is an opportune moment for teachers and teacher educators to get on board with addressing complex issues surrounding body types and bullying in their classrooms. But it isn't easy. I've been struggling as a teacher educator with how to talk about sizism.

Challenges in Talking about Sizism

There is plenty of scholarship and meaningful dialogue on the topics of racism, sexism, classism, and heterosexism, and as sensitive and challenging as these topics can be, I feel reasonably competent in my manner of weaving them into the blanket of social justice and diversity that covers all of my teaching. I approach body type discrimination, however, with the trepidation and sense of inadequacy that I used to feel in talking about race as a novice teacher. I've been thinking about why this is so, and I've come up with a few reasons and counterarguments for why I—and, I hope, you—should press on despite discomfort.

First of all, I'm mindful of my subject position as someone who is neither overweight nor underweight because of an eating disorder. Who am I to speak to these issues when I have no embodied experience to draw from? Sure, I watched one of my nieces battle bulimia for more than a decade while my sister struggled to parent her, and I am among the 80% of women who are dissatisfied with what they see in the mirror (Fox, 1997). However, I don't know what it's like to have a pathological relationship with my body, so I can claim no understanding or expertise based on experience. But this is a poor excuse for avoiding an uncomfortable topic. Though I don't know what it's like to be brown or poor or gay or disabled, I deliberately raise these identity categories as topics for critical analysis in part *because* brown, poor, gay, and disabled students may not be empowered to speak up. The same argument applies for some of my colleagues. My subject position is a privileged one in that I rarely—I won't say never—get accused of having an agenda or receive negative course evaluations as a result of my commitment to social justice, repercussions that teachers of color or LGBTQGV teachers more commonly experience when they raise issues with which they personally identify. I feel it is a responsibility, then, for people who represent the norm to, at the very least, support the efforts of others—if not lead the charge for anti-discriminatory practices.

Another reason I get nervous about raising body type issues is that invariably my classes include students with eating disorders (one in five college-aged women has one, and my classes are comprised mostly of females) as well as obese students (one in four in Indiana, where I teach, according to the CDC, though educated women are less likely to be obese). Just as the nature of dialogue around race tends to be different depending on whether it's a racially homogenous or diverse class, I'm hyper-conscious that some students might feel singled out when they'd rather remain invisible. In the past I've been able to have a private conversation with the occasional person of color in my classes, along the lines of "Look, we're going to be discussing issues of race in here, and I don't want you to feel like you have to be the spokesperson for all things Black—and yet I'm sure your perspective will be valuable. How would you like me to handle it?" But I've never had a similar conversation with a person of size. I'm at a loss for words, which leads me to my next point: there is a lack of culturally sensitive language for talking about body-type discrimination.

Fatism and *sizism* are terms that are gaining ground in popular culture and research—I received 20 or so hits in our library's electronic database during my first foray into the topic. Even a cursory read of the literature suggests there are counter-narratives to the so-called obesity epidemic—that the hoopla and hyperbole has generated a moral panic that may be more damaging than actual health risks due to being overweight. A Facebook friend's recent post advertising her newly approved class titled "Fat Studies" also raised my awareness of a growing body (no pun intended) of scholarship. However, I'm mindful that this friend embodies Saguy and Ward's (2011) observation: "The fat acceptance movement is dominated by fat, white, middle-class women, for whom body size is especially salient" (p. 61). It makes me wonder why this emerging discipline, like second-wave feminism of yore, is less relevant for working-class women or women of color.

Despite this growing movement to educate people about weight-based discrimination, describing or acknowledging someone as fat or skinny is potentially pejorative or, at best, impolite, because it draws attention to a bodily characteristic we're not supposed to notice in our classrooms. This leads me to my final point, which is that sizism isn't perceived to be an issue that needs to be addressed, particularly in schools, where bodies are systematically ignored and suppressed. Schooling is supposed to be for the mind, not the body, and teachers may feel that they have bigger concerns than their students' body images. People with atypical body types aren't protected under equal opportunity or anti-discrimination laws, either, perhaps because in our society being fat is largely perceived as a moral problem, something within a person's control, unlike the supposedly immutable categories of gender or race. This could be why LGBTQGV folks aren't protected, either. But as the center of gravity in public discourse leans toward the "inborn" end of the nature-nurture debate, it seems that more institutions are voluntarily adding inclusive language regarding sexual orientation in their policies. This gives me hope that body type discrimination might follow suit.

Opportunities for Addressing Sizism

Despite my discomfort in raising the issue of sizism in my classes, I have opened the door for dialogue by incorporating readings, both fictional and scholarly, about people of size. For example, I pair *The Misfits,* a young adult novel narrated by a fat seventh-grade boy, with "The Fan Club," a short story written by a teenager that complicates the bully/bullied dichotomy when the narrator joins the popular crowd in taunting her overweight quasi-friend. The most thorny text I use in terms of ensuing classroom discussion has been Margaret Kent Bass's (2001) essay "On Being a Fat Black Girl in a Fat-Hating Culture," an epiphany-inducing text in that it had never occurred to me that adults would be well advised to inoculate children against fatism as well as racism. Bass's parents had instilled racial pride in her as a prophylactic for the Jim Crow South, but she was wholly unprepared to deal with her peers' and even a teacher's cruel and incessant teasing about her weight. Bass, an emeritus professor at St. Lawrence University, writes eloquently about her lifelong struggle between calorie-rich Southern fare as a source of pleasure and community on the one hand, and censure and self-loathing on the other. I include this essay with other readings that synthesize the intersections among race, class, gender, and sexuality near the end of an undergraduate capstone methods course I routinely teach, when students are typically comfortable enough with each other and me to be frank in their comments. Even so, I've noticed that the dialogue surrounding this piece is marked by the heavy silences, hesitations, false starts, and disclaimers characteristic of an initial conversation about race or sexual orientation among strangers. Last semester I decided to take a more systematic look at my students' questions and reflections about the reading and discussion (to hold them accountable for the readings I assign, I require them to bring typed questions to class to generate discussion, then write a 5-minute reflection on the back as their "ticket" out of class[1]) so that I might be better equipped to manage such discussions with future students. In my class of 15 preservice English teachers—all White, middle-class young women except for one White man and two women of mixed heritage—the following five themes recurred.

1. Discomfort with talking about sizism but acknowledging it'd be helpful to address it in an English class, perhaps as part of a unit on social justice, identity, media literacy (critique of body norms), or current events (obesity epidemic).

2. New awareness of discrimination as inclusive of body types (and not just overweight ones; the consequences of being too thin, whether as a result of genetics or an eating disorder, is consistently brought up).

3. Childhood stories where they could relate to issues of sizism, either through direct personal experience or observation of a family member.

4. Ambivalence about the issue—whether it's better left to health class or counseling professionals; but if they were to tackle it, how to promote positive body images *and* healthy lifestyles, and whether these two might be mutually exclusive.

5. Concern about being perceived as having an agenda as an overweight teacher raising the issue in class.

Though the general consensus in my classes has always been that it's wrong for students to be bullied or discriminated against because of their body type, there has also been a corollary voice along the lines of "Yes, but…." I once had an African American student (not in this group) who Googled author Bass and shared her picture with the class, making the point that she *is* morbidly obese and thus should bear some responsibility for her self-image, a perspective perhaps informed by the student's own upper-middle-class, physically fit status.

A "yes, but" student from this group voiced her opinion that teachers should emphasize healthy behaviors over fat acceptance, though I didn't realize until reading her four-page reflection (they're generally one page at the most) that she felt silenced. "Although I'm being continuously shot down in this discussion," she wrote, "I feel like encouraging some healthiness is not wrong." She touched on the third and fourth themes above in her ticket, relating her personal experience to her desire to incorporate education about healthy lifestyles in her classes.

> Growing up in a single-parent home with a father who worked all day, I was an over-weight child. I got picked on a lot…. It hurts me a ton, now that I work at a local candy store, to see the same obese children in my store being quieted by their mother simply by a candy bar or two. Although it may please them now, I worry about the consequences they'll face later, whether it would be verbal comments, bullying, or even health issues.

That 9 of 15 tickets included a personal or observed experience such as this one is indicative of the relevance of the issue. I'd also wager that it wasn't for lack of experience that the remaining 6 students eschewed a personal story as much as a reluctance to share. One student wrote: "I feel like I'm probably not the type of person to reveal personal things about myself to students b/c of the vulnerability it leaves you with." She may have been alluding to an earlier (and ongoing) conversation we had in class about a caveat for being *too* authentic in sharing our stories and perspectives as we expect our students to do: it leaves us open to misinterpretation or the possibility that students might use personal information against us. Novice teachers often struggle with establishing a professional teacher-student boundary, so the question of how much of their personal lives to share is a common one.

Two students who self-identified as overweight mentioned concerns in their tickets (though, notably, not during class discussion) about addressing sizism with their students. One stated in her reflection, "I am so uncomfortable talking about 'fatism.' How can I speak to it? I am an overweight woman—will I come across bitter, hypocritical, etc.?" She had othered the issue of fatness to her father as part of her discussion question, which she also shared in class:

> The little chubby black girl [Bass] reminds me of stories my father told me of his child-hood. He was a big boned boy born in the late 1950s. Dressed in husky clothing through-out his childhood, his mother had to take him to a specialty store. Like the mother in the story, she did not think to encourage her son to participate in physical activity, but

instead fed him well and nurtured him. My grandmother, who grew up during the depression, and a product of "old country" Lithuania, was more concerned about eating well. According to my grandmother, if you didn't eat, you were unwell.

She elaborated on the cultural clash her father experienced between his home and the rest of his world, where people assumed he was fat by choice.

Elana is the other student who was concerned with how to raise awareness of weight-based discrimination without being dismissed as having a personal agenda. She related more directly to Bass in her ticket question, which I include here in its entirety because it represents the kind of deep and thoughtful reflection that deliberate engagement with the issue can engender.

> I must admit that the Bass reading really upset me, especially when she brought up her memories of being teased by peers and teachers alike because of her weight. Though she focused on the connection between her identity as a black woman and as an overweight woman, so many issues were brought to the forefront of my mind, issues that I struggle with on a daily basis as a young overweight woman myself: the issue of being overweight or obese as a moral choice, and then what being overweight signifies to others. This is why, near the beginning of the semester, I came to ask you about what I should do with my 13 year old actress [Elana was an acting coach for a local play] who kept making self-deprecatory comments about her body. I remember that phase of my life; I remember the ebb and flow of the abject self-loathing. And as I heard her say phrases such as, "I'm too fat to do that" or "I'm too fat to be pretty," I felt helpless because I didn't know what to say to her. I don't know what I would have *needed* to hear at that age, if anything would have helped at all. My question becomes, how can we advocate for body image acceptance in our curriculum? And how would it be the same as or different from advocating for other social issues (e.g., gender or sexuality)?

Elana asked in her reflection, "If I were to advocate for body image acceptance, would the fact that I'm overweight taint what I'm trying to teach?" I responded this way:

> I wouldn't think "taint" so much as "affect." Just as students tend to be more cautious in how they talk about race to a teacher of color, I think you'd have students thinking twice before making what could be perceived as an insensitive comment. That's not necessarily a bad thing...just something to be mindful of, that you may unwittingly be silencing a fair-minded/questioning perspective.

As I now re-read my response to Elana, I'm struck by my unconscious biases. I should have clarified that *White* students are reticent about discussing racism, as I speculate *average-weight* students would be about discussing sizism. Clearly I have my own work to do with respect to making culturally sensitive language an automatic part of my vocabulary.

I was delighted this semester when Elana, currently a student teacher, decided to conduct an action research project on weight discrimination with her students in which she essentially answered the questions she posed in her ticket question.

Through (1) questionnaires asking students to evaluate scenarios in which race, gender, and fat discrimination occurred, (2) a freewrite to extend their thinking on the topic, and (3) a reading and discussion of the essay "Fatso" from Peck's (2005) memoir, she successfully raised awareness of the issue of weight-based discrimination among her tenth graders. She serves as a model for tackling the taboo, and I'm so proud of her efforts. Her conclusions from her project serve as a call to action for us all.

Elana's Conclusions

From the experiences I have witnessed both as a student and as a preservice teacher, the issue of sizism and the prejudice that surrounds it—specifically in regard to weight—is one that has repeatedly affected me, my peers, and my students. The literature addressing weight stigma, prejudice, and discrimination describes the negative effect that this stigma has on the psychological, as well as the physical, well-being of fat individuals. Often the authors' suggestions for the lessening of this stigma include education, or the persistent, inclusive awareness and analysis of anti-fat prejudice in the United States.

Though teacher education programs have required pre-service candidates to take courses that account for multiculturalism and diversity sensitivities, instructors dedicate little or no time to the study of weight-based prejudice and discrimination, despite the fact that this issue is one that permeates and negatively influences student interactions inside and outside of school. Maybe this is because sizism would fall into a broader category that relates to bullying. Whatever the reason, the issue of sizism, specifically as it relates to weight prejudice and discrimination, has a negative effect on men's and women's perceptions of themselves, and from my personal interactions with students, I feel that this form of prejudice is especially harmful to adolescents and their body image. I propose that sizism is a significant and under-analyzed issue that permeates students' lives, and it should be on the agenda of any social justice teacher to require students to analyze and to think critically about their beliefs concerning fat.

My findings suggest that, though the majority of students seem to see weight discrimination to be as inappropriate as racial discrimination but less inappropriate than gender discrimination, they lack an overall awareness of the problem itself. However, their interest in the topic during my data collection, from their survey responses to our animated whole-class discussions, tells me that this is an issue to which they would pay attention and enjoy analyzing, if only instructors had the audacity to address the highly stigmatized and controversial concept of fat acceptance. Fat acceptance doesn't mean that we promote an unhealthy lifestyle; rather, it is a viewpoint that encourages diversity acceptance and challenges stereotypes used to label people of substance. Teaching this kind of topic would require instructors to analyze their personal beliefs about weight—both the conscious and unconscious—and acknowledge that most of what they believe is the result of living in a country whose aim is to declare war on obesity as it relates to the physical body rather than the intellectual and emotional mind.

Now, the purpose of this study wasn't to grind my own axe just because I happen to be fat. Rather, the purpose was to challenge the way that I think about my own and others' bodies, while also challenging the ways that my students think about themselves and those around them.

Elana's insights over the span of the two semesters I've been privileged to have her in my classes have taught me that issues of weight discrimination are a worthwhile and salient part of teacher education. I've taken to heart her observation that our limited class discussion focused exclusively on physical rather than emotional health, and I look forward to more robust dialogue in future classes. Such conversations, albeit uncomfortable, could be an important step toward addressing the kind of body type bullying that contributes to behaviors such as Butch's from my childhood days.

Note

1   I borrowed this idea from my brilliant and beautiful friend and colleague, Jill Hermann-Wilmarth, Associate Professor of Socio-Cultural Studies of Education at Western Michigan University.

References

Bass, M. (2001). On being a fat Black girl in a fat-hating culture. In M. Bennett & V. Dickerson (Eds.), *Recovering the Black female body: Self-representations by African American women* (pp. 220–230). New Brunswick, NJ: Rutgers University Press.

Bryner, J. (2010). Childhood obesity takes psychological toll, too. LiveScience. Retrieved November 9, 2012, from http://www.livescience.com/6126-childhood-obesity-takes-psychological-toll.html

Fox, K. (1997). Mirror, mirror: A summary of research findings on body image. Social Issues Research Centre. Retrieved November 11, 2012, from http://www.sirc.org/publik/mirror.html

Greenleaf, C., Chambliss, H., Rhea, D.J., Martin, S.B., & Morrow, Jr., J.R. (2006). Weight stereotypes and behavioral intentions toward thin and fat peers among White and Hispanic adolescents. *Journal of Adolescent Health, 39*, 617–627.

Griffiths, L.J., Wolke, D., Page, A.S., & Horwood, J.P. (2006). Obesity and bullying: Different effects for boys and girls. *Archives of Disease in Childhood, 91*,121–125.

James, S.D. (2009). Bullies drive girl to anorexia, says lawsuit. ABC News. Retrieved November 10, 2012, from http://abcnews.go.com/Health/WellnessNews/story?id=8367578#.UJ6D-BaM2RRw

Janssen, I., Craig, W.M., & Boyce, W.F. (2004). Associations between overweight and obesity with bullying behaviors in school-aged children. *Pediatrics, 113*,1187–1194.

Kosciw, J.G., Greytak, E.A., Bartkiewicz, M.J., Boesen, M.J., & Palmer, N.A. (2012). *The 2011 national school climate survey: The experiences of lesbian, gay, bisexual and transgender youth in our nation's schools*. New York: GLSEN.

Lumeng, J.C., Forrest, P., Appugliese, D.P., Kaciroti, N., Corwyn, R.F., & Bradley, R.H. (2010). Weight status as a predictor of being bullied in third through sixth grades. *Pediatrics, 125*(6), 1301–1307.

Peck, C. (2005). *Revenge of the paste eaters: Memoirs of a misfit.* New York: Warner Books.

Puhl, R.M., & Heuer, C.A. (2010). Obesity stigma: Important considerations for public health. *American Journal of Public Health, 100*(6), 1019–1028.

Saguy, A.C., & Ward, A. (2011). Coming out as fat: Rethinking stigma. *Social Psychology Quarterly, 74*(1), 53–75.

Taylor, N. (2011). "Guys, she's humongous": Gender and weight-based teasing in adolescence. *Journal of Adolescent Research, 26*(2), 178–199.

Weinstock, J., & Krehbiel, M. (2009). Fat youth as common targets for bullying. In E. Rothblum & S. Solovay (Eds.), *The fat studies reader* (pp. 120–126).New York: New York University Press.

Wolf, N. (1990). *The beauty myth: How images of beauty are used against women.* London: Vintage.

CHAPTER FOUR

Bullying and Students with Disabilities

The Bully, the Bullied, and the Misunderstood

Joseph John Morgan & Deanna Adams

---

*E*lsa is a sixth-grade student. When she was 9, she was struck by a car while riding *her bike through her neighborhood. Elsa sustained a serious brain and spinal cord injury as a result of this accident and had to miss several months of school in order to receive treatment. As a top student in her class, she was devastated because she was missing school and the learning she loved. Although Elsa has made great progress over the past few years, she still has to wear a special brace to support her legs and back. The injuries to her brain also caused her to have cognitive impairments, and she has begun struggling in school to relearn basic reading and math skills. Elsa's parents are worried about her. What once came so easily to their daughter now causes her much pain and strife, and the transition to middle school has not been easy. Elsa struggles with severe anxiety and no longer wants to go to school.*

In order to support Elsa in her academic foundations, she receives support from a special education teacher and a speech-language pathologist. It is common for Elsa to hear snide comments made behind her back as she walks from the resource room back to her general education classroom. As she walks through the hallways, she often hears a chorus of "dummy," "retard," and "stupid" from people who used to be her friends. Azure, her best friend from middle school, stopped her in the hallway one day and said, "You know. It really is too bad. You used to be so pretty. Now you are just about the ugliest, stupidest person I have ever met. It will be amazing if you ever pass a class again." Elsa was devastated. Another of her friends, Marie, heard this and said, "Elsa, do not worry about her. Come find me at lunch and you can sit with me and my friends."

Elsa was ecstatic. She counted down the hours until it was lunchtime. When she got to the cafeteria, she slowly made her way to Marie's table. With a smile on her face, Elsa went to sit down. Marie jumped up and said, "No way—I would never let a retard sit at my table. Go away, although with that stupid thing on your back you probably couldn't even walk." Elsa was shocked, and just stood there with her tray in her hands. Marie walked over to Elsa and knocked Elsa's tray out of her hands. "Get out of here now, you cripple!" Marie screamed in Elsa's face, as Azure smiled in the background.

After the incident at lunch, Elsa had had enough. No one at school was watching out for her—not the teachers or her fellow classmates—so Elsa decided it was time for her to stand up for herself. In the hallways, Elsa would walk up next to other students and trip them, knock their books out of their hands, and call them names. She would try to fight anyone who tried to stand up for themselves and started using some of the most negative language she could think of to call them names. Elsa began picking on younger students on the bus and on the walk home, as well as harassing people through the Internet. The principal of Elsa's school had so many complaints that he had no option but to move for an expulsion. Elsa's parents were shocked—both at the behavior their daughter was exhibiting, and the fact that the school that seemingly did nothing to support their daughter was now moving to get her expelled. When she heard the news, Elsa looked at her parents and said, "I do not want to see any of those jerks anyway." However, behind closed doors, Elsa was devastated. If she did not have school, what did she have?

The fear of bullying for students with disabilities like Elsa has risen at alarming rates on American public school campuses. The culture of these campuses has normative expectations for how students should behave, interact, and learn (Miller, 2012), and students who do not meet those expectations (for example, students who identify as LGBTQGV, or students of color who are in the minority on the public school campus) often become the targets of aggressive and violent acts. Students with disabilities follow a similar continuum to those who are bullied for not fitting into the norm. However, disability is a broad and diverse category that incorporates students with physical and sensory disabilities (for instance, motor, vision, or hearing impairments) and students with academic and cognitive disabilities (learning disabilities, intellectual disabilities, emotional and behavioral disorders, and so on), and the manifestation of disability across individuals is hugely varied.

A common thread connecting students with disabilities is that some of their characteristics deviate from the educational norm, and as a result they require individualized educational services to support their access to the public school environment. As is seen throughout Elsa's story, this deviation carries with it a high risk that students with disabilities will become involved in bullying, both as the victims and, in some instances, as the perpetrators of bullying. Keeping this in mind, it is important to explore differing views of disability, the characteristics of disabilities that are often misunderstood and connected to bullying, and how sociocultural contexts impact the interactions students with disabilities have on public school campuses. Elsa's story highlights this deviation from normative school values, as she has limited access to the school environment both physically and academically as a result of injuries sustained in a car accident. Because of these deviations, she has become the target of bullying by her peers. The current state of bullying against students with disabilities is grounded in the way disability is broadly understood by the biomedical model.

Students with Disabilities as the Victims of Bullying

Much national attention has been paid to the plight of bullying in the American public school environment, with recent statistics suggesting that approximately 30%–50% of all students have experienced bullying in some way, either as the bully or as the victim (Flynt & Morton, 2004; Rose, Espelage, Aragaon, & Elliott, 2011; Rose, Espelage, & Monda-Amaya, 2009; White & Loeber, 2008). Historically, the primary focus of research related to bullying has been on the general school population, with little focus on the bullying of students with disabilities (Estell et al., 2009). From a methodological standpoint, much of the research being conducted focuses on anonymous student self-report of bullying, which often does not provide information about a student's disability (Rose et al., 2011; Rose et al., 2009). When students with disabilities are the focus of research related to bullying, they are often analyzed as a homogeneous group without heavy consideration of the different types of disabilities (Estell et al., 2009). Rose and his colleagues, recognizing that this is a vulnerable population on public school campuses whose needs related to bullying must be understood, are currently conducting research that specifically focuses on bullying and the different types of disability among these students as they access public school environments (Rose et al., 2011; Rose et al., 2009).

There is a growing body of research indicating that students with disabilities may be the victims of bullying in public schools at higher rates than their typical peers (Flynt & Morton, 2004; Rose et al., 2011; Rose et al., 2009; Saylor & Leach, 2009). Statistics indicate that students with disabilities may be 2 to 3 times more likely than their typical peers to be targeted for bullying on public school campuses (Rose et al., 2011). Much of the research that has been conducted relating to students with disabilities as the victims of bullying has not separated students with visible disabilities (that is, disabilities whose characteristics can be seen, such as physical disabilities or vision impairments) from students with non-visible disabilities (that is, disabilities whose characteristics cannot be ascertained visually and would take more time to determine, such as students with learning disabilities or emotional and behavioral disorders) (Carter & Spencer, 2006). Although it would seem that students with visible disabilities might be more prone to being the victims of bullying, research has indicated that students with invisible disabilities are just as likely to be victimized for being different. Such was the case with Elsa, whose cognitive differences were the focus of the bullies (Carter & Spencer, 2006; Rose et al., 2011; Rose et al., 2009).

Within the elementary school context, Estell and his colleagues (2009) analyzed the impact of bullying on three groups: students with disabilities, typical students, and gifted students. Using a series of teacher and peer nominations and reports, they found that students with disabilities overwhelmingly reported being the victims of bullying at higher rates than either of the other groups. They also had the lowest teacher and peer nomination scores, indicating that they were not liked by their peers. Students with gifts and talents, on the other hand, had the lowest reports of being the victims of bullying and had the highest teacher and peer nomination scores. In other words, they were liked by their teachers and peers (Estell et al., 2009).

Another study, conducted by Rose, Espelage, and Monda-Amaya (2009), compared the bullying rates of students with disabilities enrolled in inclusive programming (learning in classrooms with their peers, at least the majority of the time), students with disabilities enrolled in self-contained programming (learning in segregated classrooms with minimal interaction with their peers), and the general population of students on middle and high school campuses. Among middle school students, they found that those with disabilities were more likely to be victimized on school campuses. Within the disability classification, students who were enrolled in self-contained programming were more likely to be the victims of bullying than students enrolled in inclusive programming. Similar trends were found for students at the high school level, although overall rates of bullying tended to be lower for older students than younger students (Rose et al., 2009). Overall, the peak incidence of bullying against students with disabilities seemed to occur in the seventh grade.

The interaction of teachers and students with disabilities is of additional concern when considering the bullying of students with disabilities in the general education environment. McEvoy (2005) found that teachers are often the perpetrators of bullying on the school campus and that they typically target students whom "others will not defend...or because of some devalued personal attribute" (p. 2) such as disability. McEvoy surveyed teachers on a high school campus and found that the vast majority felt that other teachers on the campus bullied students. Additionally, many teachers felt that teachers as bullies got away with their behavior because they called their actions "behavior management."

Dichotomous Definitions of Disability

While it is known that students with disabilities are more likely to be the victims and perpetrators of bullying in the public school environment, it is important to understand how the definitions of disability shape societal interactions with this population and how shifts in perspective may begin to create environments in which students with disabilities are provided more access, thereby shifting perspectives. The historic view of disability comes from the biomedical model perspective, in which disability is viewed as a deficit, or something that needs to be remediated or cured by a team of professionals. Within this model, professionals determine a label that describes an individual's disability—a label that tends to limit what individuals with disabilities are able to do and be. These labels are based on a specific understanding of what is "normal" within society and describe the individual's deviations from the norm (for example, the learning disability of an individual who might not access curricula in a way that is culturally expected, or the intellectual disability of an individual whose adaptive and cognitive skills differ from the norm). The biomedical model perspective's "emphasis is on the physical abnormality or deficiency that is held to be central to actions, experiences, and social identity of the individual" (Danforth, 2001, p. 352).

Within the biomedical model perspective, an individual's disability is one that is to be remediated or corrected. Disability is viewed as something inherently wrong in the individual, and therefore the job of the education professional is to determine ways to correct the disability and provide the student with academic interventions that will eliminate the disability. This model views the limitations facing an individual as within the individual, and as long as the disability is not addressed, the limitations will always remain (Danforth, 2001). Much special education practice within the public school environment is currently centered on this biomedical model perspective's definition of disability: students with disabilities must be remediated so that they can access the same environments as their typical peers (Linton, 1998; Ferri, 2008).

Standing in contrast to the biomedical model perspective's definition of disability is the social model perspective of disability, often viewed within the framework of Disability Studies (DS). The social model perspective is one that analyzes the social construction of disability instead of focusing on something that is inherently wrong with the individual person, and it views human differences, including disability, as natural differences within individuals of the species. The focus is not the disability itself, but the meaning that society places on an individual's difference (Linton, 1998; Davis, 2002; Longmore, 2003). For instance, people who wear glasses are not usually described as having a disability, but people who use wheelchairs or canes are, which has more to do with societal definitions of disability than with the people who use these devices.

Under the social model perspective of disability, the disability is not inherent in the individual person but in the complex sociocultural dynamics found in interactions among society, the environment, and the individual. The social model perspective of disability views it as contextual and fluid; a person may have a disability in one situation, but not in another. For example, a person with a learning disability in reading may have a disability in an English classroom, but not in a mathematics classroom, and a person in a wheelchair has a disability when there are stairs but not when there is an elevator. The issue for individuals with disabilities is not the disability, but their interactions with the environment and the people who construct the environment.

The difference in definitions between the biomedical model and social model perspectives is important to consider for public school educators. It is essential to remember that school is a sociocultural setting that encompasses a series of variables that are expected for students in the school environment. Students with disabilities are individuals who often have normative differences from the cultural expectations of school, and because of these differences they struggle in their interactions with teachers and peers in the public school environment. A student with attention deficits will likely struggle in a classroom that values on-task work and silence during independent instruction; a student with an internalizing emotional or behavioral disorder may struggle to make friends with typical peers during non-academic activities.

In considering the bullying of students with disabilities in public schools, it is important to understand that many public school educators maintain a biomedical model perspective of disability, viewing any difference as something that needs to be corrected within the individual. With a nod toward the biomedical model perspective of disability, pubic educators often focus on what is "wrong" with the student with a disability and how the deviation can be corrected to increase his or her access to the school environment. Conversely, disability under the social model perspective views the complicated interplay among an individual, the characteristics of the environment, and the perceptions of difference by other people within the environment, thereby understanding that the bullying of students with disabilities may be the result of this interplay and not the disability of the individual student. If public educators were to view disability under this model, then the focus of special education would become making adaptations and alterations to the environment in order to support the access of students with disabilities instead of focusing on what "deficits" need to be corrected within the student. During discussions of bullying among students with disabilities, it is important to consider the environmental factors that may be perpetuating both the victimization of students with disabilities and the perpetration of bullying on their part.

Deviations from the Norm
That May Incite Bullying Behavior

Miller (2012) indicated that bullies often target individuals who are different from the norm in some way, as "deviation away from it [the norm] might agitate social and relational aggression" (p. 107). Students with disabilities in public schools often exhibit characteristics that deviate from the norm of school behavior, and these characteristics often make them the targets of bullies. One characteristic of students with disabilities that may incite bullying behavior is a difference in implementation of social and communication skills (Carter & Spencer, 2006; Estell et al., 2009; Flynt & Morton, 2004; Rose et al., 2011; Rose et al., 2009; Saylor & Leach, 2009). Students with disabilities often have not learned the normative skills for social interactions with their peers (for example, introducing oneself or asking to join an activity), thereby ostracizing them from their peers and teachers. This lack of a normative skill set is especially apparent in students who are educated in self-contained classroom settings, as they do not have opportunities to interact with their typical peers or learn social skills that will aid them in attaining friendships (Rose et al., 2009).

Additionally, cognitive or impulse delays may be a component of the students' disabilities. As a result, students may not fully understand the social interactions of their peers or be able to pick up on subtle context communication clues—body language, facial expressions, sarcasm, or figurative language—that indicate group membership or exclusion. This difference in social communication inhibits the connections that students might make with each other and may also make them a target for bullying. Additionally, students with disabilities may not even be aware that they are being bullied by their peers and thus may not understand that it is something that should be reported (Jackson, 2002). Jackson states: "Sometimes, bullying carries on because someone may not recognize that it is bullying which they are experiencing" (p. 138).

Students with disabilities often have some physical characteristic that is different from their typical peers and that incites bullying against them (Carter & Spencer, 2006; Siebers, 2008). Carter and Spencer (2006) found that students with physical disabilities often feel ignored and isolated by their peers at school, as their physical disability and lack of accessibility may impede their interactions with typical peer activities. Flynt and Morton (2004) reported that students with physical impairments might have less stamina or different physical movements than their peers. As a result, these characteristics "may be viewed by bullies as signs of weakness" (p. 332).

In addition to physical characteristics that can label a student as different, academic and cognitive differences may also lead to bullying behavior directed at the student (Rose et al., 2011; Rose et al., 2009). Estell and his colleagues (2009) found that any student who was viewed as needing additional assistance from an adult might be more likely to be the target of bullying behavior. Students with physical, academic, and cognitive disabilities often receive adaptations and accommodations from school personnel to increase access to the general education environment. However, these adjustments, which are designed to support the needs of students with disabilities, may often be the variable that causes tension.

Those who don't use accommodations may perceive themselves to be at a disadvantage.

Students who maintain strong support networks, both inside and outside of the school environment, are less likely to be the victims of bullying (Estell et al., 2009). Strong support networks deter bullying because they provide students with individuals who will stand up for victims and support them in finding the appropriate avenues to report or deal with bullying behavior. In contrast, students with disabilities often do not have these strong support networks within the school environment, as they often struggle with making friends (Estell et al., 2009). This lack of support may also be indicative of the increased bullying rates of students with disabilities. The story of Elsa is all too common when talking about social support networks of students with disabilities in public school environments; students without social support networks often do not know who to turn to, and this can lead to aggressive and detrimental behavior.

Students with Disabilities as the Perceived Perpetrators of Bullying

Students with disabilities are also more likely to be labeled by teachers and other peers as the perpetrators of bullying behaviors among their peers (Estell et al., 2009; Flynt & Morton, 2004; Rose et al., 2011; Rose et al., 2009; White & Loeber, 2008). Of students with disabilities, those who display aggressive behaviors or lack normative social skills are most likely to be reported as being bullies (for instance, students with emotional and behavioral disorders [EBD]) (Rose et al., 2011). White and Loeber (2008) found that aggressive behaviors in the school environment and lack of social connection with typical peers were strong predictors of bullying behaviors. Rose et al. (2011) found that students enrolled in self-contained programming were more likely to engage in fighting and aggressive bullying behaviors on the school campus than their typical peers.

Rose, Espelage, and Monda-Amaya (2009) found that on middle school campuses, students with disabilities were more likely to be the perpetrators of bullying behavior than their typical peers and that students in self-contained programming were more likely than students in inclusive environments to perpetrate bullying. Similar results were found for high school students with disabilities, although the rate of bullying and fighting were lower for older students with disabilities than they were for younger ones (Rose et al., 2009). This suggests that as students progress through school grades, they are less likely to use violence and aggression to deal with social situations than they did when they were younger. It also demonstrates, again, that inclusive environments foster better interactions between those who are labeled as having a disability and those who are not. This in turn may reduce bullying behavior, since typical students have a better understanding of the nature of educational disability and what impact it has on the learning taking place within the school.

As studies of other forms of violence indicate, perpetrators of violence are or were often the victims of it. Flynt and Morton (2004) suggest that students with disabilities who are the perpetrators of bullying may be responding to their own victimization. They do so by replicating the behaviors and actions that they encounter in their own school experience, thereby making them bully-victims. The underlying idea is that, as the victims of bullying, students with disabilities learn to use aggressive behaviors to maintain a power balance within the school environment, and then turn on other students in order to exert their own power over that group (White & Loeber, 2008). Through these behavior patterns, students with disabilities become more likely to be viewed as perpetrators of aggression aimed at other students.

Misunderstandings Related to the Perpetration of Bullying by Students with Disabilities

There are several misunderstandings that must be addressed regarding labeling students with disabilities as bullies. Rose et al. (2009) found that students with disabilities in self-contained programming were more likely to perpetrate bullying behaviors during periods of transition (for example, from middle school to high school, from a more restrictive environment to a less restrictive one, or movement between classes). With this pattern in mind, it must be remembered that students with disabilities—primarily with social and behavioral problems—rely on a structured environment in the school setting. Deviations from that structure often increase their anxiety about coming to school, which in turn may encourage aggressive behaviors in the school environment.

As stated above, students with disabilities often lack access to the normative social interactions of their typical peers, cognitive understanding of problem solving in specific situations, and impulse control. This is clearly seen in the case of Elsa; she had been continuously bullied by a group of students who had formerly been her friends. Because of limited impulse control, her response was aggressive in nature and misunderstood by the school administration. What was seemingly an example of aggressive behavior displayed by Elsa may not have been actual bullying behavior, but more likely a deviation in social interaction that could be addressed through targeted intervention or instruction, or an overreaction to routine social situations that she was not familiar with (Rose et al., 2011; Rose et al., 2009). Differences in communication and a lack of understanding of verbal and nonverbal cues may result in misunderstandings between students with disabilities and their typical peers (Estell et al., 2009; Saylor & Leach, 2009). Such differences become even more apparent when students with disabilities are educated in self-contained classroom settings, as their models for social interaction tend to be other students with disabilities who have similar deviations from the norms of school interactions. The models of appropriate behavior are not always readily available for students with disabilities; thus they begin to replicate behaviors that can seem to be bullying in nature.

Finally, aggressive behaviors can often be indicative of an educational disability, and these characteristics are part of the identification process for determining who receives educational services (as in the case of students with EBD or autism) (Flynt & Morton, 2004). For this population of students, part of the educational intervention is teaching appropriate replacement behaviors and techniques that reduce the maladaptive behavior and increase the prosocial behaviors within the school environment (Rose et al., 2009). Although the aggressive behavior toward other students may seem like bullying, it is important to note that this behavior may be a manifestation of the student's disability, a functional reaction to being frustrated within the academic environment, or a response to a situation in which the student feels that he or she is being wronged or victimized. Therefore, it is important to record when aggressive behaviors occur in students with disabilities and address them through the educational plan, as they may be connected to other things that are occurring within the school environment.

Once an understanding of the definitions and common misunderstandings of students with disabilities has been achieved, it becomes important to begin to consider how social environments can be altered in order to better meet the needs of this population. Continued focus on the biomedical model perspective and the "fixing" of disability will do nothing to impact (a) the interactions students with disabilities have with public school environments, and (b) the ways that students with disabilities are perceived by their peers, as there is nothing about disability that needs to be fixed. Therefore, it is important that educators begin to shift their perspective toward understanding the sociocultural factors that impact, shape, and define disability, and how these factors can be altered to increase access and understanding.

Shifting the Social Environment for Students with Disabilities

Recent educational reform efforts that have focused on including students with disabilities in general education classrooms have created an environment in which the bullying of students with disabilities has become a central focus, as interactions between typical peers (who may not understand disability) and students with disabilities have increased in number (Rose et al., 2011). The Individuals with Disabilities Education Act, or IDEA (2004), mandates that students with disabilities be given access to the general education environment, and it charges educational teams with identifying strategies to include students with disabilities with their typical peers whenever educationally appropriate. Additionally, the Elementary and Secondary Education Act (ESEA, colloquially known as No Child Left Behind) is focused on the academic achievement of all students in the public school environment (ESEA, 2001). The ESEA holds schools and districts responsible for showing academic growth for all students in the public school environment, including students with disabilities. In order to meet the mandates of the IDEA and the ESEA, schools across the country are including students with disabilities in the general education environment. These rates are now at their highest levels since the inception of special education (Scruggs, Mastropieri, & Okolo, 2008). The increase in inclusion has called into question the interactions between students with disabilities and their peers, and research has begun to focus on the social structures that impact the education of students with disabilities.

There is some indication that by changing their environment to be more inclusive and welcoming of difference, the incidence of bullying of students with disabilities can be decreased. Saylor and Leach (2009) implemented an inclusion program for students with disabilities and their typical peers that focused on collaboration through teaching about different types of disabilities. At the end of the inclusion program, students with disabilities reported lower rates of bullying than they had at the beginning of the program; however, the frequency of reported bullying was still significantly higher for students with disabilities than for typical peers (Saylor & Leach, 2009).

Legal Aspects of Bullying Related to Students with Disabilities

There are legal ramifications for the bullying of students with disabilities, since federal law governs much of special education and the rules of access for people with disabilities (Maag & Katsiyannis, 2012). The Office of Civil Rights (OCR) (2010), a division of the U.S. Department of Education (USDOE), states that bullying based on race, color, national origin, sex, or disability constitutes discrimination, and schools can be held responsible if they are aware of bullying but do not act to reduce the hostility of the environment for students. The OCR (2010) indicates that once a student with a disability reports bullying activity, the school has the responsibility to investigate and take steps to address it. If students with disabilities who are bullied in public schools feel as though they are in a hostile environment and that the issue is not being addressed, they may be able to file a due process complaint against the school for failing to guarantee a free and appropriate public education (FAPE), which is a pillar of the IDEA (Maag & Katsiyannis, 2012). In addition to this statement from the OCR, which provided administrative direction on the interpretation of federal law and the methods for dealing with bullying of students with disabilities within the public school environment, students with disabilities are also protected under Section 504 of the Rehabilitation Act of 1973, which explicitly prohibits discrimination on the basis of disability (Maag & Katsiyannis, 2012). Under Section 504, failure to address bullying based on disability is a violation of a student with disability's civil rights.

Precedent has been set within the judicial branch of the federal government to direct and support schools in determining what action to take if a student with a disability is being bullied (Maag & Katsiyannis, 2012). The courts have found that schools are culpable for the impact of bullying on the education of students with disabilities if they were aware that the bullying was taking place but did nothing to address the situation (cases include *Davis v. Monroe County Board of Education* [1999], and *M.P. by K. and D.P. v. Independent School District No. 721* [2003]) (Maag & Katsiyannis, 2012). In the case of Elsa, it is unclear whether the staff at her school had been aware of the bullying that was occurring. If indeed they were and did not act on it, according to federal mandate they would be in violation of her rights to FAPE. In that case, the court's options for censuring the public school include the development of a corrective action plan, the provision of compensatory education, and/or reimbursement to parents for outside tutoring services (Maag & Katsiyannis, 2012).

For students with disabilities who are the perpetrators of bullying, it is essential that Individualized Education Program (IEP) teams identify these areas of concern and address them through the IEP using positive behavioral supports and other educational interventions. The IDEA requires that any deficits in students' performance that inhibit their access to the general education environment be identified and addressed within the IEP (2004). Students with disabilities who display aggressive behaviors in school should be assessed using functional behavioral analysis (FBA) strategies in order to develop a behavioral intervention plan (BIP) that teaches an appropriate replacement behavior. Since much of the behavior related to the perpetration of bullying is linked to a lack of normative social interactions, it is important that a plan be developed to address these interventions and try to teach students with disabilities more appropriate ways of interacting with their peers. For Elsa, the aggressive behaviors she showed are clearly related to her identified disability. The incident at lunch should precipitate a functional behavioral analysis and the development for interventions related to impulse control and social skills that might better allow her to interact with her peers in the general education environment.

Shifting the Tide of Bullying to Support Students with Disabilities

In order to stem the tide of bullying in relation to students with disabilities, it is important for preservice and inservice teachers to understand (a) the social construction of disability, (b) the characteristics of individual students with disabilities, (c) the environmental structure of the school environment, and (d) how these variables interact with each other to create situations in which bullying can occur. Students with disabilities are more likely than their typical peers to be both the victims and the perpetrators of bullying because of characteristics and behaviors that often deviate from the normative structure of the school environment, as well as strategies they have developed due to inaccessible or segregated school placements. In order to appropriately address cases of bullying related to students with disabilities, public educators must be aware of these interactions and work tirelessly to ensure that the school environment is structured in a way that supports all students so that everyone has access to a safe, welcoming, and appropriate educational environment.

Elsa's story shows that, if educators take the time to explain disability both to the student who has been identified as having a disability as well as his or her peers, an awareness of disability can develop that may mitigate the sociocultural context that limited Elsa's interactions with a typical environment. By helping students understand disability and how it may lead to characteristics that deviate from the "normative" social environment, educators can ensure that students like Elsa are attending school in environments that are understanding and supportive of their needs.

References

Davis, L.J. (2002). *Bending over backwards: Disability, dismodernism & other difficult positions*. New York: New York University Press.

Carter, B.B., & Spencer, V.G. (2006). The fear factor: Bullying and students with disabilities. *International Journal of Special Education, 21*, 11–23.

Danforth, S. (2001). A pragmatic evaluation of three models of disability in special education. *Journal of Developmental and Physical Disabilities, 13*(4), 343–359.

Elementary and Secondary Education Act of 2001, 20 U.S.C. 6301 Sec. 1 et seq.

Estell, D.B., Farmer, T.W., Irvin, M.J., Crowther, A., Akos, P., & Boudah, D.J. (2009). Students with exceptionalities and the peer group context of bullying and victimization in late elementary school. *Journal of Child and Family Studies, 18*, 136–150.

Ferri, B.A. (2008). Doing a (dis)Service: Reimagining special education from a disability studies perspective. In W. Ayers, T. Quinn, & D. Stovall (Eds.), *The handbook of social justice in education*. Mahwah, NJ: Lawrence Erlbaum.

Flynt, S.W., & Morton, R.C. (2004). Bullying and children with disabilities. *Journal of Instructional Psychology, 31*, 330–333.

Individuals with Disabilities Education Improvement Act, H.R. 1350, 108th Congress (2004).

Jackson, L., & Panyan, M. V. (2002). *Positive behavior supports in the classroom: Principles and practice*. Baltimore: Paul H. Brooks.

Linton, S. (1998). *Claiming disability, knowledge and identity*. New York: New York University Press.

Longmore, P. (2003). *Why I burned my book and other essays on disability*. Philadelphia: Temple University Press.

Maag, J.W., & Katsiyannis, A. (2012). Bullying and students with disabilities: Legal and practice considerations. *Behavioral Disorders, 37*, 78–86.

McEvoy, A. (2005). *Teachers who bully students: Patterns and policy implications*. Paper presented at the Hamilton Fish Institute's Persistently Safe Schools Conference. Philadelphia, PA, September 11–14.

Miller, s. (2012). Mythology of the norm: Disrupting the culture of bullying in schools. *English Journal*, *101*(6), 107–109.

Rose, C.A., Espelage, D.L., Aragon, S.R., & Elliott, J. (2011). Bullying and victimization among students in special education and general education curricula. *Exceptionality Education International*, *21*(3), 2–14.

Rose, C.A., Espelage, D.L., & Monda-Amaya, L.E. (2009). Bullying and victimisation rates among students in general and special education: A comparative analysis. *Educational Psychology: An International Journal of Experimental Education*, *29*, 761–776.

Saylor, C.F., & Leach, J.B. (2009). Perceived bullying and social support in students accessing special inclusion programming. *Journal of Developmental and Physical Disabilities*, *21*(1), 69–80.

Scruggs, T.E., Mastropieri, M.A., & Okolo, C.M. (2008). Science and social studies for students with disabilities. *Focus on Exceptional Children*, *41*(2), 1–24.

Siebers, T. (2008). *Disability theory*. Ann Arbor: University of Michigan Press.

U.S. Department of Education, Office of Civil Rights. (2010). Dear colleague letter: Harassment and bullying. Retrieved January 20, 2013, from http://www2.ed.gov/about/offices/list/ocr/letters/colleague-201010.html

White, N.A., & Loeber, R. (2008). Bullying and special education as predictors of serious delinquency. *Journal of Research in Crime and Delinquency*, *45*, 380–397.

CHAPTER FIVE

Black Ritual Insults

Causing Harm or Passing Time?

Tyrone Rivers & Dorothy Espelage

Student 1: Someone said you look like a black Skittle.
Student 2: Someone said you look like a Puma shoe!
Onlookers: (laugh)
Student 1: Why yo eyes look'n at each other? You look serious when you happy.
Student 2: Why you shaped like a pound cake?
Onlookers: (laugh)

Bullying and Victimization Among Black Youth

A significant gap in the bullying literature at present is the lack of scholarship surrounding ethnically diverse populations (Espelage & Horne, 2008). In Peskin, Tortolero, and Markham's (2006) sample of Black and Hispanic middle and high school students, Blacks had higher rates of group teasing, harassing others, teasing others, and upsetting other students for enjoyment compared to Hispanics. Blacks also had higher rates of being teased and called names. All of these variables are characteristics of Black ritual insults. An earlier study conducted by Nansel et al. (2001), based on a nationally representative sample, found that Hispanic/Latino students reported bullying others more than White or African American students, whereas African Americans reported peer victimization more than Whites or Hispanic/Latinos. A recent study by Wang, Iannotti, and Nansel (2009) found that African American students were more frequently involved in bullying others (physical, verbal, and cyber) as compared to Whites and Hispanic/Latinos.

However, when victimization is measured more broadly and in contexts outside of the school, the experiences of Black youth look different than in studies that just measure bullying. For example, Turner and colleagues (2011) assessed six types of victimization, including peer physical assault (for example, being hit, kicked, punched, or attacked with or without a weapon) and physical intimidation (being grabbed, chased, or forced to do something against one's will), among a nationally representative study of 2,999 students between the ages of 6 and 17. Findings indicated that Black youth experienced more physical assaults than their White counterparts (31.5% vs. 20.7%). Further, Black youth from 10 to 13 years old had particularly elevated rates of polyvictimization, meaning they reported multiple forms of victimization by peers, family, or in the community (Finkelhor, Shattuck, Turner, Ormrod, & Hamby, 2011). While studies have shown that Black youth experience the most pervasive types of bullying, a phenomenon exists between or intraculturally among Black youth.

Roasting or Ritualistic Insults Among Black Youth

A way in which Black youth manage multiple experiences of victimization is to engage in what is called roasting. In the Black community, roasting behavior (that is, Black ritual insults) has become widely popular; however, scholars largely overlook this activity in the bullying literature. One exception was Graham and Juvonen's (2002) study of peer harassment among African American, Hispanic, and multiethnic students in an urban middle school. Results indicated that African American youth in the sample received more peer nominations for aggressiveness. Graham and Juvonen mentioned the phenomenon of Black ritual insults, its prosocial functions, and how other racial groups may misunderstand it as verbal harassment. However, these authors did not discuss the potentially adverse effects of roasting, and it should not be assumed that roasting always improves African American friendships. Within-group variability should be accounted for. Though roasting is indeed an oral tradition that has a long history among Black individuals, our research indicates that not all individuals enjoy being roasted, and for that reason some adolescents do not roast others. More research needs to be conducted on this topic to understand the differential impact of this activity on adolescents.

What Are Black Ritual Insults?

Black ritual insult contests can be defined as talking about someone in a group of three or more people through clever insults (Smitherman, 1977). Played for fun or to be mean, this Black oral tradition dates back to American slavery (Smitherman, 1977) and even to Africa (Chimenzie, 1976). Across the country (Percelay,

Dweck, & Ivey, 1995; Smitherman, 2000), the game or activity is known by different names—*roastin'* is what it is called in the Southeast and on the popular urban media website WorldStar Hip Hop. *Heatin'* is what it is called in the Chicago area. *Signifying* and *playing the dozens* are older terms, the latter referring to ritually insulting one's mother or relatives (Garner, 1983; Smitherman, 1977). The name of this oral tradition usually changes with each generation, but the fundamentals of the activity remain the same (Labov, 1972; Smitherman, 2000). "Roasting" will be used throughout this chapter to reflect this activity.

Hubert "Rap" Brown (1974), former leader of the Student Nonviolent Coordinating Committee (SNCC), described a roasting session (defined here as two or more people or groups roasting each other in competition) and the intent of a ritual insult contest in his autobiography *Die Nigger Die!*

> [W]hat you try to do is totally destroy somebody else with your words. It's that whole competition thing again, fighting each other. There'd be sometimes 40 or 50 dudes standing around and the winner was determined by the way they responded to what was said. If you fell all over each other laughing, then you knew you'd scored.... The real aim of the dozens was to get a dude so mad that he'd cry or get mad enough to fight.... Signifying is more humane. Instead of coming down on somebody's mother, you come down on them. (p. 206)

As alluded to by Brown, roasting is viewed largely as a competition in the Black community. Participants aim to recite the funniest joke and get the biggest reaction from their nearby audience of peers. The person who makes the crowd or group laugh the hardest wins the session.

Although the intent of roasting is to arouse a negative emotional response from one's competitor, scholars note that the jokes are not meant to be taken seriously (Garner, 1983; Lefever, 1981; Smitherman, 2000). Roasting is supposed to be taken in good humor (Garner, 1983; Smitherman, 1977). In other words, "it's not personal, it's [just] business" (Smitherman, 2000, p. 223). In the opening roasting session, for instance, Student 1's reference to the dark skin of Student 2 through the metaphorical use of a black Skittle is not supposed to be taken seriously by Student 2. Likewise, Student 1 is not supposed to take it personally when Student 2 references his weight by comparing him to a pound cake. Further, Smitherman (1977) stated that the insults must be impersonal in order to maintain control in a roasting session and prevent fights. For example, it is disrespectful to talk about an ailing or deceased relative, so the opening example could lead to a physical fight if, for instance, Student 2 is sensitive about his complexion and begins to take the jokes about himself personally.

Labov (1972) asserted that the difference between personal insults and ritual insults can be identified by the responses they are met with: "A personal insult is answered by a denial, excuse, or mitigation, whereas a sound or ritual insult is answered by another sound" (p. 298). However, Kochman (1983) argued that roasting "insults may still be personal (true) even though they are not denied" (p. 331). In a roasting session, play becomes serious when an insult is met with a denial. The responsibility to maintain the play framework rests solely with the recipient. So, in the opening vignette, it is up to Student 2 to respond with a ritual insult of his own to maintain the play framework. If a recipient responds to being roasted by roasting back, the play continues. But if that person responds with a defensive denial, an argument can ensue. For instance, if Student 2 responded to Student 1's initial insult by saying, "I'm not even that dark!", Student 1's joke would no longer fit into the category of "ritual insult." The joke is now personal. However, the person in competition loses if he or she responds with a denial, because roasting is supposed to be answered with more roasting (whether the initial joke be personal or impersonal). It is important to note that as the jokes get more and more personal, it becomes increasingly difficult for recipients to not take what is being said about them seriously.

Are Black Ritual Insults Harmless?

Roasting behavior is very popular in the Black community (Abrahams, 1990; Cole, 1974; Dollard, 1939; Kochman, 1969; Percelay et al., 1995). However, scholars in the developmental literature largely overlook this activity, and the current function and outcome of roasting among early adolescents is not understood. Thus, we conducted two studies with middle school students to explore the contemporary dynamics of roasting. Study 1 included 12 Black males (7 seventh graders and 5 eighth graders) who shared their thoughts, experiences, and the psychosocial effects of roasting through focus groups and a self-reported survey. Study 2 included a diverse sample of 141 seventh- and eighth-grade male and female students (54.6% identified as African American/Black, 15.6% identified as multiracial, and 5% identified as Hispanic/Latino; *Males n* = 69) who responded to a survey developed for this study that intended to measure roasting attitudes, behaviors, and motivations, and also the relationship among roasting, depression, and students' sense of belonging in school.

The theoretical framework guiding this research was the verbal aggressiveness model (Infante & Rancer, 1996). From this perspective, roasting is viewed as verbal aggression. Verbal aggressiveness is defined as "attacking the self-concepts of others in order to inflict psychological pain, such as humiliation, embarrassment, depression, and other negative feelings about self" (Infante & Wigley, 1986, as cited in Infante & Rancer, 1996, p. 323). Both roasting and verbally aggressive messages include teasing, ridicule, attacks on personal appearance, obscenities, and gestures. Individuals who engage in high levels of verbal aggressiveness use these messages more frequently than individuals who engage in low-level aggressive messages. Additionally, individuals who are high in verbal aggressiveness appear less sensitive to the aforementioned messages when on the receiving end, because they do not view verbally aggressive messages as hurtful.

Many themes were revealed in Study 1. Consistent with the literature, roasting was found to occur among friends, strangers, groups, and family, but a heretofore-unmentioned type of roasting, which takes place between teachers and students, was also revealed. Roasting perceptions and behaviors varied among students. Some reported having a positive attitude toward roasting, while others reported having a negative attitude. The themes revealed that students roast others for fun, for revenge, to protect themselves, to defend themselves, to build character, and because someone does or says something outside of the norm that merits being roasted. Further (and adding to the literature), roasting can have adverse psychosocial effects on students: it can lower their self-esteem, hurt their feelings, instigate physical fights, and prevent them from learning in class.

General descriptive statistics were conducted to identify trends for the 12 students: Although 100% (12 of 12) reported that they did not like being roasted, 50% (6 of 12) reported that they enjoyed roasting other individuals. More specifically, 41.7% (5 of 12) reported that they enjoy roasting their friends, and 33.3% (4 of 12) reported that they enjoy roasting people they do not know. In addition, 66.6% (4 of 6) of students who do not enjoy roasting other people reported that they feel less self-confident after being roasted, while 100% (6 of 6) of students who enjoy roasting others reported that they do *not* feel less self-confident after being roasted. There was some evidence that roasting is a common activity. For example, 83.3% of students (10 of 12) reported having roasted someone in the last 7 days, and 58.3% of students (7 of 12) reported having roasted two or more people at once during this time. Further, 83.3% of students (10 of 12) reported that they roast others to defend themselves (i.e., roast others after being roasted/attacked), and 41.7% of students (5 of 12) reported that they roast others to protect themselves (that is, to keep from being roasted/attacked). In addition, 66.6% of students (4 of 6) who *enjoy* roasting other people do so to protect themselves, while only 16.6% of students (1 of 6) who do *not enjoy* roasting other people do so to protect themselves. In terms of frequency, for those students who enjoy roasting other people, 83.3% of them (5 of 6) had not been roasted in the last 7 days. However, one student who reported that he does not enjoy roasting other people was roasted by others "10 or more times" in the last 7 days. In addition, three students who do not enjoy roasting others were roasted by someone "1 or 2 times" in the last 7 days.

In Study 1, there was preliminary evidence that roasting is supported by the verbal aggressiveness model (Infante & Rancer, 1996). Focus group participants who enjoy roasting are generally individuals who are high in verbal aggression. They roast more often and are not as psychologically affected when roasted, perhaps because they do not view verbally aggressive messages as hurtful. It can also be argued that developing "thick skin" from being roasted is equal to being "desensitized" to verbally aggressive messages. In contrast, those who do not enjoy roasting are considered low verbal aggressives. They roast much less frequently (if at all), and they are more inclined to be adversely affected psychologically after being roasted. Students who feel less self-confident after being roasted said that they do not participate in roasting activities in order to protect themselves (in other words, they do not initiate roasting episodes or sessions). Perhaps these students lack roasting ability.

Study 2 included a self-report survey with a larger group of male and female middle school students. Students completed survey items/scales assessing their perceptions of roasting and the impact of roasting. A majority of the participants (75.4%) do not like it when others roast them. However, 73.5% reported roasting someone else in the 7 days before the study. Most of the participants (64.5%) try not to do or say anything that will make others roast them. Over half (52.5%) feel bad inside after roasting someone else—that is, they feel guilty for saying what they said to the other person. Most participants (60.9%) also do not believe that saying "I'm just playing" to someone before roasting that person excuses a potentially hurtful joke. In other words, in contrast to the literature (Percelay et al., 1995; Smitherman, 2000), the play context of roasting does not justify hurtful remarks. In the 7 days prior to our survey, 51.4% of the participants roasted someone else because they were angry (8.6% of these students roasted someone else 10 or more times because they were angry). Many of the participants (65.3%) reported that when other students start roasting in class, it distracts them from learning. Many of the students (66.4%) also reported that teachers/administrators should stop students from roasting in school. Finally, 70.9% of the students reported that school would be a better place if no one roasted.

In Study 2, students completed measures concerning traditional verbal bullying and physical fighting. Correlational analyses yielded positive significant relations between roasting and verbal bullying perpetration and physical fighting. Attitudes supportive of roasting were also associated with greater verbal bullying perpetration and fighting perpetration. Further, holding attitudes supportive of roasting was associated with feeling less guilty after roasting sessions and episodes. Based on the results of Study 1, there is a basis for the idea that students who hold attitudes supportive of roasting are likely to roast others who are not their friends. Pro-roasting attitudes were also associated with less change in self-confidence when students were roasted by someone else. In contrast, feeling socially anxious around others who are roasting was associated with less bully perpetration and fighting perpetration, but it was also associated with greater feelings of diminished self-confidence when roasted. Further, reports of more experiences of general peer victimization were significantly associated with social anxiety and diminished self-confidence as a result of roasting.

Correlational analyses in Study 2 also indicated that holding attitudes supportive of roasting was associated with less school sense of belonging. These findings support the notion that students who are disengaged with their school might engage in roasting in order to belong or to pass the time. However, more research needs to be conducted with longitudinal data in order to understand this correlation. Perhaps roasting is a way for these students to distract themselves in class when (a) they do not like the subject being taught, (b) they do not like the teacher, or (c) they do not understand how to do the work. The opening vignette in this chapter could very well take place in the classroom, and by studying these exchanges, teachers can learn how to identify, intervene, and redirect behavior.

Conclusion

The studies described in this chapter represent an effort to begin a discussion centering on culture-specific bullying. Roasting is framed within the context of a game where participants are expected to endure the pain caused by insults. These insults may include attacks on an individual's personal attributes, clothing, social status (or lack thereof), and family members, to name a few. When consenting individuals engage in roasting games, it may be interpreted as a fun activity. However, when non-consenting individuals become targets of roasting behaviors, these episodes mimic bullying behaviors in many ways. In order to help improve the social climate in schools, students (and adults) who favor roasting need to be sensitive to the line between consenting and non-consenting individuals and respect a non-consenting individual's wish to not engage in roasting behavior.

Regardless, Berdie's (1947) participants, all of whom admitted to habitually roasting others, described the activity as "*mean, low, nasty,* and in general not socially acceptable" (p. 121). Johnson (1941) stated that "being put in the dozens is one of the worst things that can happen to someone" (as cited in Golightly & Scheffler, 1948, p. 104). Finally, author Ossie Guffy (1971) recalled a childhood memory of her grandfather telling her and her friends his thoughts on ritual insults after catching them play as kids.

> "When I was coming up," Grandpa said, "I heard about that game, only I heard about it the way it used to be, and I heard how it started and why it started. It was a game slaves used to play, only they wasn't just playing for fun. They was playing to teach themselves and their sons how to stay alive. The whole idea was to learn to take whatever the master said to you without answering back or hitting him, 'cause that was the way a slave had to be, so's he could go on living. It maybe was a bad game, but it was necessary. It ain't necessary now." (Cited in Lefever, 1981, p. 79)

For centuries, slave mothers and fathers made disparaging remarks to their children in order to protect them from hostile slave masters (Leary, 2005). Yet what began as a necessary adjustment to a cruel and unsafe society was later passed down through the generations to a time when the benefits might not outweigh the costs. Leary (2005) comments that some behaviors adopted for survival in slavery times, but still used today, can keep the Black community from flourishing. Roasting may be among these behaviors, which should be "replaced with behaviors which promote and maximize [the Black community's] progress" (p. 16). Further, the principle of being cognizant of the words one uses against another person would obviously be useful not only in the Black community but in all communities, especially within primary and secondary schools. This could lead to improved student-to-student and student-to-teacher interactions.

But given the value placed on high verbal ability in the Black community, a challenge to educators, researchers, and policymakers will be how to maximize the benefits gained from roasting while also eliminating its costs. Some suggestions raised here are:

1. Apply culturally responsive teaching practices (Brayboy & Castagno, 2009; Santamaria, 2009; Villegas & Lucas, 2007) by allowing students more verbal creativity in assignments (for example, verbal presentations).

2. Decrease down time in classrooms where roasting is an issue, because boredom fuels roasting perpetration.

3. Implement a zero-tolerance policy for roasting in classrooms. There is usually zero tolerance for saying "gay" and "homo" to describe things or people, but there is nothing to prevent a student from tearing down a classmate's self-esteem through roasting. This should not be the case.

4. Teachers should have candid discussions with students about roasting (how it started, why it started, its place in society) and its power to hurt others. Just because the activity is largely portrayed as harmless in the media does not make it so.

5. Adults in the school need to set the example. If the adults are roasting each other and also the students, they cannot expect the students to refrain from roasting others, either.

Teachers need to recognize roasting when they see it and understand that not all students benefit from roasting, and involvement takes away from students' feeling of safety and security in schools and challenges their readiness to learn. Students and teachers need to talk about how someone who cannot roast feels about the pressure to roast. First and foremost, everyone who works with youth needs to be aware of ritual insults and the detrimental effects that it might have on academic outcomes for students. Unfortunately, in many U.S. public schools, teachers and administrators do not understand roasting and therefore do nothing about it. Thus, raising awareness through professional development is needed. More research on the topic must be a priority, too, since prevention strategies need to be developed to minimize the adverse outcomes associated with roasting.

References

Abrahams, R.D. (1990). Playing the dozens. In A. Dundes (Ed.), *Mother wit from the laughing barrel* (pp. 295–309). Jackson: University Press of Mississippi.

Berdie, R.F. (1947). Playing the dozens. *Journal of Abnormal and Social Psychology, 42*, 120–121.

Brayboy, B.M.J., & Castagno, A. (2009). Self-determination through self-education: Culturally responsive schooling for indigenous students in the USA. *Teaching Education, 20*(1), 31–53.

Brown, H.R. (1974). Street talk. In T. Kochman (Ed.), *Rappin' and stylin' out* (pp. 205–208). Urbana: University of Illinois Press.

Chimenzie, A. (1976). The dozens: An African-heritage theory. *Journal of Black Studies, 6*, 401–420.

Cole, R.W. (1974). Ribbin', jivin', and playin' the dozens. *Phi Delta Kappan, 56*, 171–175.

Dollard, J. (1939). The dozens: Dialectic of insult. *American Imago, 1*, 3–25.

Espelage, D.L., & Horne, A.M. (2008). School violence and bullying prevention: From research-based explanations to empirically based solutions. In S.D. Brown & R.W. Lent (Eds.), *Handbook of counseling psychology* (pp. 588–598). Hoboken, NJ: John Wiley.

Finkelhor, D., Shattuck, A., Turner, H.A., Ormrod, R., & Hamby, S.L. (2011). Polyvictimization in developmental context. *Journal of Child & Adolescent Trauma, 4*(4), 291–300.

Garner, T. (1983). Playing the dozens: Folklore as strategies for living. *Quarterly Journal of Speech, 69*(1), 47–57.

Golightly, C.L., & Scheffler, I. (1948). "Playing the dozens": A note. *Journal of Abnormal and Social Psychology, 43*, 104–105.

Graham, S., & Juvonen, J. (2002). Ethnicity, peer harassment, and adjustment in middle school: An exploratory study. *Journal of Early Adolescence, 22*, 173–199.

Guffy, O., & Ledner, C. (1971). *Ossie: The autobiography of a Black woman.* New York: W.W. Norton.

Infante, D.A., & Rancer, A.S. (1996). Argumentativeness and verbal aggressiveness: A review of recent theory and research. *Communication Yearbook, 19*, 319–351.

Infante, D.A., & Wigley, C.J. (1986). Verbal aggressiveness: An interpersonal model and measure. *Communication Monographs, 53*, 61–69.

Johnson, C.S. (1941). *Growing up in the Black belt.* Washington, DC: American Council on Education.

Kochman, T. (1969). "Rapping" in the Black ghetto. *Trans-Action, 6*(4), 26–34.

Kochman, T. (1983). The boundary between play and nonplay in Black verbal dueling. *Language Socialization, 12*, 329–337.

Labov, W. (1972). Rules for ritual insult. In T. Kochman (Ed.), *Rappin' and stylin' out* (pp. 265–314). Urbana: University of Illinois Press.

Leary, J.D. (2005). *Post traumatic slave syndrome: America's legacy of enduring injury and healing.* Milwaukie, OR: Uptone Press.

Lefever, H.G. (1981). "Playing the dozens": A mechanism for social control. *Phylon, 42*, 73–85.

Nansel, T.R., et al. (2001). Bullying behaviors among US youth: Prevalence and association with psychological adjustment. *Journal of the American Medical Association, 285*, 2094–2100.

Percelay, J.L., Dweck, S., & Ivey, M. (1995). *Double snaps.* New York: Quill.

Peskin, M.F., Tortolero, S.R., & Markham, C.M. (2006). Bullying and victimization among Black and Hispanic adolescents. *Adolescence, 41*, 467–484.

Santamaria, L.J. (2009). Culturally responsive differentiated instruction: Narrowing gaps between the best pedagogical practices benefiting all learners. *Teachers College Record, 111*(1), 214–247.

Smitherman, G. (1977). *Talkin and testifyin: The language of Black America*. Boston: Houghton Mifflin.

Smitherman, G. (2000). *Talkin that talk: Language, culture and education in African America*. New York: Routledge.

Turner, H.A., Finkelhor, D., Hamby, S.L., Shattuck, A., & Ormrod, R.K. (2011). Specifying type and location of peer victimization in a national sample of children and youth. *Journal of Youth & Adolescence, 40*(8), 1052–1067.

Villegas, A.M., & Lucas, T. (2007). The culturally responsive teacher. *Educational Leadership, 64*(6), 28–33.

Wang, J., Iannotti, R.J., & Nansel, T.R. (2009). School bullying among adolescents in the United States: Physical, verbal, relational, and cyber. *Journal of Adolescent Health, 45*(4), 368–375.

CHAPTER SIX

Bullying and Harassment Prevention in the Lives of Latina and Latino Students

Rodrigo Joseph Rodríguez

"Today I still bear that scar on my chest like a scarlet letter." —David Ray Ritcheson (1988–2007), from testimony to the U.S. House of Representatives, Judiciary Committee, April 17, 2007

"Your influence and the relationships that you build with your students, along with an unconditional positive regard towards them, will speak more for your level of work than any test score ever could." —Juan Sánchez (2011, p. 66)

On April 23, 2006, in the suburbs of Houston, David Ray Ritcheson was beaten unconscious and sexually assaulted by two teenage White supremacists. He was a student at Klein Collins High School (Spring Independent School District) in Spring, Texas, and 16 years old when these violent acts occurred. David was a talented and beloved student, a former football running back and star athlete, the freshman homecoming prince, and a participant in several other extracurricular activities. In spite of these accomplishments, David was tormented in and out of the classroom, and his schooling experiences were filled with fearful, hurtful, and brutal attacks.

On that April day, David Henry Tuck and Keith Robert Turner dragged David, a Latino youth, into a backyard, where they taunted him with racial slurs. They punched and kicked him, attempted to carve a swastika into this chest, burned him with cigarettes, sodomized him with a patio umbrella pipe, and poured bleach onto his open wounds. For their crimes, Tuck and Turner were convicted and imprisoned for aggravated sexual assault.

Following invasive surgeries and a prolonged recovery, David's awareness about bullying and hate crimes sparked his commitment to justice and safer spaces everywhere, regardless of differences or disabilities among people. Confined to a wheelchair, David worked with courage and strength alongside the Anti-Defamation League for the founding of an anti-hate and -bullying prevention program at Klein Collins High School. His work was not solely limited to his hometown of Spring, Texas; he was on a citizen's mission to awaken us about hate crimes and school violence across the country and even in our very own backyards. On April 17, 2007, David appeared as a student, survivor, activist, and ambassador before the U.S. House of Representatives Judiciary Committee's Subcommittee on Crime, Terrorism and Homeland Security in support of the Local Law Enforcement Hate Crimes Prevention Act of 2007.

Although David attempted to return to school, the physical and emotional pain and peer pressure at school and in society became too great for him as a survivor. He struggled with the trauma and feelings of isolation, alienation, and victimization associated with the violence he had endured at the hands of his peers, which sj Miller references in Chapter 1 as complex post-traumatic stress disorder (C-PTSD). On July 1, 2007, David committed suicide by jumping to his death from the Carnival Ecstasy cruise ship in the Gulf of Mexico. David was not alive to witness the passage of the Matthew Shepard and James Byrd, Jr. Hate Crimes Prevention Acton October 22, 2009, signed into law by President Barack Obama on October 28, 2009.

David's activism as a student and survivor led to changes introduced by schools and legislative bodies to enforce the protection of our citizens. Thus far, a total of 49 states have passed and implemented anti-bullying measures, and new school policies are being developed to protect students and families. This chapter will briefly highlight Latino education and challenges, approaches initiated by teachers for culturally diverse thinking and learning, and classroom-tested strategies to support and guarantee safe and positive learning experiences for Latino students and their peers.

Demographic Trends and Their Impact on Bullying of Latina and Latino Students

Latinos constitute the fastest-growing segment of the U.S. population, and Latino students, who account for more than 22% of our public elementary and secondary school population, form majorities in many public school districts across the country (García Bedolla, 2012; Jensen & Sawyer, 2012). In 2010, 11 million Latino students were enrolled in U.S. public schools (National Center for Education Statistics, 2011b). Latino families are linguistically diverse and can identify as monolingual Spanish, monolingual English, or bilingual English and Spanish speakers at varying levels of proficiency.

Growth in the U.S. Latino[1] population is taking place nationwide, but most notably in the West and the South. For instance, Latino enrollment increased from 2.3 million in 1989 to 4.9 million in 2009 in the West, which represented 40% of total enrollment in that year. In the South, the number of Latino students increased from 1.5 million in 1989 to 3.9 million in 2009 (National Center for Educational Statistics, 2011a). Contreras (2011) describes these demographic changes as the "browning of America—a United States that has rapidly become both multicultural and multilingual" (p. 2). Along with this growth, culturally responsive learning and teaching needs for public school teachers and English language learners must become part of redesigned curricula, instruction, and policy. Advocacy and activism are essential pillars of change, especially as demographic trends affect access to schooling, resources, and capital.

Given these increasing numbers of Latino students, educational environments must be responsive to the changing population. When needs are left unattended, bullying behavior is likely to manifest. The challenges facing many Latino students are far greater than those facing their peers, with patterns of bullying and harassment appearing in our news feeds every week. Latino and Asian American students experience bullying, harassment, and victimization at statistically similar rates as their White peers (Peguero, 2009). Some of the bullying and harassment can be attributed to racial and ethnic stereotypes and students' perceptions and interactions. In addition, Latino students face disparities and barriers to obtaining a quality education in the face of steady dropout rates. The research led by Peguero and Williams (2011) found that victimization is stratified by race, ethnicity, and gender, and that stereotypes moderate provoke bullying and other peer harassment among racial and ethnic youth.

Peguero's most recent research (2012) identified four influences that increase the vulnerability of youth, including Latino youth, to being bullied at school: (a) race and ethnicity, (b) being an immigrant, (c) gender, and (d) sexual orientation. Moreover, researchers have found that stereotypes can be linked to socioeconomic status, student test scores, generational immigration status, and interscholastic sports participation. Issues of immigration and the politics of exclusion and inclusion recently became more heated as the U.S. Census Bureau reported that non-White births in the United States have become the majority, and the Deferred Action for Childhood Arrivals Process was approved in June 2012. Terms applied to immigrant youth, such as illegal, undocumented, and remedial, are labels that increase segregation practices and alienation in our schools (Patel, 2012).

A spectrum of challenges and variables connected to frequencies of bullying, peer harassment, and peer victimization appear in the schooling experiences of Latino students at the middle and high school levels. Bauman and Summers (2009) studied both relational and indirect victimization between students "being the target of aggressive actions designed to damage relationships and social status. Examples are social exclusion, rumor spreading, and withholding friendship" (p. 516). Bauman and Summers further identified the prominence of relational victimization through passive and emotional distress in early adolescence (middle school); as schools "impose harsh sanctions for overt aggression, covert and indirect forms increase." The enforcement of sanctions and policies often emphasizes punishment and corrective measures related solely to overt aggression instead of education about, and prevention of, covert and indirect bullying, peer harassment, and peer victimization.

In response to intracultural bullying, and as a means of broadening the discussion from the general population to specific groups, research led by Mendez, Bauman, and Guillory (2012) documented exchanges between a small sample of Mexican immigrants and Mexican American students in a predominately Latino high school in Washington State. The study found evidence of bullying based on language acquisition and preferences (English vs. Spanish) and sense of superiority "within an ethnic group, particularly those related to varying levels of acculturation, foster[ing] an environment conducive to bullying" (p. 298). These issues must be addressed in order to create schooling spaces that are safe and inclusive for Latino students and their diverse culture.[2]

In her research study *Subtractive Schooling: U.S.-Mexican Youth and the Politics of Caring* (1999), Angela Valenzuela explained Mexican-origin students' attitudes toward schooling as follows: "While cultural values like respect (*respeto*) encourage deference and docility, a sense of powerlessness or a belief that they are not 'entitled' to openly defy school authority just as powerfully explains their comportment, especially for the more recently arrived [immigrant students]" (pp. 13–14). In the schooling process, teacher awareness of these themes, realities, and issues can inform how they plan and deliver instruction and engage students to maximize their strengths as well as student and teacher ways of knowing, seeing, and reading the world they must navigate for survival and success. Most important, we can teach students about their rights and responsibilities toward each other to combat school climates and peer behaviors that make them feel disrespected and unsafe. For David Ray Ritcheson, however, respect and deference alone could not have spared him from the assault and the bullying he endured. He was harassed by classmates on and off the school grounds. The morning he was brutally assaulted, both he and his assailants were under the influence of drugs. His ability to defend himself was weakened by drugs and alcohol, and the individuals around him who might have helped him did not take immediate action to ensure his safety and well-being.

In *Crossing Boundaries: Teaching and Learning with Urban Youth* (2012), Kinloch posed the following question: "How is power defined in the presence of categories—poor, working-class, wealthy, White, of color, and so on—and what are the educative consequences of relying on those categories?" (p. 11). Categories such as these have ramifications in learning and social spaces if we do not confront and dispel them. David suffered through various categories that limited who he wished to become, independent of the school's and society's social boundaries and norms. In addition, David's ambiguous sexual orientation, perceived as ambiguous, and his ethnic membership contributed to harassment by peers and a series of ongoing assaults.

For Latino students[3] in particular, the dominant, normative concept is evident in their schooling and based on histories of racial, ethnic, and linguistic stratification in the U.S. educational and social system (Peguero, 2012; Peguero & Williams, 2011; Valdés, Capitelli, & Alvarez, 2010; Valenzuela, 1999). Legal challenges mounted by non-dominant racial and ethnic groups seeking equity, equality, and access are numerous and ongoing. The legal and social challenges presented can be examples of what responsible individuals and teachers—as individuals and collectively—have done and continue to do to (a) challenge injustice in the form of bullying, harassment, and violence, and (b) gain inclusion and thence access to equal services and resources in schools and communities (Yabko, Hokoda, & Ulloa, 2008). David's advocacy of legislation to protect young people and vulnerable populations against bullying, peer harassment, and hate crimes is an example of responsible citizenship and action in our local public schools and communities.

Schooling and Vulnerabilities of All Students

Racial, ethnic, and gender-based conflicts have been dominant themes in U.S. school history from the New England Puritans to the Obama era. In fact, economic inequities and real estate disparities are often the basis of disputes among residents over redrawn school boundary lines, which often trigger migration by more affluent citizens to wealthier school districts. These conflicts, disputes, and disparities bring mixed, emotional responses and perspectives about the role of public schooling and who the vulnerable students are.

Access to sports by females was mandated through Title IX in 1972, yet 40 years later most girls in urban and low-income communities lack access to athletic programs. Spring (2011) argues, in retrospect:

> Violence and racism are a basic part of American social and school history. From colonial times to today, educators have preached equality of opportunity and good citizenship while engaging in acts of religious intolerance, racial segregation, cultural genocide, and discrimination against immigrants and nonwhites. Schooling has been plagued by scenes of violence. (pp. 7–8)

Which messages do we seek as teachers to imprint on the everyday lives of our students in order to foster care and empathy for themselves and their fellow humans? The challenge begins with our schools' curriculum and instruction, which should teach the negative consequences of bullying and peer harassment across race, ethnicity, status, gender, and sexual orientation.

Demographic changes can bring both crisis and opportunity to our schools. Our society, which describes itself as post-racial with justice for all, must challenge stereotypes that stratify our schools and institutions, as well as poverty that disenfranchises youth and families. Conchas and Vigil (2012) contend that "Race and ethnicity matter; however, poverty and racism remain the devastating linchpins of inequality. Latinos, Native Americans, Blacks, Whites, and Asians in disenfranchised neighborhoods struggle to access the hopes and dreams of those born into privilege" (p. 1). These struggles for equality enter our schools, and we must be aware and ready to teach students of all backgrounds, including those with special needs. What can we do, then, to shift the tide away from bullying Latino students?

Disrupting the Norm and Belief Structures

In "Mythology of the Norm: Disrupting the Culture of Bullying in Schools" (2012), Miller describes a culture that promotes desired behaviors, appearances, stances, statuses, and utterances as follows:

> Deviation from the norm may pathologize the individual who then must bear the weight of its consequences, which sometimes manifest in the form of a diagnosis, a pill, a hospital treatment, being bullied, internalizing negative self-constructs, or, even worse, *suicide/ bullycide* [emphasis in original].... Unless interrupted and disrupted institutionally, this concept will continue to have power to provoke and reinforce bullying behavior in our schools. (p. 107)

Our work as both teachers and students is to be aware and vigilant of power-based relations that require us to interrupt and disrupt situations such as those described by Miller. For instance, students who are members of various racial, ethnic, immigrant, and linguistic groups and who identify as lesbian, gay, bisexual, or transgendered are susceptible to bullying and harassment from peers—and sometimes from teachers who lack background or experience with today's diverse populations. As a result, we see the persistence of what Bomer (2011) calls the "gatekeeping functions of language," as well as other language and power patterns that emphasize exclusion, deficiency, and hierarchies (p. 271). As teachers, we must plan instructional opportunities and school-wide programming that focus on intentional, inclusionary approaches for educational progress in a democratic society. Our students must connect learning, language, and schooling experiences to their intellectual, emotional, and social responsibility toward adulthood.

To educate and safeguard students, teachers who identify as preservice, beginning, experienced, and veteran must become aware of school policies and practices that have affected minority groups in the United States, including legislation to counter discrimination and unequal access to public and private schooling and academic resources. Conversely, access to media outlets that communicate people's struggle for justice in the United States can help us involve students through empathy and critical thinking. With a growing body of teaching resources now available in print and online formats, we can plan to embed anti-bullying, anti-hate, and LGBTQ issues into our English language arts curriculum and instruction, as well as support disciplinary literacies and the reading of world literatures.

Preservice teachers who work with diverse student populations such as Latinos must become familiar with generational and acculturation differences among Latinos such as (1) linguistic diversity; (2) definitions of family, ethnic, and popular cultures; (3) perceptions of respect and authority; (4) identity influence from migration, immigration, and U.S.-born youth; and (5) distinctions between schooling and education. Many Latino households maintain Spanish as a heritage language, but the odds are that elementary and secondary schools will not be open to linguistic and cultural diversity in curricula and instruction. Definitions of family continue to evolve as American society changes its views of norms and equality, while economic sustainability calls for new ways of surviving with limited and middle-income levels. All of these realities affect youth development, socialization, health, and wellness, as well as opportunities for academic achievement. Future educators must be prepared to address these realities.

The causes of bullying and peer harassment can be complex, but we know the behavior patterns and relationships of bullies and harassers that create vulnerabilities for all. Latino students can be both perpetrators and victims of bullying and harassment, although this is not an ethnic or culturally based behavior but more one that is influenced by society, institutional structures, and perceived behavioral norms. As teachers, we must remain informed and connected about direct and subtle practices that are based on dominance and coercion in our classrooms and schools.

Meyer's (2009) research defined gendered harassment as "any behavior that acts to shape and police boundaries of traditional gender norms: heterosexual masculinity and femininity" (pp. 1–2). Our role as teachers must be to plan instructional opportunities and school-wide programming that focuses on intentional, inclusive approaches to redefining norms, definitions, and expectations that create hostile environments for learning and socialization. Our students can connect their learning and emotional experiences to their social responsibility toward adulthood that requires them to act on behalf of the most vulnerable, who are not always protected in society.

Ascribed gender roles are protected and sanctioned by institutionalized systems. Practices to mediate and control gendered behaviors create power dynamics that can further alienate, marginalize, and oppress our Latino students. Anzaldúa (1999) explained:

> Culture is made by those in power—men. Males make the rules and laws; women transmit them. The culture expects women to show greater acceptance of, and commitment to, the value system than men. The culture and the Church insist that women are subservient to males. (pp. 38–39)

Our task as teachers is to maintain awareness about institutions and systems that create values and beliefs that work against Latino students, and to work toward all of our students' well-being and personal development.

Who are the bullies and victims in our schools? How do we identify them? To answer these questions and extend the discussion further, Blackburn (2012) states:

> Many people in U.S. schools are, in more subtle ways, both victims and bullies, particularly around norms related to gender and sexuality. To pretend otherwise fails to capture and, thus, to address adequately the complexity of homophobia. The protect-and-punish approach also distracts from the real change that needs to happen, that is, the dismantling of oppressive institutions, including schooling. (p. 2)

The thematic approach often used is that of knowledge as power, yet our schooling practices and everyday rules do not empower Latino students to combat oppressive norms and peer habits in our schools. Our institutional knowledge and practices must be questioned in order to determine how we ourselves are participants in creating unsafe, unresponsive, and irrelevant environments for learning.

Expectations of masculinity among Latino males can often include social pressure by enforcing a definition of what constitutes manhood in performances of machismo with bravado, including hypersexualization through archetypes, stereotypes, patriarchy, and matriarchy (Abalos, 2002). Definitions and expectations of masculinity, maleness, and manhood all influence behaviors that are present in our schools. The bullying and peer harassment are often linked to gender expectations and sexual orientation and are not solely based on racial and ethnic stereotypes. David experienced firsthand how these definitions and expectations created hostile environments for him in school and brutal violence in out-of-school settings. Klein (2012) argued:

> Masculinity expectations in the form of heterosexism are a crucial but underexamined motivation for school shootings and school violence generally. While gender norms have presumably relaxed in some ways, they remain oppressive, and gay bashing is still one of the most prevalent and devastating forms of school bullying. It affected most of the school shooters. They were called "queer" and "faggot" as they walked through the school halls; they were tormented emotionally and in many cases threatened or roughed up physically. (p. 82)

Being aware of these realities and the intersections of various social constructions can help us as teachers to recognize the dynamics at play in informing perceptions and possibly behaviors that are meant to dominate peers perceived as different, weak, or even stronger than others. As a result, the conditions and environments required to maintain safe spaces for learning become more complex. Self-identification by students and traditional social-sexual boundaries may need to be reconfigured.

The vulnerabilities of Latino students are greater when teachers are uncomfortable and underprepared, or ignore topics because of personal, political, or religious beliefs. To increase comfort, preparation, and safety, we need to become informed about what measures our colleagues are taking to work across school settings. For instance, Morgan, Mancl, Kaffar, and Ferreira (2011) identified strategies implemented by classroom teachers to create safe environments for students with disabilities who identify as lesbian, gay, bisexual, or transgender. Each of those five strategies has an application to working with Latino students as well.

1. Recognize that students with disabilities have sexuality.

2. Discourage the use of non-inclusive and derogatory language.

3. Develop classroom rules and processes that address homophobic pejoratives.

4. Incorporate LGBT information into the curriculum.

5. Address personal bias.

The strategies apply to any effort to redesign curricula and instruction to make them culturally relevant and responsive to all learners in our schools. David was perceived as an outcast by some of his peers (there was a perception that he was gay), yet he was not defined by the categories and norms imposed upon him through schooling. His friends aided him on many occasions, but the bullying and peer harassment were insurmountable. He sought refuge in himself and refused additional support and professional counseling from a harsh society that was both culturally irrelevant and unresponsive to his needs.

What can we do as teachers to protect our vulnerable Latino youth? How can we create safe environments in which Latino students can explore their ethnic, cultural, and sexual identities? Sexual identity harassment as well as gendered harassment can become pervasive in our schools if we do not implement and enforce anti-bullying policies. Latino students—indeed all students—must be informed about acceptable, respectful, and lawful behaviors in and out of the classroom so that we can eliminate all manifestations of bullying and harassment. Socially ascribed gender norms, attitudes about sexuality, and social expectations of Latino students can lead to varying levels of harmful bullying and peer harassment.

Dignity for All

In their book *Bullying Prevention and Intervention: Realistic Strategies for Schools* (2009), Swearer, Espelage, and Napolitano challenge eight myths about bullying and victimization that some of our teacher colleagues may believe, such as "Bullying is a 'normal' part of growing up" (p. 6). This particular myth excuses professionals, teachers, students, and parents from acting in our shared mission to create safe learning environments and dignity for all. The approach to bullying as "normal" affected David and his acculturation to schooling norms that further added stressors, burdens, and wounds to his life as a young learner and citizen. Notwithstanding the pressures for school accountability from the general public in other areas, all schools must include safe, inclusive learning environments for all students. Indeed, the pressurized atmosphere of high-stakes testing and accountability standards connected to test scores and performance-based salaries cannot undermine the social-emotional conditions and violence created by bullying and peer harassment in the schools (Juvoven, Wang, & Espinoza, 2011).

In our efforts to change norms and initiate a dialogue in our classrooms, we can shift learning conditions that are based solely on the assimilationist power struggle to "fit in" and conform, especially for Latino students. David's story reminds us that we must take action for justice and everlasting change. Change takes place if we plan and act, because this is a matter of protection and safety for our students and their learning. As teachers we can do the following:

1. Know the rules that govern schooling and classroom policies/practices and how these conform to our values and beliefs.

2. Build awareness about safe, inclusive learning environments among colleagues, students, and parents.

3. Listen to students' ways of thinking, speaking, and knowing, including their linguistic innovations.

4. Speak up in various ways through instruction and the everyday connections we build into our classrooms.

5. Exercise the respect we seek from our students and redirect them to adopt student-to-student engagement based on mutual respect.

Our efforts at inclusion can create spaces of belonging for *all* students that meld their unique identities with their sense of self and purpose for learning and growing.

Through these efforts we can maintain the dignity of our teaching life by prioritizing care and respect for all learners and learning, including Latino students who, like many of their peers, must learn under some of the harshest circumstances, climates, and environments. We can model additive, inclusive learning on a belief held by educator and scholar María E. Fránquiz (2010), who stated:

"A premise underlying all my work is that when interpersonal relationships, curricula, and institutional structures do not place value on the native languages, histories, and cultures of students, literacy resources for learning are subtracted and academic resiliency suffers" (p. 95). Students know what we value, and our beliefs and convictions are easily read in Braille with tactile and perceptive precision by our students and colleagues alike.

Rigby (2012) argued that "many species, including our own, have survived and indeed thrived because of an inbuilt predisposition among its members to cooperate and work together for the good of all" (p. 6). David envisioned the humane treatment of the most vulnerable in society. He imagined learning and living free of scarlet letters and wounds. Preventive anti-bullying measures could have helped David to survive and thrive, but we knew and did so little then. David's spirit and resilience, although taken so abruptly from us, challenged us to change how we think, believe, respond, and act.

No human should endure the brutality and sexual assault that occurred on April 23, 2006. Like David, we as individuals and communities can act so that no student wears a scarlet letter. As teachers we can lead instruction and facilitate discussions that foster a more caring, responsive school culture. The horrific crime David endured is a reminder to Americans about the violence experienced daily by people of all ages, abilities, backgrounds, colors, gender expressions, and sexual orientations. It is also a call to action for vulnerable young people in our schools and communities. We can challenge the thinking that allows students to justify either bullying or harassment of peers who do not conform to their social preconceptions. To do nothing only confirms the existence of a conspiracy and culture of silence among teachers and students. Many educational and prevention programs either ignore this issue or favor surface-level discussions with the student body about what is considered the norm or normalcy by societies and institutions of power. These groups dictate the status quo by defining acceptable practices and supporting them through unwritten rules and curricula, subliminal messages, and emotional abuse.

Today our work as educators can be directed at creating safer learning spaces. These should encompass culturally relevant and responsive teaching for all students that include "an unconditional positive regard" for their sense of self, identification, and expression. We can work together with our school colleagues to end institutional practices of bullying and peer harassment that endanger the lives of our students so that they can learn with dignity in an environment that is safe, accepting, and nurturing of their growth and development. As President Obama (2010) reminded us in the "It Gets Better" project:

> You are not alone. You didn't do anything wrong. You didn't do anything to deserve being bullied…. [T]hings will get better. And more than that, with time you're going to see that your differences are a source of pride and a source of strength. You'll look back

on the struggles you've faced with compassion and wisdom. And that's not just going to serve you, but it will help you get involved and make this country a better place. (Cited in Savage & Miller, 2011, p. 9)

Reminders like this one abound in society at large, and we can use them to teach students the meaning of humanity as David envisioned it in his championing of a hate crimes prevention law. We must bring David's story and his letter of advocacy and action into our classrooms as tools for social change and justice against manifestations that hinder our progress and humanity.

Notes

1   The term *Latino* is used to describe male and female persons who are either U.S. or non-U.S. born with ancestral heritage from any Latin American or Caribbean country and are identified as an ethnic group by the U.S. Census Bureau. The U.S. Latino population is diverse and by no means monolithic.

2   The term *culture* is used here as defined by Riggs and das Nair (2012): "Our take on culture includes individual and collective identities carved out from various social markers of culture, which an individual may be able to recognise, acknowledge, affiliate with (and therefore be able to 'articulate'), but may also include those aspects to which he/she feels connected, in a manner which defies reason, and which cannot be communicated through conventional forms of signs and symbols. In our reference to culture, we embrace a wide array of cultural positions and/or identities, which could include race, religion, ability, class, and so forth. Importantly, we are mindful of the immense diversity that exists within cultures, and our intention is to signal that any singular approach to working with any given cultural 'group' will always fail to truly encompass the breadth of experiences that shape what we refer to here as 'culture'" (p. 10).

3   From this point forward, all references to "Latino students" will reflect both Latinas (females) and Latinos (males).

References

Abalos, D.T. (2002). *The Latino male: A radical definition.* Boulder, CO: Lynne Rienner Publishers, Inc.

Anzaldúa, G. (1999). *Borderlands/La frontera: The new mestiza* (4th ed.). San Francisco, CA: Aunt Lute Press.

Bauman, S., & Summers, J.J. (2009). Peer victimization and depressive symptoms in Mexican American middle school students: Including acculturation as a variable of interest. *Hispanic Journal of Behavioral Sciences, 31*(4), 515–535.

Blackburn, M.V. (2011). *Interrupting hate: Homophobia in schools and what literacy can do about it.* New York: Teachers College Press.

Bomer, R. (2011). *Building adolescent literacy in today's English classroom.* Portsmouth, NH: Heinemann.

Bradshaw, C.P., & Waasdorp, T.E. (2009). Measuring and changing a "culture of bullying." *School Psychology Review, 38*(3), 356–361.

Conchas, G.Q., & Vigil, J.D. (2012). *Street smart school smart: Urban poverty and the education of adolescent boys.* New York: Teachers College Press.

Contreras, F. (2011). *Achieving equity for Latino students: Expanding the pathway to higher education through public policy.* New York: Teachers College Press.

DeWitt, P. (2012). *Dignity for all: Safeguarding LGBT students.* Thousand Oaks, CA: Corwin and National Association of School Psychologists.

Fránquiz, M.E. (2010). Traveling on the biliteracy highway: Educators paving a road toward conocimiento. In N.E. Cantú & M.E. Fránquiz (Eds.), *Inside the Latin@ experience: A Latin@ studies reader* (pp. 93–109). New York: Palgrave Macmillan.

García Bedolla, L. (2012). Latino education, civic education, and the public good. *Review of Research in Education, 36*(12), 23–42.

Gómez, M., & Arroyo, M.L. (2012). *Bullying: Replies, rebuttals, confessions, and catharsis. An intergenerational and multicultural anthology.* New York: Skyhorse Publishing.

Jensen, B., & Sawyer, A. (Eds.). (2012). *Regarding educación: Mexican-American schooling, immigration, and bi-national improvement.* New York: Teachers College Press.

Juvonen, J., Wang, Y., & Espinoza, G. (2011). Bullying experiences and compromised academic performance across middle school grades. *Journal of Early Adolescence, 31*(1), 152–173.

Kinloch, V. (2012). *Crossing boundaries: Teaching and learning with urban youth.* New York: Teachers College Press.

Klein, J. (2012). *The bully society: School shootings and the crisis of bullying in America's schools.* New York: New York University Press.

Mendez, J.J., Bauman, S., & Guillory, R.M. (2012). Bullying of Mexican immigrant students by Mexican American students: An examination of intracultural bullying. *Hispanic Journal of Behavioral Sciences, 34*(2), 279–304.

Meyer, E.J. (2009). *Gender, bullying and harassment: Strategies to end sexism and homophobia in our schools.* New York: Teachers College Press.

Miller, s. (2012). Mythology of the norm: Disrupting the culture of bullying in schools. *English Journal, 101*(6), 107–109.

Morgan, J.J., Mancl, D.B., Kaffar, B.J., & Ferreira, D. (2011). Creating safe environments for students with disabilities who identify as lesbian, gay, bisexual, or transgender. *Intervention in School and Clinic, 47*(1), 3–13.

National Center for Education Statistics. (2011a). *The condition of education, 2011.* Retrieved January 24, 2013, from http://nces.ed.gov/pubs2012/2012045.pdf

National Center for Education Statistics. (2011b). *Digest of education statistics, 2011.* Retrieved January 24, 2013, from http://nces.ed.gov/programs/digest/d11/

Nelson, J.L., Palonsky, S.B., & McCarthy, M.R. (2013). *Critical issues in education: Dialogues and dialectics* (8th ed.). New York: McGraw-Hill.

Obama, B. (2010, October 21). Remarks of President Barack Obama: Video for the "It Gets Better Project" [video transcript], Washington, DC. Retrieved January 24, 2013, from http://www.whitehouse.gov/it-gets-better-transcript

Patel, L. (2012). *Youth held at the border: Immigration, education, and the politics of inclusion.* New York: Teachers College Press.

Peguero, A.A. (2009). Victimizing the children of immigrants: Latino and Asian American student victimization. *Youth & Society, 41*(2), 186–208.

Peguero, A.A. (2012). Schools, bullying, and inequality: Intersecting factors and complexities with the stratification of youth victimization at school. *Sociology Compass, 6*(5), 402–412.

Peguero, A.A., & Shekarkhar, Z. (2011). Latino/a student misbehavior and school punishment. *Hispanic Journal of Behavioral Sciences, 33*(1), 54–70.

Peguero, A.A., & Williams, L.M. (2011). Racial and ethnic stereotypes and bullying victimization. *Youth & Society.* Retrieved January 24, 2013, from http://yas.sagepub.com/content/early/201 1/10/22/0044118X11424757

Poteat, V.P., & Rivers, I. (2010). The use of homophobic language across bullying roles during adolescence. *Journal of Applied Development Psychology, 31,* 166–172.

Reyes, J. A., & Elias, M.J. (2011). Fostering social-emotional resilience among Latino youth. *Psychology in the Schools, 48*(7), 723–737.

Richert, A.E. (2012). *What should I do? Confronting dilemmas of teaching in urban schools.* New York: Teachers College Press.

Rigby, K. (2012). *Bullying interventions in schools: Six basic approaches.* London: Wiley-Blackwell.

Riggs, D.W., & das Nair, R. (2012). Intersecting identities. In R. das Nair & C. Butler (Eds.), *Intersectionality, sexuality and psychological therapies: Working with lesbian, gay and bisexual diversity* (pp. 9–30). San Francisco: John Wiley & Sons.

Ritcheson, D.R. (2007, April 17). Statement of Mr. David [Ray] Ritcheson, hearing on H.R.1592, the "Local Law Enforcement Hate Crimes Prevention Act of 2007," House Judiciary Committee, Subcommittee on Crime, Terrorism, and Homeland Security. U.S. House of Representatives Committee on the Judiciary. Retrieved January 24, 2013, from http://judiciary.house.gov/hearings/April2007/041707ritcheson.pdf

Sánchez, J. (2011). Opportunity or a deposit: Serving children linguistically. In L.W. Watson & C.S. Woods (Eds.), *Go where you belong: Male teachers as cultural workers in the lives of children, families, and communities* (pp. 63–66). Boston: Sense Publishers.

Savage, D., & Miller, T. (Eds.). (2012). *It gets better: Coming out, overcoming bullying, and creating a life worth living.* New York: Plume.

Shaheen, S., & Churchill, A.H. (Eds.). (2010). *Truths and myths of cyber-bullying: International perspectives on stakeholder responsibility and children's safety.* Berlin: Peter Lang Publishing Group.

Strohmeier, D., & Noam, G.G. (2012). Bullying in schools: What is the problem, and how can educators solve it? In D. Strohmeier & G.G. Noam (Eds.), *Evidence-based bullying prevention programs for children and youth: New directions for youth development* (special issue of *New Directions for Youth Development, 133,* pp. 7–13). San Francisco: Jossey-Bass; John Wiley & Sons.

Swearer, S.M., Espelage, D.L., & Napolitano, S.A. (2009). *Bullying prevention and intervention: Realistic strategies for schools.* New York: The Guilford Press.

Valdés, G., Capitelli, S., & Alvarez, L. (2010). *Latino children learning English: Steps in the journey.* New York: Teachers College Press.

Valenzuela, A. (1999). *Subtractive schooling: U.S.-Mexican youth and the politics of caring.* Albany: State University of New York Press.

Yabko, B.A., Hokoda, A., & Ulloa, E.C. (2008). Depression as a mediator between family factors and peer-bullying victimization in Latino adolescents. *Violence and Victims, 23*(6), 727–742.

CHAPTER SEVEN

Cyber-Digital Bullying

sj Miller & Stephanie Beyer

Have you ever received a message like this on Facebook or MySpace, in a text or email, or through another type of digital device? "Everybody in O'Fallon knows how you are. You are a bad person and everybody hates you. Have a shitty rest of your life. The world would be a better place without you." Well, Megan Meier did, and this is the story of how she succumbed to bullycide three weeks before her 14th birthday.

Megan, an eighth-grader from Dardenne Prairie, Missouri, was like many 13-year-old love-struck females. She was bubbly, full of life, goofy, and self-conscious about her weight. She appreciated swimming, boating, dogs, and rap music, and was boy crazy. She'd had some darkness surrounding her struggles with weight and had contemplated suicide in third grade, but ever since had been under the care of a psychiatrist and was on several prescription medications. She was beginning a new grade at a new school and trying to make a fresh start after having shed 20 pounds—she even found the confidence to break ties with a girl down the street who was an on-again, off-again friend. Around the same time, Josh Evans, a 16-year-old who'd moved close by, had contacted her on MySpace to be added as a friend. Megan's mother approved of the "friend add" because their correspondence, according to Megan's mother, was seemingly innocent. Every day after school, Megan enthusiastically logged on to check for messages from her new friend, Josh.

One day Megan received a message from Josh that seemed out of character for their budding friendship. It read: "I don't know if I want to be friends with you anymore because I've heard that you are not very nice to your friends." Megan's mother intervened and cut off her access to MySpace because of Megan's ex-friend down the street, whom she knew had created fake profiles before. Megan pushed for another chance as her 14th birthday approached, and her mother caved in.

On October 16, 2006, while her mother was out on an errand, Megan logged on to MySpace to look for responses from Josh. Horrified and in tears at what she saw, she began to call her mother and relay that there were such comments as: "Megan Meier is a slut! Megan Meier is fat!" Megan retaliated against the posts with vulgarity of her own. Later that evening, Megan's mother and father offered what support they could to console her. Unbeknownst to them, while they were making dinner, Megan went up to her bedroom closet and hanged herself.[1]

Josh Evans had never moved to the area. In fact, there was no Josh Evans. A single mother who lived down the street from the Meiers, with a daughter the same age as Megan, told Mr. and Mrs. Meier that Lori Drew, the parent of Megan's ex-friend, and some other adults had created the fake profile for Josh. Lori wanted to get back at Megan for rumors she had spread about her daughter. Posing as Josh, she and others asked for personal information to gain her confidence and then posted that information to deliberately humiliate her.

Although the case has gone to trial, no charges have ever been brought against the family involved in Megan's death. Missouri prosecutors found that they could not charge Drew in connection with Meier's death because there was not enough evidence. The case then went to federal court in 2008, and Drew and others were convicted of violating MySpace's Terms of Service by accessing a computer that was not theirs and by using it to inflict emotional distress. Drew appealed the decision, and a judge overturned the verdict, arguing that the Terms of Service were vague at best, and that anyone violating a Terms of Service agreement could be subject to prosecution.

Like Megan, most students are in danger of becoming targets of cyber-digital[2] bullying because of the ubiquity of technology in their daily lives. In fact, the American Academy of Pediatrics claims that cyber-bullying is the most common online risk for teens. Likewise, because of the availability of technology both inside and outside of school, bullies have the means to inflict pain on others 24 hours a day. These attacks outside of school hours often remain unseen by school personnel, because they enable bullies to enter a classroom or school anonymously and affect a child's ability to perform. Understanding what cyber-digital bullying is and developing cyber-digital literacy tools are two meta-strategies that we believe can help eliminate some of these attacks.

What Is Cyber-Digital Bullying?

We recognize that while the U.S. House of Representatives has a definition for cyber-digital bullying, that definition is temporal at best due to the rate at which new technologies and social networking platforms are being created and made accessible to the population. Currently, as stated in the introduction to this book, cyber-digital bullying is a relatively new phenomenon and is defined under H.R. 975 (House of Representatives) as "conduct undertaken, in whole or in part, through use of technology or electronic communications (including electronic mail, internet communications, instant messages, or facsimile communications) to transmit images, text, sounds, or other data."[3] Cyber-digital bullying causes deliberate, intentional social cruelty to victims by threatening, harming, humiliating, or engendering fear and helplessness in the victim (Strom & Strom, 2005). Cyber-digital bullying can also take the form of falsely identifying the self by "knowingly impersonating another person as the author of posted content or messages on the Internet in order to trick, tease, harass, or spread rumors about the other person."[4] Like bullying, cyber-digital bullying manifests in direct and indirect ways and is a form of injury that is essentially no different from physical fighting.

Table 1: Direct and Indirect Forms of Cyber-Digital Bullying

Cyber-Digital Bullying	Direct Bullying	Indirect Bullying
The intent is to inflict social cruelty on victims *repeatedly* by threatening, harming, humiliating, and engendering fear and helplessness in the victim through the use of electronic and communication technologies.	•text messages •emails •social networking sites •mobile phones •chat rooms •blogs •IM •pictures •video clips •forwarding •writing confidential emails or messages	•sending lewd or nude images to others (*sexting*) •posting hurtful information on blogs •spreading rumors online or through texts •hacking into an account and sending damaging messages •pretending to be someone else in order to hurt someone •portable gaming devices •3-D virtual, and social gaming sites •interactive sites such as Formspring and ChatRoulette

Note: Direct action is bullying against the victim, while indirect action often—but not always—involves anonymity through "verbal, emotional, sexual, or passive-aggressive behaviors" (Ferrell-Smith, 2003, p. 2).

Some cyber-bullies hurt their victims without the aid of any technology at all. In these situations, cyber-bullying is an indirect factor in harming students. Keith and Martin (2004) note that females learn behaviors from cyber-bullying and engage in "relational aggression." Instead of "duking it out" (p. 225) like boys would on the playground, girls are notorious for disturbing the natural relationship/friendship flow in their eco-systems It is important to be aware of this type of bullying, because it has the potential to be just as psychologically detrimental as a push on the playground (see specific examples in Table 2).

The Realities of Cyber-Digital Bullying

Cyber-digital bullies may be sensation seekers drawn to the immediacy of the impact that bullying can have on its victim. Cyber-digital bullies do not necessarily premeditate their actions; sometimes they are spontaneous. Often the victims of cyber-digital bullying do not know that information about them has circulated through digital tools or, if they do, who the offender is. The anonymity that can come with cyber-digital bullying can create an unseen audience, one that even becomes complicit in the bullying (Shariff, 2005). Cyber-digital bullying also leads to a higher prevalence of sexual harassment, because the victim is less likely to seek help for fear of drawing more attention to the public humiliation. It allows students who may be fearful of behaving in person in sexually explicit ways to hide behind technology.

Known Incidences of Cyber-Digital Bullying

Bullying through cyber-tools has greatly increased the incidence of bullying of students. Today the most prevalent means of cyber-digital bullying for teens reported in the United States in order of access, popularity, and frequency are cell phone use, text messaging (NCH: The Children's Charity, 2006), chat rooms, computer text messages, and email (Patchin & Hinduja, 2006). This phenomenon has been included in the proposed Megan Meier Cyberbullying Prevention Act (House of Representatives 1966, 111th Congress), which cites these findings:

1. Four out of five of United States children aged 2 to 17 live in a home where either they or their parents access the Internet.

2. Youth who create Internet content and use social networking sites are more likely to be targets of cyberbullying.

3. Electronic communications provide anonymity to the perpetrator and the potential for widespread public distribution, potentially making them severely dangerous and cruel to youth.

4. Online victimizations are associated with emotional distress and other psychological problems, including depression.

5. Cyberbullying can cause psychological harm, including depression; negatively impact academic performance, safety, and the well-being of children in school; force children to change schools; and in some cases lead to extreme violent behavior, including murder and suicide.

6. Sixty percent of mental health professionals who responded to the Survey of Internet Mental Health Issues report having treated at least one patient

with a problematic Internet experience in the previous five years; 54 percent of these clients were 18 years of age or younger.[5]

Statistics from the National Crime Prevention Council and Harris Interactive reveal that more than 40% of teens are victims of cyber-digital bullying but that only 10% report it to their parents. When students were asked why they were less inclined to report bullying to their parents, they responded that they were fearful that the parents would suspend their privileges to access technology. The National Center for Educational Statistics (2011) reports that for those who were cyber-bullied, 73% said it had occurred once or twice during a given period, 21% said it had occurred once or twice a month, and 5% said it had occurred once or twice a week. Five percent of female students reported being cyber-digitally bullied compared to 2% of male students.

Statistics from Hinduja and Patchin's (2012) research of 4,400 randomly selected 11- to 18-year-olds revealed that 20% had been victims of cyber-bullying and 20% had cyber-bullied, while 10% had been both the victim and the offender. They also found that those teens who "hyper-network"—those who spend more than 3 hours per school day on online social networks—are 110% more likely to be victims of cyber-digital bullying. These alarming statistics stem from a lack of tangible consequences for those who engage in cyber-digital bullying. In fact, statistics for those who have admitted to cyber-digital bullying self-report that if there were increased surveillance, monitoring, teaching about the practice, or cyber-support for what students did vis-à-vis their access to technology, perhaps the incidence of cyber-digital bullying would decrease. Given this reality, how does one know if his/her/per[6] child or student is a victim or perpetrator of cyber-digital bullying?

There are warning signs when a child or teen is a victim of cyber-digital bullying. The child or teen

- unexpectedly stops using their computer or cell phone

- seems nervous or anxious when an instant message or email appears

- seems uneasy about attending school or going somewhere in general

- begins to show symptoms of anger, depression, or frustration after using the computer or cell phone

- is circumspect or avoids discussion about using the computer or cell phone

- demonstrates withdrawal from social networks and family members.

Further signs that your child is engaging in cyber-digital bullying behaviors include:

- abruptly switching screens, or closing programs, or shutting down the screen when you approach

- becoming anxious and even hostile when computer or cell phone privileges are revoked or restricted

- circumventing restrictions on using the computer or cell phone

- seeming to have multiple online accounts and using pseudonyms

Enacted and Proposed Cyber-Bullying Legislation

There are a limited number of studies describing the psychosocial impact of cyber-digital bullying on youth. It is highly probable that victims of cyber-digital bullying also experience face-to-face bullying, which makes it nearly impossible for them to have a safe haven. We know from the research that students who are bullied are at risk for depression, loneliness, low self-esteem, anxiety (Hawker & Boulton, 2000), and low levels of mental health that can take the form of suicidal ideation (Rigby, 2005). Add to this the lack of a safe haven, and they are likely to be put at even greater risk for these symptoms.

The question that many parents and educators have about cyber-digital bullying, given the prevalence of bullying in the lives of today's youth, is this: What measures are being taken at the state or national level to stop it? While we still have no federal legislation against cyber-digital bullying, there are 34 states that have enacted laws against cyber-digital bullying in schools.[7] These laws are an outgrowth of state cyber-stalking and cyber-harassment laws that have been prompted by recent concerns about protecting minors from online bullying or harassment. According to the National Conference of State Legislatures, all states today have enacted some form of "cyber-stalking" or "cyber-harassment" laws that explicitly include electronic forms of communication.[8] And, in the absence of federal law, each state must rely on these very laws for prosecuting those who harass, threaten, or bully others online.[9] We regard this lack of federal law on cyber-digital bullying as highly controversial, because safety should be at the forefront of students' educational experience and not be left to the discretion of states.

Redirecting Cyber-Digital Bullying Behavior: Cyber-Literacy

Working teachers and preservice teachers understand firsthand that their students often use cyber-tools to communicate information on a daily basis, so what can they do to redirect cyber-digital bullying behavior? Providing cyber-literacy tools can be a proactive strategy for teaching students about how they may inadvertently bully one another (see Table 2). And for those students who are being bullied but are afraid to seek support, we offer some ideas that could be used in what we refer to as "cyber-support."

Cyber-Literacy Lesson Plans

In order to help students recognize their possible complicity in cyber-digital bullying, we recommend studying currently proposed cyber-digital bullying laws side-by-side with the definitions of the different types of cyber-bullying/harassment/stalking, and how cyber-digital bullying extends beyond the school walls. This will help them to recognize any knowing or unknowing complicity in fostering bullying behaviors. We also recommend helping them understand the bullying laws in their own states, the related criminal and school sanctions, and the details of their own school's policy. In fact, if a policy is not in place, perhaps students can get involved in helping to develop a state- or school-wide policy. We recommend helping students see that, while there may not be legislation in some states or even in their own, laws are temporal and can (and will) change depending on what cases move through the courts. We also recommend studying why the Megan Meier Cyberbullying Prevention Act to amend Title 18 is still stalled on the House Floor. Representative Linda Sanchez of California has suggested that federal cyber-digital laws are failing because some see them as an infringement on First Amendment speech rights, while others see them as opening up a can of worms regarding what is deemed harassing or hurtful (Szoka, 2009). Some citizens don't want Title 18 to change, because the result would be to censor them from sending "incendiary" emails.

Another form of cyber-literacy is the teaching of "Netiquette" (proper school use of the Internet) alongside cyber-bullying education. We offer these specific suggestions for lesson plans:

- Use books (see Appendix C in Chapter 10 for suggestions) that frequently have cell phone and text interaction to demonstrate to students (middle school students especially) how harmful texts can be by sending a simple, seemingly innocent text. Students often forget the power of their own voices, especially when they cannot be physically heard. Remind them about the power of voice by having them read *Lord of the Flies* and emphasizing the conch shell, or by taking their voice away from them for a period of silence. This should help show how powerful their words truly are.

- Discuss the possibility of misinterpretation. This can be done by picking dialogue (from a text or play) with little natural inflection and asking three students to volunteer to recite it. Ask two of the students to wait outside while the third reads through the text until each of the three has been given the chance to read. This goal can be accomplished by instructing each volunteer to read it "sarcastically" or "excitedly." This will show how easily text can be manipulated, especially a text message that could inflict harm.

- Develop a unit plan with the theme of permanence to develop a connection between this concept and the Internet. Begin with quotes about permanence (possibly introducing "Nothing Gold Can Stay" by Robert Frost), and then move on to topics such as "How are physical things destroyed?" and lead into "If a computer breaks, does the information disappear?" or "If you delete something online, does it ever really go away?" Getting your students to discuss this will allow them to internalize the concept and apply it to their online posts. If they thought their Facebook posts would last forever, they probably wouldn't post as many of them.

- Encourage students to think about different ways they could use the vast quantity of information that is available to them through technology to promote good. Incorporate human service projects into the curriculum and offer extra credit when students bring in examples of Netiquette or good online behavior, in the news or in their personal lives (explaining that appropriateness is important in school).

- Teach often the elements of cyber-digital bullying offered in the introduction to this book, and provide opportunities for discussion of and reflection on misunderstanding.

- Reflect on the cyber-bullying law in your state, district, or school. If there isn't one, invite your students to do research and create a campaign to enact a cyber-digital bullying law.

- Study the text of the Megan Meier Cyberbullying Prevention Act and create a plan to track its progress or support its passage. Section 881 of the law reads: "Whoever transmits in interstate or foreign commerce any communication, with the intent to coerce, intimidate, harass, or cause substantial emotional distress to a person, using electronic means to support severe, repeated, and hostile behavior, shall be fined under this title or imprisoned not more than two years, or both."[10]

- Study court cases of cyber-digital bullying and conduct mock trials on the cases.

- Study FCC regulations and laws related to schools.

Teaching Cyber-Support

Although therapy and psychological counseling are routine in society today, many stigmas still surround this coping method. Oftentimes it is the threat of acquiring a label like "crazy" or "unstable" that prevents individuals from seeking psychological guidance. This is certainly an issue with youth today; many students are bullied and, as a result, would benefit from counseling. However, they are reluctant to do so because entering therapy would seem like a perverse justification for bullying: "This kid deserves to be bullied; he's seeing a shrink. He must be crazy."

How can educators deal with this? How can we encourage troubled students to admit that they need help and actively seek it out? There are several potential solutions. For instance, the possibility of incorporating virtual or "cyber-therapy" into the classroom could be explored. Although this method of therapy is not yet popular in school districts, companies are exploring its use for soldiers returning from war with post-traumatic stress disorder who may not be willing to engage in face-to-face therapy. By directing them to an online version of therapy, they enable soldiers to escape a public stigma, much as students would be able to do while receiving private and discreet services. Similarly, a program like this could literally mean the difference between life and death for a student. The possibility of incorporating "virtual therapy" into the classroom could help students and bullies alike to deal with their issues in an anonymous way that would protect them from scrutiny and further bullying from their classmates.

Virtual therapy settings "appear and feel to users like they're inhabiting a relatively real setting" (DeAngelis, 2012, p. 49). These virtual realities are capable of creating a completely student-generated environment that stands to help victims by recreating situations and facing their own fears. Some of the websites that design this technology make it possible for patients to create replicas of scenes that they have experienced. This gives students the opportunity to confront their fears head-on by creating a virtual lunchroom or school bus setting that would allow them to revisit bullying incidents. That element of control could be essential in helping them to recover.

This technology has been used in the workplace to deal with issues of interpersonal relationships (DeAngelo, 2012, p. 49). The virtual aspect renders touchy situations easier to address, making it a perfect solution for bullying in schools. The possibility of incorporating "virtual therapy" in the classroom would give students and bullies alike the opportunity to deal with their issues in an anonymous manner that would protect them from scrutiny and additional bullying from their classmates.

Because this technology is gaining in popularity, psychologists are developing appropriate HIPAA guidelines that would address virtual forms of therapy. Student protection remains the number one concern, and, if virtual therapy were to be adopted in school systems, it would only be feasible if we were certain that student identities would be protected. This technology could be essential in fighting fire with fire in the war against cyber-digital bullying.

There are several companies currently offering online counseling services and therapy-related computer software. Virtually Better, Inc. (www.virtuallybetter.

com) provides products that address psychological wellness, including Virtual Iraq for post-traumatic stress disorder. Metaverse+ (www.metaverseplus.com) is a website that "provides information, training and research summaries for psychologists who want to learn how virtual reality and other interactive communications technology can be applied to…clinical psychology" (De Angelo, 2012, p. 51). The technology exists for this type of counseling but lacks a prototype that would focus on our nation's students. It is popular among veterans' associations and is gaining popularity in the business world. School systems are next, and this type of technology is well worth pursuing for the sake of students.

Because of technology, many students live in constant fear of receiving a hurtful Facebook comment alert at 3 o'clock in the morning. They cannot simply get on a bus and escape their terrorizers, at least not the way they were once able to. Technology has become an accomplice, a fellow bully, in this constant struggle between the oppressed and the oppressor—a silent partner that allows for 24-hour torture. With that in mind, educators must seek places of refuge for their students. How can we take technology and turn it from something that harms into an ally? This can be done through what has been dubbed "cyber-support": websites designed to help students who are victims of bullying and other methods of personal torture by offering resources for support. "Cyber-support" is a term associated with sites that offer help and hope to bullied students.

The website It Gets Better (www.itgetsbetter.org) is designed to assist bullied students in the LGBTQGV community, but while the site is the perfect example of cyber-support, it is one of the few such resources available. This website is a video board for LGBTQGV students who think that their adolescent life (and the torture that comes from being an openly gay teenager) is the last word on the tone that has been set for their lives. The videos are posted by LGBTQGV people who were bullied in their own high school days but who lived to tell their stories. Their videos are 30-second messages of hope that explain that high school is a phase, one that everyone must survive, and that their life will improve after graduation day. These videos offer confident role models, sometimes even celebrities (including Lady Gaga and President Barack Obama), who wish to share their own stories in an effort to convince suicidal teens that life is worth living. More of these websites need to be created; more places need to pop up that support not only LGBTQGV students but any group that feels it is being marginalized by an oppressor.

Most people today are familiar with the popular social networking website Twitter. Twitter allows members to create messages of up to 140 characters and send them into the "webiverse." Tweets usually attempt to be humorous or interesting so that members "retweet" the messages to more members. Oftentimes Tweets can be used inappropriately and—you guessed it—as a form of bullying. A recent study found that "out of the 250 million public tweets sent each day, the program usually identifies about 15,000 bullying-related messages" (Webley, 2012, p. 1). The program is an algorithm that recognizes words that have negative connotations and generally relate to bullying. While some students might be comfortable Tweeting negative comments about their peers' outfit choices, one student decided to use Twitter for the greater good. A high school football player from Osseo High School in Minnesota created a Twitter account called @OsseoNiceThings. Instead of spreading hatred, this student decided to Tweet things that would encourage and support his classmates (Douglas, 2012, p. 1). Through the efforts of students who are willing to create supportive online communities to help their classmates, cyber-digital bullying could be majorly rejected. Although cyber-support will never eradicate cyber-digital bullying, it can raise spirits and create friendships instead.

Because few resources for pure cyber-support currently exist online, an interesting approach to the concept would be to ask students to create their own websites. Students would be asked to consider topics they feel strongly about: disabilities, women's rights, LGBTQGV rights, and so forth. They would then consider different ways that their chosen groups are marginalized in society. At the end of the unit, their assignment would be to design a website, modeled along the idea of itgetsbetter.org, that would allow a certain group or combination of groups to come together to seek refuge They would create a common place where people who share common interests could go and communicate with other people who are marginalized. The website could be designed around chat rooms (stipulating that anti-group comments or conversations would not be tolerated) or message boards. Students who knit could create a website that calls on fellow knitters to make blankets and baby clothes for unwed mothers who have taken abuse and criticism from society. Or it could be as simple as setting up a chat room for members of the chess team who are bullied. The possibilities are endless: creating 30 new websites each year would mean 30 more places offering security and hope for bullied individuals. This unit would also give students a chance to express their creativity and individual concerns about the world. It would be most appropriate for juniors and seniors in high school (or even college-level students), but with some tweaking, younger students could engage in this type of project as well. By harnessing the individual talents of our students, we offer them the opportunity to express their feelings and learn how to treat their peers with respect. At the same time, we enable them to touch the lives of millions of people.

Cyber-Literacy for All: Shifting a School Climate

It is possible to lessen the frequency of cyber-digital bullying by changing the climate in schools toward bullying. We offer several suggestions to that end. First, the students who most often come into contact with technology—those in audio-visual clubs or computer clubs, students who do school news or TV, or any other grouping of students who have easy access to computers and know how to use them—could create a larger organization that develops an anti-bullying cyber-digital manifesto. These students could teach about cyber-digital bullying through posters, visits to classrooms, and leaflets, and could then request that others in the school pledge not to engage in cyber-digital bullying.

Another possibility is that newspaper or journalism teachers could develop a webspace/website aimed at teaching about cyber-digital bullying and providing access to sources for cyber-support or virtual therapy. The space/site would be maintained by students in their courses who would be responsible for a blog or for keeping information on the site current . Wikis are also an option; by implementing a classroom Wiki, classes would be able to control different pages under an umbrella site. They would also be controlled by a master password, over which the teacher would have ultimate control. Peer-to-peer support might offer an incentive to students who would otherwise be too intimidated to reach out to adults. A final possibility is to approach the school board and push for a tougher policy on cyber-digital bullying. Teachers could invite administrators, parents, and students involved in these efforts so that the change comes from within. Taught together, cyber-literacy and cyber-support can be tools for systemic change in our schools.

Missouri, Megan Meier's home state, to this day lacks anti-bullying and cyber-bullying laws that can trigger criminal charges. Nor do school policies extend to off-campus behavior. This leads us to the question: If cyber-digital bullying laws were in place that extended beyond the school walls and into the home, would casualties like Megan Meier (and too many others to count) be averted altogether? Instead, we are left in the wake of their deaths with reminders that we have so much work to do locally and nationally to educate ourselves about the ever-increasing presence of digital technology and its impact on today's youth.

Notes

1 For Megan's full story, see http://www.meganmeierfoundation.org/megansstory.php

2 Although the official term is cyber-bullying, we take license to say cyber-digital as an instantiation of the bullying. We use the term cyber-bullying when it is referenced in the literature and cyber-digital when it is our work.

3 GovTrack.us. Retrieved May 8, 2011, from http://www.govtrack.us/congress/billtext.xpd?bill=h112-975

4 GovTrack.us. Retrieved May 8, 2011, from http://www.govtrack.us/congress/billtext.xpd?bill=h112-975

5 GovTrack.us. Retrieved July 5, 2012, from http://www.govtrack.us/congress/billtext.xpd?bill=h111-1966

6 We use the invented pronoun *per* to honor students whose identities are gender non-conforming, gender variant, or transgender. We alternate it with s/he at various times throughout the book. While there are other pronouns such as "hir," "ze," and "they," which also refer to gender non-conforming, gender variant, or transgender people, using *per* is an intentional stylistic decision.

7   See http://www.ncsl.org/issues-research/educ/cyberbullying.aspx

8   *Cyber-stalking* is the use of the Internet, email, or other electronic communications to stalk, and generally refers to a pattern of threatening or malicious behavior. Transgressions range from misdemeanors to felonies. *Cyber-harassment* involves a credible threat and usually pertains to threatening or harassing email messages, instant messages, or to blog entries or websites dedicated solely to tormenting an individual.

9   For more information see http://www.ncsl.org/issues-research/telecom/cyberstalking-and-cyberharassment-laws.aspx and http://www.cyberbullying.us/

10 See http://www.govtrack.us/congress/bills/111/hr1966/text

References

Bhat, S.C. (2008). Cyber bullying: Overview and strategies for school counselors, guidance officers, and all school personnel. *Australian Journal of Guidance and Counselling, 18*(1), 53–66.

Covenant Eyes (2012). Breaking free blog: Honest discussions about Internet temptations. Retrieved July 7, 2012, from http://www.covenanteyes.com/2012/01/17/bullying-statistics-fast-facts-about-cyberbullying/

DeAngelis, T. (2012). A second life for practice? *Monitor on Psychology, 43*(3), 48–51.

Douglas, S. (2012). High school football player starts kindness campaign on Twitter. Retrieved January 28, 2013, from http://www.thebiglead.com/index.php/2012/08/18/high-school-football-player-starts-kindness-campaign-on-twitter/

Ferrell-Smith, F. (2003). *School violence: Tackling the schoolyard bully. Combining policy making with prevention.* Denver, CO: National Conference of State Legislatures, Children and Families Program.

Hawker, D.S.J., & Boulton, M.J. (2000). Twenty years' research on peer victimization and psychosocial maladjustment: A meta-analytic review of cross-section studies. *Journal of Child Psychology and Psychiatry, 41*(4), 441–455.

Hinduja, S., & Patchin, J. (2012). *Cyberbullying research center.* Retrieved July 5, 2012, from http://www.cyberbullying.us/research.php

Keith, S., & Martin, M. (2004). Cyber bullying: Creating a culture of respect in a cyber world. *Reclaiming Children and Youth, 13*(4), 224–228.

National Center for Educational Statistics. (2011). *Student reports of bullying and cyber-bullying: Reports from the 2007 school crime supplement to the national crime victimization study.* Retrieved August 11, 2011, from http://nces.ed.gov/pubs2011/2011316.pdf#page=1

National Conference of State Legislatures. (2012). *State cyberstalking and cyberharassment laws.* Retrieved July 5, 2012, from http://www.ncsl.org/issues-research/telecom/cyberstalking-and-cyberharassment-laws.aspx

NCH: The children's charity. (2006). Preventing child abuse: Internet safety FAQ—Is it true that children can be bullied online and via mobiles? Retrieved July 5, 2012, from http://www.nch.org.uk/information/index.php?i=134#78

Patchin, J.W., & Hinduja, S. (2006). Bullies move beyond the school yard: A preliminary look at cyber bullying. *Youth, Violence and Juvenile Justice, 4*(2), 148–169.

Rigby, K. (2005). Bullying in schools and the mental health of children. *Australian Journal of Guidance and Counselling, 15*(2), 195–208.

Shariff, S. (2005). Cyber-dilemmas in the new millennium: School obligations to provide student safety in virtual school environment. *McGill Journal of Education, 40*(3), 457–477.

Strom, P.S., & Strom, R.D. (2005). When teens turn cyberbullies. *The Education Digest, 71*(4), 35–41.

Szoka, B. (2009, October 1). Cyberbullying hearing yesterday: Education, not criminalization or intermediary deputization. Retrieved November 30, 2012, from http://techliberation.com/2009/10/01/cyberbullying-hearing-yesterday-education-not-criminalization-or-intermediary-deputization/

United Press International. (2008, April 9). *Survey*. Retrieved July 5, 2012, from http://www.upi.com/Health_News/2008/04/09/Survey-Cyber-bullying-affects-US-teens/UPI-38231207776077/

Webley, K. (2012, August 17). Using Twitter to crack down on bullying. *Time*. Retrieved January 27, 2013, from http://newsfeed.time.com/2012/08/17/using-twitter-to-crack-down-on-bullying/

The Consequences of Bullying and Anti-Bullying Interventions for Individual and School Success

Leslie David Burns

So far we have described the identities of the most vulnerable students in our nation's public schools and explored many of the ways and reasons they are bullied on a regular basis. In this chapter we turn our attention to a discussion of the real consequences of such bullying and the scientific reasons we use to argue for combating bullying through prevention, intervention, and policy oversight.

Let's review some of the statistics we have reported. Three out of every four children in our public schools say they have either been bullied themselves, bullied their peers, or both (Nansel et al., 2001). *Seventy-five percent!* One out of every four schools, even using the most conservative estimates, reports that bullying happens on a daily basis (Crary, 2010). Fully one-third of all adolescents report they either witness or experience bullying every day. Sixty-nine percent believe their schools respond poorly or fail to intervene and prevent bullying at all, even when it is identified and reported. These are merely the results of self-reports by children, so the actual incidence of bullying is probably higher.

It cannot be denied that bullying is endemic to our public schools, and perhaps even a defining experience of school life for most children. For too many it may be *the* defining experience of childhood and public education. It is important to note that the statistics reported above represent all students regardless of their identities or statuses. Members of minority groups who differ from heterosexual, White, ablest, and socioeconomic norms experience much higher rates of bullying. More importantly, 90% of children, regardless of their identities or statuses, understand and report openly that bullying causes social, emotional, or academic problems (Markow & Fein, 2005). Let us ask ourselves: How much bullying is acceptable? How much is too much?

More significantly, how does bullying affect what we claim is the essential need for safe and positive classroom/learning environments for children in our schools? Such classrooms are not referred to as "safe" and "positive" simply because such safety is a legal obligation. Their conditions, based on hard science and statistical analyses of data about the requirements for optimal student success, are not just morally and ethically nice. They provide the essentials for increasing students' self-efficacy—their perception that they are capable of success. In the diverse schools we all work in, generating that self-efficacy is described as a "Herculean task," even without worrying that children will be persecuted for their differences (Cruikshank, Bainer, & Metcalf, 1995, p. 32). Allowing classrooms to become psychologically threatening places for young people is antithetical to nearly everything we claim we want from our schools, everything we want for our children, and everything we want young people to learn and do as they grow into adulthood.

None of the findings reported above include the statistics for LGBTQGV students, or Blacks, Latinos, or other minority or marginalized groups. When these are unaccounted for, imagine the scope of effects bullying actually has in school life every minute of every day. Social stratification via "cliques" and subcultures is so ingrained in American school culture that any citizen can easily name the classic, persistent groups that bully and get bullied based on their status in school hierarchies. American pop culture is rife with amplifications and caricatures of these groups and their members to the point that most people in U.S. society find their inclusion a matter of commonsense. Bullying and being bullied are considered normal and even important rites of passage for the transition from childhood to adulthood. Films and television programs like *The Breakfast Club, Heathers, Mean Girls, American Pie, Sixteen Candles, Glee, Freaks and Geeks, Scream, The Karate Kid, Easy A, That 70's Show, Rushmore, Revenge of the Nerds, South Park, The Simpsons, Diary of a Wimpy Kid, The Perks of Being a Wallflower,* and even the *Harry Potter* series—several considered revolutionary and even classic texts—reinforce and even rely on the notion that no school or youth narrative is complete without a cast that includes nerds, jocks, prom queens, wannabes, freaks, stoners, rich kids, metalheads, slackers, band geeks, "the" Black kid, "the" handicapped kid, the ugly girl, the fat kid, the Asian math geek, the preppy bully, and countless other stock characters. Even in television programs such as *Glee,* where traditionally persecuted characters are celebrated for overcoming the confines of "normalcy," such characters' behaviors and identities are rooted in stereotyped observations. Their necessarily superficial treatments reinforce the power relations and divisions between diverse groups and encourage us to continue assigning each other to them.

It may *feel* natural. It may *seem* normal. It may even happen because there are kernels of truth to all stereotypes. And yet...

If we really mean what we say when we claim *all* people are equal and *all* people have the right to life, liberty, and the pursuit of happiness, we must ask ourselves: Why does it matter who a person is or seems to be? Why does it matter that someone is different in his or her culture, values, beliefs, sexuality, race, gender, social class, fashion/style, or interests in our world? If we embrace our nation's most coveted rights, the answer is clear. These things *do not matter*. And they *would* not matter except that we have allowed a culture of normativity to become so powerful that we use bullying to police and sanction people whose identities, backgrounds, and/or preferences stray from whatever dominant notion of "normal" might be active at any given place and time.

When we allow the policing of false normalcy via bullying in school, everyone suffers. Everyone loses the ability to focus on and succeed in the actual purposes of education. We literally waste time, energy, emotion, and, most importantly *thought* on planning and executing bullying behaviors, managing them, ignoring them, or, worst of all, enduring, avoiding, and escaping the resulting conflicts. These claims are not matters of opinion, nor are they moralizing. They are based on scientific findings from experimental research (Steele, 2010). The central consequence of allowing bullying in our schools is that we systematically reduce every person's capacity to succeed. We reduce every person's ability to participate in and contribute. Bullying is rooted in threats to individuals' identities, and research from social psychology demonstrates irrefutably that such threats have powerful, negative effects on *everyone's* abilities to perform and learn. In the next section we review how *stereotype threat* (Steele, 2010) helps explain the consequences of bullying, and how it also underscores the positive benefits of interventions that prevent, sanction, and eliminate bullying in our schools.

Bullying and Stereotype Threat

There is a reason the phrase "Out of the mouths of babes" is a cliché in our society. Children often speak the truth or know things intuitively that adults are reluctant to acknowledge. But the 90% of children who report that bullying harms their emotional health, physical health, and ability to succeed in school turn out to be absolutely correct. Their reports are supported by hard science and the findings from rigorously controlled experiments about what happens when we threaten a person's identity (Steele, 2010). According to Steele, stereotype threats are defined as real or perceived threats that lead to concerns that one will be judged or treated negatively based on false assumptions about one's identities. Based on the concept that Steele and his colleagues have established and explored, even unspoken or potential threats to a person's identity have significant negative effects on that person's abilities to think clearly and perform at high levels.

For example, Steele's research and subsequent experiments include studies like the following. Two groups of men and women who scored in the top 15% on the mathematics SAT were placed randomly into two groups. Members of each group were placed in rooms by themselves and given a test of their mathematical skills. However, in order to assess the effects of stereotype threat on women in the experiment, female members of the experimental group were casually told, "You may have heard that women don't do as well on difficult standardized math tests…" (Steele, 2010, p. 38). The women who were *not* offered this "reminder" scored well— as one would expect expert mathematicians to score no matter what gender they claimed. The women who heard the implied threat (you are not men and won't do as well as men will) scored significantly lower than their peers— male or female. More dramatically, the women in the control group who did *not* experience any stereotype threat performed just as well as their male counterparts (Benbow & Stanley, 1980, 1983).

Similarly, a group of White male mathematicians from Stanford University whose average score on the mathematics portion of the SAT was 712/800 were given a difficult math test and casually told that Asian males score higher than White males. Based solely on hearing this implied threat—that White males cannot compete with Asian males—the experimental group scored *three times* lower on average than White males in the control group who were not threatened (Aronson et al., 1999). As a final example, Stone and colleagues (1999) placed Black men in random groups and introduced them to a miniature golf course. One group was told to play the course as best they could as a test of their natural athletic ability. The other was told they would be tested for "sports strategic intelligence." As hypothesized, the Black men who simply played the course performed at average levels. Those who were threatened implicitly by the stereotype that Black males are not good at strategic problem solving performed, on average, four strokes worse their counterparts—a dramatically significant statistical difference.

The conclusions from these experiments are clear, and they have been replicated many times across practically all racial and gender groups, at least. When given opportunities to perform tasks without prior assumptions about ability or intelligence related to their social identities, most people will perform at optimal levels. But if and when people are positioned and allowed to feel stereotyped, different, inferior, or even threatened by an *implied* stereotype that suggests they are unable, abnormal, or inferior, those people will perform worse and even fail. The findings persist even when the person in question is asked to perform tasks he is already highly skilled at performing. It is true whether the person is a member of a traditionally powerful group, a contextually dominant group, a minority group, or a persecuted group.

Stereotype threat harms the ability of all people to succeed, and it stands at the heart of all bullying behavior. As Miller (2012) notes, because social norms are so powerful, any deviation can stir up aggression, fear, and conflict. "When a person is not readily understood or identified, [other people may feel] a psychological need to minimize, hurt, or make the person disappear altogether" (p. 107). Even more disturbing is the finding that a person will respond to these threats even when they are not overt. When bullying occurs, stereotype threats are not only made overt but also become the focus of life in school for victims and bullies alike. And when stereotyping leads to bullying, it forces all participants to waste thought and energy on the threats and attacks rather than using that thought and energy to learn, practice, grow, and succeed in school. Bullying has a direct effect on our ability to focus on the actual goals of public education whether we are teachers, administrators, bullies, or victims of bullying. Bullying interrupts our ability to think.

Bullying and Cognition

Based on neurological research, human brains have the capacity to deal with a limited number of ideas, problems, tasks, or concepts at one time via short-term memory (Cruikshank, Bainer, & Metcalf, 1995). This fact is commonly assumed in discussions of memory and the notion that the average person's brain can only "hold" seven to nine items at once in short-term memory. An example of how this phenomenon is honored is the fact that telephone numbers are purposely limited to seven digits (Cruikshank, Bainer, & Metcalf, 1995, p. 54). Limiting them in this way makes them easier to remember for longer periods, repeat them, and thereby transfer them to long-term memory for use over time. This is a simplistic representation, but it gets the idea across. However, when we apply this same notion to participating in a diverse public school classroom, we can begin to understand the enormously powerful implications it has for our abilities to learn and grow in more complicated scenarios. We can also begin to appreciate how ability to learn is harmed when bullying is one of the social variables at play in the learning context.

At a minimum, any student in a public school classroom already has a huge amount of data to process, an incredible array of stimuli, and countless rules to follow (Jackson, 1968/1990). Some of these data, stimuli, and rules are made explicit, and some are assumed to be obvious, even when they are not. Students must contend with the expectations of a teacher—often many teachers—and those expectations vary from day to day and even from moment to moment, depending on tasks, purposes, individual moods, and more. A student has to deal with the fact that she is not at school by choice, but because she is forced to go. She must deal with the fact that she is surrounded by other children, some of whom are different than she is in speech, dress, race, gender, sexual orientation, religion, social class, size, language, behavior, and more. This list could extend much further, but let's simply add to this already-complex social context the fact that the primary expectation is that all the students in the school are supposed to focus on learning how to read, write, speak, listen, do math, study history, learn science, follow rules, share, collaborate, answer questions, take tests, follow rules, be polite, and succeed in all those areas while satisfying both the teachers' and peers' demands that they meet all of the various definitions of "good" (in other words, "like us") that are involved. This is an impossible task even under the best possible conditions.

Now imagine you are a child in such a class, and for some reason you stand out as "different." Maybe you are the only Black, Latina, or White kid. Maybe you are the only boy or girl. Maybe you are a boy who likes to wear bright colors that other students believe are only supposed to be seen on girls. Maybe you are a boy who doesn't enjoy sports. Maybe you are an athletic girl who is perceived as being too masculine because you are highly competitive. Maybe you are gay or lesbian, or perceived as either even though you are actually heterosexual. Maybe you have not yet determined your sexual identity and you are exploring it by trying out different ways of expressing yourself when the majority of the class is heterosexual. Maybe you are different from the teacher, too.

Right or wrong, many of us have experienced being different at one point or another during school. Alternately, we have noticed people who are different from what we believe is "normal" and treated those people differently than those who are more like us.

It could be that this different treatment is revealed through overt acts of bullying, or through cumulative microaggressions that eventually mark a student as different, marginal, or otherwise outside the mainstream. Children will pick on a peer for being different, or weaker, or because that peer is an isolated and easy target who violates their assumptions about how people ought to look, be, think, or do. They might physically abuse that peer. They might verbally attack him and call him names. They might make fun of her for the way she dresses or how she talks. They could exclude her because she enjoys a different style of music, or because he likes to dance and sing instead of play sports.

All of these are acts of bullying. It is a truism in the field of discourse analysis that when a group member strays too far from the norms of the dominant members, or if a member fails to demonstrate sufficient solidarity or likeness with the dominant group, the members of that group will pressure or even sanction the deviant until s/he conforms to their norms (Gee, 1996). If the perceived deviant fails or refuses to comply, s/he will be persecuted, marginalized, excluded, or even kicked out of the discourse group. S/he will be bullied.

Those who appear to refuse or fail to play the game will be kicked off the team by their peers. At school this happens constantly. For too many of us, schools are places where we think such experiences and acts are not just normal, but necessary rites of passage into adulthood. Bullying experiences are (in many minds) natural, normal childhood experiences believed to build character, toughen us up, and prepare us for a "real world" where life is hard and we have to do what's expected of us in order to succeed.

The Roles of Teacher Expectation in School Bullying

The games students play in school are also played by (or even enforced and refereed by) teachers (Gee, 1996). As Lortie (1975) found in his classic study of the profession, many teachers are motivated to take up a teaching career by a desire to continue their experiences of school, embrace its predictable social structures, and value its seemingly comfortable and common-sense sources of normalcy in their own lives. For such teachers, school is a comfortable and secure space, a place where they fit in, and a place to be conserved. Their goal is often to ensure that students become like them—to think, speak, act, feel, and believe as the teacher does.

Other teachers come to the profession because they feel an almost religious mission to fix children whom they believe are needy, broken, misguided, or lost—in other words, children who do not fit their conceptions of normal. And, as Lortie found, nearly all teachers enter the profession with the desire to work with children who are not "ill nor especially disadvantaged" (1975, p. 27). In other words, they seek to work with children they perceive as normal and to avoid working with children who are different from them, whether in terms of race, ability, sexuality, behavior, or otherwise. When such teachers discover the realities of contemporary public schools in the United States, many are more than disappointed to learn not only that most of their students are *not* like them, but also that *most* of their students are different from them in numerous ways. Recent statistical surveys of teachers in the United States show that the demographics of the profession have not changed much in several decades (Feistritzer, 2011). The majority of teachers—about 85% overall—are still White, middle class, and female (Feistritzer, 2011), and they have certain culturally based expectations of how children in their classes should appear and behave (Gee,1996). This is especially true in early grades, but not significantly different in the upper grades, where the teaching forces still includes only about 15% of people who differ from the norm in that they might be male, a racial minority, former members of a different social class, or something other than heterosexual.

The characteristics of teachers and their personal conceptions of what is normal about schools and students matter. Long-standing bodies of research about teacher expectations show that when a teacher views students as normal and therefore able, that teacher is significantly more likely to give those students more help, more praise, higher grades, more chances, better access, and fewer punishments (Chickering, 1969; Anyon, 1981,1997; Claridge & Berliner,1991;

Cochran-Smith, 1995, 2000; Danielewicz, 2001). When the children are viewed by the teacher as different or abnormal in any way, the teacher is significantly more likely to punish those children, ignore them, assign them lower grades, label them as resistant or learning disabled, and provide them with less choice, collaboration, and validation for their work and worth. In these ways, teachers not only can be bullies, too, but they can and do support and perpetuate bullying among students. They may also encourage the phenomenon of bystanders who notice bullying but do nothing to intervene, even though they realize it is harmful.

In terms of cognition, then, any child in any classroom with these conditions faces an overwhelming cognitive overload even before having to try to learn new academic concepts and skills that are measured in a competitive format. Is it any wonder that a child who feels different and is treated as abnormal by her peers and even her teachers might struggle? Is it really a surprise when a boy who is unfairly punished and picked on because he is a racial minority might feel angry enough to lash out or stop trying, and in doing so seems to confirm the suspicions of his bullies that they were right all along? And is it any wonder that, faced with so much cognitive overload, many children who are bullied perform at a level as much as a full grade point lower than their supposedly "normal" peers (see Chapter 2)? The single greatest consequence of bullying and allowing bullying in schools is that it literally harms all students' abilities to learn, achieve, and succeed.

Our primary argument that bullying must be stopped is based largely on moral arguments and ethical positions when considered at its most basic level. And it *is* a moral and ethical imperative that all children be treated equally and allowed to live, learn, and grow without fear that they will be scorned, threatened, or excluded for simply being who they are. That argument is the bedrock of democratic thinking and civilization in our society. It is an argument about the sanctity of human dignity, and that argument is nothing to take lightly or dismiss as "politically correct" mumbo jumbo about boosting kids' self-esteem, being warm and fuzzy, or building some kind of utopia.

That said, the imperative that we end bullying behaviors and prevent school cultures that allow bullying to take place is also a scientific one. When we allow bullying, we unwittingly but systematically decrease our ability to achieve a truly democratic, free society. We unwittingly but systematically prevent *all* children from performing, learning, growing, and reaching their highest potentials. We unwittingly but systematically prevent all this because we actively create social conditions in which people must constantly think about how to avoid standing out, taking risks, revealing their true selves, being different, fitting in, avoiding trouble, overcoming embarrassment, and all the other unproductive behaviors required to contend with a culture of bullying that is pandemic. It really is so bad that children too often decide that their only option in avoiding these problems is suicide—or what we have called bullycide in this book.

If our society and our education system were attentive to the ways in which bullying impairs the cognitive loads of students and their teachers, we could improve school success almost overnight. This assertion is confirmed by findings from scientific research about motivation and engagement in learning and school. In the next section we will describe how an engaging classroom that supports diverse identities can and does correlate with higher rates of success for all. In addition, we explore how these scientific findings might be implemented to establish healthy and supportive environments that prevent bullying, enable intervention, and carefully attend to the systematic support of all learners.

Bullying and Research About Motivation and Engagement

In the field of cognitive psychological research, several factors have been studied and found to correlate almost perfectly with increased student motivation, engagement, and success in school (Guthrie & Wigfield, 2001). These factors include having a caring teacher who believes that all students can learn and achieve at high levels, providing students with explicit learning goals, teaching children how to collaborate, providing them with texts and topics that they find interesting and relevant to their own lives and identities, giving them authentic opportunities to talk about and apply concepts and skills they will use in the real world, and teaching them explicit strategies for learning along with lots of practice using those strategies in psychologically and physically safe spaces. Additional research shows that when educators take the time to learn about their students' "funds of knowledge"—the knowledge they bring to school with them about their identities, their home lives, their communities, their popular cultures, and their prior experiences—they can use that knowledge to put academic learning into context for those students and frame new knowledge so that it reflects children's identities and increases their motivation and engagement even more (Moll & Gonzales, 2001; Mojeetal, 2004; Hall, Burns, & Edwards, 2010).

Discussions about how to motivate and engage students, even when based on research, are too often framed in terms of making school activities more "fun." When that happens, the actual scientific findings are distorted and misused, or even dismissed. Learning in school that is based on the simplistic notion that we need to make it more "fun" for kids both misses the point and cheapens the meaning of the research that led people to that conclusion in the first place. If children have fun in school, it is because the learning tasks teachers design for them are relevant, useful, and therefore interesting. And if they are "fun" as a result of those factors, that's a good thing, but it is not the goal. The relevance, interest, and usefulness of school tasks and learning are actually found to correlate almost perfectly with increased success, the desire to learn more, and increased achievement. A perfect correlation (one that approaches causality) is statistically expressed as a score of "1." Research on the conditions of motivation and engagement named above has been found to result in a correlation of 0.8—a scientific fact that cannot be overlooked if we seek to design classrooms that are psychologically safe and therefore conducive to learning (Guthrie & Wigfield, 2001). To emphasize this, we briefly discuss each of the conditions found to improve student motivation and engagement. Then we relate these scientific findings to the consequences of bullying (or the failure to prevent it).

Lightening the Load: Creating a Safe, Bully-Free, Engaging Classroom

As we noted earlier in this chapter, creating a safe and supportive classroom environment is not merely a nice thing to do, nor is it simply based on the idea that we want all kids to have positive self-esteem. In fact, the concept of a safe and supportive classroom is central to educational success. What does it mean to make a classroom environment "safe"?

First, a safe classroom is more than physically safe. Of course we must ensure that the arrangement of furniture is efficient and provides both safe and orderly points of exit, entry, and movement within the learning space. We must also ensure that students of all ages have access to the resources they need in ways that will guarantee to the extent possible that no child will have an accident while obtaining or using resources and facilities. These matters should go without saying. But in addition, a physically safe environment is one in which acts of physical violence or other aggressive behaviors are not just prohibited and punished but prevented on the basis of a clear social contract. Thus, it is impossible to engineer a safe learning environment without focusing on the concept of psychological safety for all participants.

Psychological safety entails the secure understanding, belief, faith, and agreement among all students, teachers, administrators, and support staff that no individual will be—or even feel—at risk of becoming a victim of violence or abuse. In other words, all participants must agree to work systematically at eliminating stereotype threats. Any condition or circumstance that may threaten an individual's identity—perceived or real—can and should be addressed as much as possible. We do not argue that it is always possible to identify or anticipate every possible stereotype threat that might crop up in a given classroom or school. We do argue, however, that all educators and students are obligated to respond to such threats when they occur, or when they are revealed, whether they result in obvious harm or not. When we do not intervene and respond, we implicitly allow and even encourage stereotype threats and bullying—and in doing so we decrease an individual's ability to learn. We increase students' cognitive loads and prevent them from using their thought and energy to focus on learning and interacting in productive and positive ways.

This kind of psychological safety is not just about protecting potential victims of bullying. It protects those who would otherwise act as bullies, too. When any individual—adult or child—operates as a bully and/or capitalizes on the notions of a given stereotype threat, that person is also wasting cognitive capacity, emotional/physical energy, and time that would be better spent focusing on learning and succeeding in school. In this light, psychological safety is not about protecting some children and punishing others. It is about supporting *every* member of the school to perform at his or her optimal capacity.

A teacher can explain this to students even when working with very young children. For example, the teacher in any classroom and at any grade level could begin engineering a safe classroom community by saying something like the following:

> We have two big jobs in this class, and I need your help with both. The first job is to work together so you learn and succeed in school, and so you can grow and achieve your goals in life. I believe every person in this room is smart and able to do great things. Our first job is to make sure you all hear that and realize it every day: You can learn and you can do great things. I need your help to make sure that happens. That's our first job.
>
> But we have a second job, too—another job that helps make sure we all succeed. Our second job is to make sure no one ever interferes with our ability to learn and grow. We all have to feel safe. That means we have to make sure no one in this class ever worries about being hurt or treated badly for being themselves. We have to make sure everyone here treats each other with respect. We all have to respect ourselves, too. I need your help with that.
>
> We are all different, sometimes even when we seem to look or think the same. It's okay to be different. In fact, one of the best ways to learn and grow is to be around lots of different kinds of people who look different, act different, and think differently. We all have things we believe, things we think are good or bad, right or wrong. We are all good at some things and maybe not so good at others. Some things come easy for us, and some are really hard. Some of us like certain things that others don't like, or believe in things that other people here don't believe. That's okay. It's good! We're going to respect those differences, because when we don't we might treat each other badly. We might make fun of each other. We might pick on somebody or tease him or her. We might bully them or leave them out, or we might be mean just because they seem different to us.
>
> That's not okay in this classroom. I need you to help me make sure it doesn't happen. When it does, it gets in the way of our success. If you ever feel like someone is hurting you—whether it's by hitting you or teasing you or leaving you out, you can tell me. If you see these things happening to someone else in class, you need to tell me so I can help everyone stop it and make it better. And if you do any of these things to someone else, you need to know that I am going to stop you. I won't stop you because I am mad at you, or because I am being mean. I won't bully you, either. First I'll remind you of what we're talking about now. If that doesn't fix the problem, I'll talk with you about why you are acting like a bully, and if we can't fix that problem together, then I will get you even more help. We will go talk with the counselor, or the principal, and we'll go talk with your parents—maybe all of them at the same time. I'll do that because I can't let anyone get in the way of our learning and growth, including yours. That's our job in this class, and

these are the things that will make it safe for everybody here to be themselves, feel safe, and succeed.

The teacher language modeled above demonstrates the findings from science about engaging and motivating students as well as embodying the characteristics of a "caring teacher"—that is, a teacher who truly believes that all his students can succeed and that he can work together with any child to reach that goal. When the teacher cares and the students know it and see it every day, it is often the single most powerful factor in students' overall success in school (Rosenthal & Jacobson, 1968/1990; Good, 1987).

The second factor in creating a safe environment is providing children with explicit goals. This requires telling the children not only what to do, but why doing it matters and why it will help them both in school and the real world (Marzano, Pickering, & Pollock, 2001). We cannot simply say, "Because I said so," or "You'll need this later in school or college or work." We have to have good reasons for asking children to do things in school, and we need to frame those explanations in ways that the children feel are important, real, and relevant to their actual lives and goals. Too often, teachers and adults assume that their beliefs about what kids need to know and do are obvious and relevant to the kids. That's not always true, and it is not fair to punish them when they don't understand or when they resist because an activity or a skill seems (to them) pointless or boring. Instead, it's our job to make the purposes of what we do in school explicit to them. If we don't, our students can't engage. They will be too busy dealing with the cognitive load required to understand "why," and as a result they will become more likely to *dis*engage. When they disengage, they will stand out as different and less able than their peers, leading to increased potential for bullying or exclusion (Guthrie, Coddington, & Wigfield, 2009; Hall et al., 2010; Hall, Burns, & Greene, 2013).

The third condition for engineering a safe and engaging environment entails explicitly teaching children how to collaborate. Often—too often—teachers presume that working in groups is a simple, straightforward, commonsense activity. It is not. It requires explicit instruction about the roles, interchanges, practices, and purposes of that activity. Many children, especially children who are used to classrooms and schools that are structured by tracking, ability grouping, and clique-ish social hierarchies may actually never have received any instruction about how to collaborate—at least not with students who are different from them. But that instruction is extremely valuable, increasing student achievement by up to 28% when taught and practiced on a regular basis (Marzano et al., 2001). Why? Students often feel safer working in smaller groups where their cognitive loads are lightened because they are less concerned with getting the "right" answer by themselves, or being wrong and risking public humiliation, or being attacked by a peer bully (Hall et al., 2013). Moreover, collaborative learning in smaller groups and pairs enables students who are different from one another to know and understand each other better through routine and predictable interactions. The more they get to know and understand each other and collaborate toward shared goals, the less strange they seem to each other. The less strange they seem, the less different they feel. And the more we minimize difference (or celebrate its power) through collaboration, the more we reduce incidences of bullying and stereotype threat. Consequently, increased and systematic use of collaboration correlates scientifically and strongly with increased student success for all children.

The fourth and fifth conditions for engineering a safe and engaging classroom require schools and teachers to provide students with a variety of texts and choices of activity that reflect their cultures and identities for use in real life (Hall et al., 2010). Again, schools and teachers too often presume to know what's best for students and pre-determine what students *ought* to find interesting and relevant. This is possibly because those texts and values are traditional, or perhaps because the teachers themselves found them to be personally relevant and interesting when they were young. But children often do not share adult interests or perspectives, and it is frankly condescending to dictate what any person ought to find interesting and then express frustration when they do not agree and fail to engage with school content. If we wish to claim that we are educators invested in responding to the needs of children, we must balance tradition with resources and activities that the students themselves believe are interesting. For those tasks and topics to be interesting, students must see themselves and aspects of their own lives and identities reflected in those texts and activities. That means *all* children. We realize that there is no single text that can reflect the identities of every child all the time in any sizable classroom. But teachers and schools can and should select resources that reflect as wide a variety of identities as possible and represent them in positive and valued ways (Moje, 2008; Moje et al., 2004). That means teachers must identify and use resources that reflect variety in gender, race, social class, body type, sexuality, ethnicity, geography, language use, and more. It also means creating learning tasks and assessments that are framed so that students can understand tasks and demonstrate applied knowledge in ways that balance traditional academic work with ways of knowing and doing that originate in the students' home cultures and everyday ways of knowing and being. Again, this kind of student recognition and valuing is proven to increase academic achievement and success by as much 6% to 28% (Marzano et al., 2001).

The sixth and final condition for engineering a safe, engaging environment in which all students can learn and thrive is to provide them with explicit instructions about how to use learning strategies. As with collaboration, it is a mistake to assume that children know, for example, how to ask questions (or even what questions to ask) while trying to learn a new concept or skill. They may also not understand that asking questions is not a sign of weakness, but a sign of strength—a sign of an engaged and successful learner. We cannot simply tell children to read and write and think and discuss. We must teach them the strategies people use to do these things in school and in life. When we make learning strategies explicit for all students and help them understand that *all* learners use strategies to grow and improve, we make it safer for all children to participate actively in the life of the classroom and become what Aukerman (2007) terms *primary knowers*. Primary knowers are students whose knowledge is treated as valuable for use by the entire class and who are positioned by the teacher to share their skills and understandings in ways that are celebrated, praised, and used to help the entire group succeed.

Like the other conditions discussed above, helping students learn and practice strategies and become primary knowers situates all classroom members to collaborate, become familiar with one another, and succeed because of their active membership. The term *familiar* is not accidental here. It means "like a family." By definition, familiarity leads not only to tolerance of difference, but an appreciation of it and an expectation that diversity is essential for success. When that's the case, bullying becomes an act that all members of the classroom family will not only avoid, but also actively prevent.

Conclusion: It Shouldn't Have to Get Better

We have noted the highly influential and successful LBGTQ movement "It Gets Better" (Savage & Miller, 2012). That program has resulted in hundreds of video messages made by adults who experienced bullying during school before moving on to succeed in life. Their message to children like them is to hang in there, to be resilient, and to rise above bullying because after school ends, life will get better and the bullying will stop. It's a hopeful message, and "It Gets Better" has been a light in the darkness for many children who have been victimized based on their sexual orientation. However, research on workplace bullying shows that bullying does not stop when school ends. It is actually a well-documented problem in scientific studies of workplace productivity (Salin, 2003a, 2003b; Lillemor, Strandmark, & Strandmark, 2006).People who learn to bully and who are not stopped from bullying others during childhood do not suddenly stop bullying when they become adults and enter the workforce. To the contrary, they learn from their experiences that bullying is a tactic that leads to increased power and success in adult life. It is no wonder they continue to behave as they do, and such action is no less damaging in adult life than it is in childhood. In adult life, it is often called *discrimination* instead. But discrimination often gets limited to issues of race and gender in workplace policy and discourse, while bullying based on other differences goes largely unaddressed. Regardless, it does not always get better for victims of bullying just because they leave school. Some things never change. Sometimes things get worse. But let's be even more honest and forthright here: It should never have to "get better" in the first place.

Bullying is *not* by necessity a rite of passage or a natural part of growing up. It *is* ingrained as a part of our traditional cultures of childhood and schooling. We rely on stereotypes to make sense of the world, and school is a place in which students learn to see the world in particular ways. It is a near cultural universal in America that children in our schools are ascribed identities and placed in certain stereotypical groups by peers, teachers, other adults, and the school system itself (Gee, 2000–2001).

But even though it may be common and even seemingly universal, bullying is *not* natural. It is an unhealthy practice that has achieved the status of common-sense to the point that we not only view it as "normal" but also talk about it as a rite of passage that we expect every person to endure. That is a problem for us all to address as citizens in a diverse and globalized society. Further, ending bullying is *not* a matter of political correctness. The branding or denigration of anti-bullying programs and related projects as politically correct, simplistic, naïve, or idealistic attempts to police human thought and behavior is a shallow argument that must be confronted and called out for what it is. The strategy of dismissing anti-bullying programs as "political correctness" is itself a bullying strategy.

Anti-bullying projects are about establishing and supporting equal rights and equal opportunity for all people, not just a lucky few or even a supposedly homogeneous majority (which does not exist and probably never did). The slur of "political correctness" is an attempt by people who do not wish to acknowledge difference to maintain whatever power they believe they have attained, especially over others who are not like them.

Arguments claiming that the prevention of bullying involves a plot to destroy our society embrace a socially constructed and socially sanctioned set of violent behaviors and thoughts. They harm victims and slander their targets on purpose. They are not just morally wrong. They are antithetical to the science about how to systematically increase the success of our contemporary society that we have described in this chapter.

Bullying has consequences for our schools. It prevents students from meeting the goals we demand they achieve. It fundamentally damages our communities and violates our professed national values. It even has consequences for the success of people who perpetrate bullying. It has deep implications for how people, schools, and society must operate as a matter of design to make the American Dream a real, attainable goal for everyone, instead of a sucker's game in which the deck is stacked against diversity and replaced with the marked cards of compliance, privileged membership, and exclusive power as the only real avenues to success.

When bullies are allowed or empowered, they will spend their time, thought, and energy consolidating power over others, fighting those who disagree with them, and preventing the work of teaching, learning, and achieving in our education system. They will violate the foundational tenets of our society. The consequences of bullying and failing to create environments that intervene against it amount to no less than the elimination of our rights as citizens to pursue life, liberty, happiness, and the American Dream. Those consequences are unacceptable, and we can reduce and eliminate them if we try.

In the following chapters we will explore in greater depth what it takes to address these consequences through national policy legislation and teacher education.

References

Anyon, J. (1981). Social class and school knowledge. *Curriculum Inquiry, 11*(1), 3–42.

Anyon, J. (1997). *Ghetto schooling: A political economy of urban educational reform.* New York: Teachers College Press.

Aronson, J., Lustina, M.J., Good, C., Keough, K., Steele, C.M., & Brown, J. (1999). When White men can't do math: Necessary and sufficient factors in stereotype threat. *Journal of Experimental Social Psychology, 35,* 29–46.

Aukerman, M.S. (2007). When reading it wrong is getting it right: Shared evaluation pedagogy among struggling fifth grade readers. *Research in the Teaching of English, 42,* 56–103.

Benbow, C.P., & Stanley, J.C. (1980). Sex differences in mathematical ability: Fact or artifact? *Science, 210,* 1262–1264.

Benbow, C.P., & Stanley, J.C. (1983). Sex differences in mathematical reasoning ability: More facts. *Science, 222,* 1029–1031.

Chickering, A.W. (1969). *Educationandidentity.* San Francisco: Jossey-Bass.

Clarridge, P.B., & Berliner, D.C. (1991). Perceptions of student behavior as a function of expertise. *Journal of Classroom Interaction, 26*(1), 1–8.

Cochran-Smith, M. (1995). Uncertain allies: Understanding the boundaries of race and teaching. *Harvard Educational Review, 65,* 541–569.

Cochran-Smith, M. (2000). Blind vision: Unlearning racisim in teacher education. *Harvard Educational Review, 70,* 157–190.

Crary, D. (2010,March 10). Columbine school shooting spawned effective anti-bullying programs. *Huffington Post.* Retrieved January 27, 2013, from http://www.huffingtonpost.com/2010/03/03/columbine-school-shooting_n_484700.html

Cruickshank, D.R., Bainer, D.L., & Metcalf, K.K. (1995). *The act of teaching.* New York: McGraw-Hill, Inc.

Danielewicz, J. (2001). *Teaching selves: Identity, pedagogy, and teacher education.* Albany: State University of New York Press.

Feistritzer, C.E. (2011). *Profile of teachers in the U.S. 2011.*Washington, DC: National Center for Educational Statistics.

Gee, J.P. (1996). *Social linguistics and literacies: Ideology in discourses.* New York: Routledge.

Gee, J.P. (2000–2001). Identity as an analytic lens for research in education. *Review of Research in Education, 25,* 99–125.

Good, T.L. (1987). Two decades of research on teacher expectations: Findings and future directions. *Journal of Teacher Education, 38*(4), 32–47.

Guthrie, J., Coddington, C., & Wigfield, A. (2009). Profiles of reading motivation among African American and Caucasian students. *Journal of Literacy Research, 41*(3), 317–353.

Guthrie, J.T., & Wigfield, A. (2001). Engagement and motivation in reading. In M.L. Kamiletal (Ed.), *Handbook of reading research* (Vol. 3, pp. 403–422). Mahwah, NJ: Lawrence Erlbaum.

Hall, L.A., Burns, L.D., & Edwards, E.C. (2010). *Empowering struggling readers: Practices for the middle grades*. New York: Guilford.

Hall, L.A., Burns, L.D., & Greene, H. T. (2013). Creating inclusive spaces for struggling readers. In E. Ortleib and E. Cheek (Eds.), pp. 219-240. *School-based interventions for struggling readers, K-8: Literacy research, practice and evaluation*, volume 3. New York: Emerald Group Publishing Limited.

Jackson, P. (1968/1990). *Life in classrooms*. New York: Teachers College Press.

Lillemor, R.M., Strandmark, H., & Strandmark, M. (2006). Health consequences of workplace bullying: Experiences from the perspective of employees in the public service sector. *International Journal of Qualitative Studies on Health and Well-Being,1*, 109–119.

Lortie, D. (1975). *Schoolteacher: A sociological study*. Chicago: University of Chicago Press.

Markow, D., & Fein, J. (2005). *From teasing to torment: School climate in America—A survey of students and teachers*. Gay, Lesbian & Straight Educational Network. New York: Harris Interactive.

Marzano, R., Pickering, D., & Pollock, J. (2001). *Classroom instruction that works: Research-based strategies for increasing student achievement*. Upper Saddle River, NJ: Pearson Education, Inc.

Miller, s. (2012). Mythology of the norm: Disrupting the culture of bullying in schools. *English Journal, 101*(6), 107–109.

Moje, E. (2008). Foregrounding the disciplines in secondary literacy teaching and learning: A call for change. *Journal of Adolescent and Adult Literacy, 52*(2), 96–107.

Moje, E., Ciechanowski, K.M., Kramer, L., Ellis, L., Carrillo, R., & Collazo, T. (2004). Working toward third space in content area literacy: An examination of everyday funds of knowledge and discourse. *Reading Research Quarterly, 39*(1), 38–70.

Moll, L., & Gonzalez, N. (2001). Lessons from research with language-minority children. In E. Cushman, E. Kintgen, B. Kroll, & M. Rose (Eds.) *Literacy: A critical sourcebook* (pp. 156–172). New York: Bedford/St. Martins.

Nansel, T.R., et al. (2001). Bullying behaviors among US youth: Prevalence and association with psychological adjustment. *Journal of the American Medical Association, 285*, 2094–2100.

Oakes, J. (1985). *Keeping track: How schools structure inequality*. New Haven, CT: Yale University Press.

Rosenthal, R., & Jacobson, L. (1968/1990). *Pygmalion in the classroom: Teacher expectation and pupils' intellectual development*. New York: Holt, Rinehart and Winston.

Salin, D. (2003a). Bullying and organizational politics in competitive and rapidly changing work environments. *International Journal of Management and Decision Making, 4*(1), 35–46.

Salin, D. (2003b). Ways of explaining workplace bullying: Are views of enabling, motivating, and precipitating structures and processes in the work environment. *Human Relations, 56*(10), 1213–1232.

Savage, D., & Miller, T. (Eds.). (2012). *It Gets Better: Coming out, overcoming bullying, and creating a life worth living*. New York: Plume.

Steele, C.M. (2010). *Whistling Vivaldi and other clues to how stereotypes affect us*. New York: Norton.

Stone, J., Lynch, C.I., Sjomeling, M., & Darley, J.M. (1999). Stereotype threat effects on Black and White athletic performance. *Journal of Personality and Social Psychology, 77*,1213–1227.

CHAPTER NINE

The Broader Contexts of Bullying

Disrupting Bullying Through Preventive and
Interventionist Policy

sj Miller

W e live in a time in which both social diversity and bullying seem to have accelerated, peaked, and entered a kind of golden age. To think of bullying as having such widespread and institutionalized tolerance is unsettling, especially since we know that bullying is strongly correlated with what would otherwise be celebrated as the expansion of social differences as an asset in nearly every other aspect of our social system. Perhaps future generations will experience bullying to a lesser degree. It may become extinct altogether if we are able to diminish the cultural and social tropes that enable bullying to occur and emphatically promote the valuable opportunities that entail increased diversity in our society. We recognize that for all of the stories and statistics we have shared here, our American culture's complicity in supporting bullying as a rite of passage, along with its failure to enact changes that end such support, not only condones bullying and allows it to continue but also sends messages about who and what we value as a nation and as civilized human beings. Because there are holes in anti-bullying programs and in current state laws against bullying that result in institutions' failure to fully include all students, the patterned absences of information that enable gaps in curriculum and policy, gaps in discourse, and lack of social services for at-risk students continue to manifest as normative aspects of the social fabric and processes we have allowed to function as common sense in our school environments. When such norms remain unnamed and/or unchallenged, these policies and negative status quos that neglect inclusion and support for all students enable microaggressions to occur as an integral and normalized curriculum—an educational program—that supports and sustains homophobic, genderistic,[1] monoethnic, and heteronormative practices.

Beyond passing federal anti-bullying legislation, we recommend looking closely at systems that sustain and/or perpetuate the occurrence of bullying as a result of social values or environmental conditions that can be identified as ableist,[2] sexist, transphobist, genderist, heterosexist, racist, and even "religist,"[3] whether those values and conditions exist intentionally or not. A systems-based anti-bullying approach for any school must be conscious of how discourses from the top down about what is "normal" create binaries and determine who is included (or not), who is labeled as normal (or not), who is treated as superior (or inferior), and who is deemed desirable (or not). We believe our strategies for eradicating bullying, which we offered in Chapter 1, allow local communities to transcend these binaries because they are proactive, preventive, and interventionist acts. In Chapter 10 we will revisit each one of these considerations in order to highlight how students, parents, teachers, school counselors, and larger communities can interrupt cycles of bullying, disrupt them, and end them once and for all.

Federal Anti-Bullying Policy: Moving Toward a Systems Approach

We begin by presenting a vision for comprehensive anti-bullying reform that, if implemented, would have the potential for eliminating bullying in all schooling contexts across the United States. *Idealism* may be defined as the eternal pursuit of excellence, and we wish to emphasize that pursuing excellence is emphatically not naïve or unrealistic. Pursuing ideals involves, first, the understanding that perfection is never attainable, and that we can never stop striving to make things better. Further, idealist efforts related to anti-bullying mean that we can never stop examining and re-examining social diversity, societal responses to that diversity, and anti-bullying programs designed to support and promote difference in our schools. When we allow ourselves to presume that an anti-bullying program is working and has "solved" the problem, it is very likely that we will begin to overlook the real needs of our children and our schools in relation to tolerance and support for *all* students. But although the pursuit of ideal models is a never-ending project, that fact does not render the project worthless. Indeed, we argue that the never-ending need to support diversity becomes more important to highlight than ever.

While several countries have been successful in reducing bullying by using a range of localized programs, we have chosen here to highlight projects in Norway and the United Kingdom that have tied bullying to national legislation and instituted accountability systems. Such mandates have led to reductions in reported incidents of bullying in schools across both countries. Norway, specifically, has reported the lowest rates of bullying in the world as a result of national policies that address the problem. The lack of comparable success for U.S. federal, state, and local anti-bullying laws is an indicator that, unless there are shifts within our country at large, the school cultures we have in place to socialize students will continue to enable, encourage, and escalate microaggressions and bullying even in schools where educators actively work against such behaviors. Without powerfully mandated penalties for bullies and those who allow bullies to act as they do, we are likely to see bullying not only to continue but also to increase significantly in our society. We would not (indeed, we cannot) recommend simply importing programs that have worked well in other countries, or even compare bullying statistics or interventionist strategies across nations because of contextual differences in behaviors, cultures, attitudes, and demographics. Yet there are aspects of Norwegian and Anglo approaches that are useful to consider in our work with schools and bullying in the United States. What seems to reverberate across national contexts is that bullying—regardless of other variables—affects children's academic, social, emotional, psychological, and physical health (Crick & Bigbee, 1998; Olweus, 1984, 1993; Rigby, 2000).

Bullying and Norwegian Policies

In 2002, the prime minister of Norway launched a government-led, multi-partner "National Manifesto Against Bullying in Schools" based on a zero-tolerance approach that asserted that "positive and caring communities, with firm and determined adults, could prevent, identify and stop bullying" (Tikkanen & Junge, 2004). Norway's education law aims to guarantee pupils a positive school environment wherein they have the right to grow and learn in a bully-free space. Norwegian schools and their personnel are required to intervene whenever bullying occurs and are supported in adopting any program that works for their particular school.

One initiative, the Zero Program, is a preventive, bullying-reduction program developed by the Centre for Behavioral Research at the University of Stavanger. The goal of the program is to ensure that school employees execute a zero-tolerance policy against bullying by utilizing their authority as professionals. The program involves (1) training all professionals (not just teachers) working in the school; (2) providing an information packet about bullying, including suggestions for classroom management and parental involvement that are easy to implement and follow; (3) providing parents with an information packet about bullying that describes the prevalence, types, causes, effects, indicators, and methods that are most important to consider when addressing allegations or actual incidents of bullying; and (4) working with students to create an atmosphere of tolerance and celebration of social diversity and understanding of human variation as normal. Such a program provides strategies to counter bullying and encourages members of the school community to become involved in peer and adult leadership focused on inclusion. In sum, the Zero Program and others like it help school employees recognize bullying, solve issues related to bullying acts or environments, prevent future bullying, and make prevention an integral part of a school's everyday climate. This program and others like it are based on an organizational model that taps into the school's resources and daily functions to integrate non-bullying discourses into the daily life and talk of the school and its participants. Conversely, anti-bullying project models designed to operate from outside a school, or those that are used sporadically and temporally as quick fixes or "one-shot" solutions, lack the capacity for full integration as parts of a school's culture and tend not to hold up, be effective, or become sustainable, integrated models like the Zero Program does.

Norway's ideological approach to inclusive schooling reflects equity and equality for all, a condition that has been written into law since 1974 as the Salamanca Statement, and is an approach that guarantees "a school for all" with the intention of ensuring optimal success for all citizens. In Norway, much of the success of federal anti-bullying work may be attributable to the fact that such policies and their mechanisms of implementation are housed in a dedicated Ministry of Education whose mission is explicitly framed as the manager of development and change in society. The ministry is predicated on the notion that educational institutions "play important roles as cultural agents and purveyors of culture. Development and change must go hand in hand with conservation and transfer of tradition and values" that support the success of all citizens (Ministry of Education and Research, 2007). The Norwegian authorities have had great success integrating this into a national ideology of anti-bullying that has led to the government providing financial support and incentives, taking direct action when needed, and continuously monitoring the success and outcomes of anti-bullying initiatives in schools.

Anti-Bullying in the United Kingdom

Much of the early anti-bullying work in the United Kingdom stems from the pioneering efforts of Dan Olweus, whose work in Norway focused on a rash of school-related suicides.[4] Olweus began a large-scale anti-bullying project in 1970 that is now regarded as the first scientific study of bully/victim problems in the world. His model has informed anti-bullying programs worldwide ever since, and the United Kingdom has appropriated his work in requiring that all schools have anti-bullying policies. The United Kingdom's Department for Education website, which offers dozens of resources for parents, students, teachers, administrators, researchers, and community members,[5] states: "It is compulsory for schools to enforce measures that will encourage good behaviour and prevent all forms of bullying." School policies must define bullying explicitly and must include definitions that address racist, sexist, and homophobic bullying, describe reporting procedures, specify methods of documentation, delineate sanctions for different bullying acts, list specific anti-bullying strategies, and specify the methods a school will use to prevent future incidents (Smith, Smith, Osborn, & Samara, 2008, p. 2). The United Kingdom's anti-bullying reforms began under the government-funded Sheffield Anti-Bullying Project of 1991–1994 with the anti-bullying pack from the Department for Education in Skills (DfES) titled *Don't Suffer in Silence*, which the government recommends for use in all school-wide anti-bullying policy implementation (Smith et al., 2008). Initially, under the School and Standards Framework Act (SSFA) of 1998, this policy required head teachers to encourage good behavior and respect for others and to prevent all forms of bullying. It became *the educator's* legal responsibility to prevent all bullying by students. This policy led to a broader definition of those who can and should be held legally responsible for anti-bullying in the Education and Inspections Act (EIA) of 2006. That act requires head teachers to make rules and impose appropriate sanctions for bullying behavior. One benefit of this national law is that all schools must have a definition of bullying in their policies and clearly spell out that definition not only to students and professionals but also to parents. Some weaknesses of this model include a lack of clarity as to the roles of school personnel other than the head teacher, poor management and lack of clear procedures for handling bullying records, and a lack of clear preventive measures related to bullying.

Potential Opportunities for Adapting Norwegian and U.K. Models for U.S. Anti-Bullying Programs

Norway and the United Kingdom have provided some excellent models and structures that can be emulated in our own country's fight against the bullying pandemic. At the federal level, both the United Kingdom and Norway require clear and explicit support for anti-bully programs in their departments of education. These departments and/or ministries provide funding, ongoing assessment, professional development programs, resources and public information outlets, and follow-up procedures for documenting, tracking, sanctioning, and preventing bullying behaviors. Fortunately, bully prevention is on U.S. President Barack Obama's own policy radar. In a recent daylong conference in March 2011, Obama stated:

> A third of middle school and high school students have reported being bullied during the school year. Almost 3 million students have said they were pushed, shoved, tripped, even spit on. It's also more likely to affect kids that are seen as different, whether it's because of the color of their skin, the clothes they wear, the disability they may have, or sexual orientation.[6]

In association with the Department of Education, the National Parent Teacher Association, the National Education Association, the American Federation of Teachers, the National Association of Student Councils, and the National School Boards Association, President Obama has allocated $132 million in the 2012 federal budget for combating violence and bullying and providing grants to state and local governments under the Department of Education's "Successful, Safe, and Healthy Students" program. As a result, the Department of Education hosted its first-ever National Bullying Summit in August 2010, and the government now has a website (StopBullying.gov) that provides resources for children, teens, young adults, parents, educators, and community members for defining bullying, recognizing it, and getting help to report and prevent it when they see it in their schools and communities. The website is new and basic, but it is a beginning.

The Possibilities of a U.S. Ministry for Anti-Bullying

If anti-bullying measures pass under H.R. 975: the Anti-Bullying and Harassment Act of 2011, and H.R. 1648: the Safe Schools Improvement Act of 2011, schools and districts receiving federal funds will be required to adopt codes of conduct specifically prohibiting bullying and harassment, report information about incidences of bullying and harassment, notify parents and students annually about incidents of bullying and prohibited conduct in their school communities, and establish procedures for students and parents to file complaints regarding such conduct. These acts also require the U.S. Secretary of Education to conduct and report on evaluations of anti-bullying programs in elementary and secondary schools. At the state level, the new legislation will require a Commissioner for Education Statistics to collect data and determine the incidence and prevalence of bullying and harassment in elementary and secondary schools in the United States. These legislative acts would also ensure that schools and districts implement prevention programs and require states to report data on bullying and harassment to the Department of Education, including procedures and outcomes for intervention.

Creating a Ministry of Anti-Bullying within the U.S. Department of Education similar to those used in model countries like Norway and the United Kingdom could help streamline issues related to eradicating bullying in our schools. Such a ministry could be used to study and review successful models of anti-bullying programs from around the world, study them scientifically, and analyze them for elements that could be appropriated for improving anti-bullying work in the United States. The ministry could establish hotlines and support systems, disseminate resources, evaluate and recommend training programs, post new knowledge and information, highlight intervention strategies, and guide follow-up protocols that are readily accessible to parents, students, teachers, administrators, researchers, and community members who are seeking to make their schools safe, healthy, and productive places for children to learn, grow, and succeed in contemporary society.

Mandatory Anti-Bullying Courses and Programs in K–12 Schools

Another possibility for interrupting bullying is to seamlessly integrate an anti-bullying curriculum based on real-time issues in pre-K–16 schooling courses. The strategy of such courses would be both interventionist and proactive and would include the voices of students, educators, school personnel, district-wide personnel, families, and the community at large. It would combine a careful analysis of scientific research and a practical implementation of findings related to bullying, including responsive teaching, inclusive schooling, and the building of healthy, positive school environments that support academic achievement. The courses could be taught by school or guidance counselors, school psychologists, diversity experts, or even by teams of teachers in a particular school who design anti-bullying strategies and pay special attention to prevention, pro-action, and intervention. The curriculum could focus developmentally on the new Common Core State Standards as they relate to the Health and Wellness Standards for K–12 schools.[7] Courses could induce students to produce critical reflections about unconscious and conscious manifestations of microaggressions in their experience and how those impact their collective success as learners and people, especially through the use of current technologies such as social networking software. The curriculum would need to be tailored to the real-time needs of students and their particular situations, and would eventually need to expand from a focus on individual behavior to community, national, and global issues/contexts. Specifically, scaffolding interpersonal and social issues that lead to bullying could include topics that treat positive and negative uses of power, strategies for assertive communication and conflict resolution, understanding the manifestations of prejudice, understanding how equity and inequity manifest, and studying topics related to human rights, social justice, and restorative justice. Whenever possible, such curricula should connect to family, the community, and the nation at large.

Some concrete methods for teaching at all K–16 levels could include:

- guest speakers
- reading texts, plays, and media representations of the topic
- performing in school and community plays
- doing prejudice-reduction activities
- participating in online anti-bullying modules
- exploring through role playing
- creating and maintaining anti-bullying campaigns for schools or communities
- participating in peer-led interventions, peer mediation, and school-wide networking
- leading writing projects that capitalize on the publication of multi-media, letter writing, and art
- networking with other schools locally, nationally, and abroad

Combating bullying is a much larger project than even the U.S. Department of Education can tackle on its own. It will take a collective effort from local, state, and national groups and communities to overhaul the current educational, cultural, and political climate that created the conditions for pandemic bullying in the first place. And that work, even through a federal agency, will require a considerable investment of time, energy, organization, and persistence in order to succeed. Nonetheless, as we seek to engage an ideal, such long-term investments are neither impossible nor unrealistic. But they must be ongoing in order to be worthwhile. And they *are* worthwhile.

A Systems Approach

A systems approach to bullying treats school environments as blends of multiple and complex interactions including individual, social, and larger contextual markers. Such an approach requires all parties to help alter the school culture so that it highlights the dangers and negative consequences of bullying. It should include principals, teachers, student peers (through peer counseling, mentoring, and partnering), guidance counselors, and all other personnel involved with the school environment. Additional partners and actors could include, but not be limited to, parents, school board members, community partners, and community members with vested interests in the health and success of their local schools. In fact, schools could ask visitors to read and sign a binding document that discusses anti-bullying policies and requires compliance with those policies from anyone operating on school property or at school-related functions. A systems approach must also be supported by broader structural financial initiatives and other incentives that enable it to continue, expand, adapt, and shift as the social diversity of the school and its community changes over time.

A systems approach should begin with either a nation wide, district wide, or school wide needs assessment that addresses how bullying manifests, who is targeted for bullying, why, and how bullying is enabled, tolerated, and/or condoned. By analyzing anonymous surveys and systematically collected anecdotal data, professionals could help shape national and district-wide anti-bullying curricula. This approach would be most successful when there are long-term commitments from all members and concrete policy procedures that can be measured and/or assessed over time. In that way, changes and responses can be identified and used to adapt to new and unexpected types of bullying issues.

Financial Incentives

One way to eradicate bullying is to award special or additional federal dollars to school districts (and states) that demonstrate sustained, collective reductions in the incidence of bullying. States, districts, and schools would be expected to utilize a systems approach to show how they create healthy and safe climates, how constituents participate in that process, how intervention and prevention occur, and how follow-up is managed and documented. Such changes can even be matriced and tracked state by state so that if particular communities are able to decrease bullying over time, they can earn rewards as AB-States (anti-bullying states). AB-States would then receive additional federal dollars earmarked for investment to enhance and continue their programs.

School Climate

How can a school climate shift when the surrounding social and cultural structures that establish national policies and discourses are definitively exclusive of many, if not all, minority groups in at least some ways and occasionally for some reasons? The individual, social, and broader contextual values that continue to shape and inform decisions related to social diversity in school policies must be altered before schools (let alone governments) can even attempt to eliminate the root causes of bullying.

The national climate in the United States recreates social inequities and privileges heteronormative and gendered behaviors and attitudes over others. Bansel and colleagues (2009) claim that "while acts of bullying are unacceptable, they are nonetheless reiterations of the dominant order…rather than acts that run counter to that order" (p. 66). For changes to be sustainable, anti-bullying work should be pursued alongside violence intervention in order to interrupt how systems of power manifest in school climates through neglect and/or willful ignorance, circumstances that make bullying possible in the first place. This means that attention should also be focused on the bully as much as it is on the bullied, while we simultaneously critique the "cultural systems that reproduce and sanction the cultural production of violence, intimidation or harassment" (Payne & Smith, 2011, p. 6).

While it will be some time before all people in our country have equal rights, and while we have yet to establish any federal anti-bullying policies, some schools have taken on the issue and are attempting to push back against the inequities that lead to bullying in the first place.

Anti-Bullying Discourse

There are currently 49 states (South Dakota is the lone holdout) that have laws addressing bullying, harassment, and hazing. Of those 49 states, 25 have laws that specifically address cyber-bullying, while 35 have laws that address hazing. The website Bully Police USA,[8] hosted by a watchdog group of parents and other community members, grades and lists what it sees as effective bullying programs and offers resources for establishing anti-bullying policies and laws, updates about current anti-bullying state and federal legislation, and testimonials from various people about issues related to bullying. While the site pays homage to the Olweus Bullying Program, there are several other programs it recommends if a school, district, or state wants to adopt anti-bullying policies. According to the website Bully Police USA,[9] an effective anti-bullying law should include:

1. the word "bullying" in the text of the bill/law/statute

2. clear anti-bullying laws, not mere school safety laws

3. clear definitions of bullying, harassment, and other associated terms (hazing, etc.)

4. recommendations for making policy and models of effective policy language and/or implementation procedures

5. required participation by all education specialists at all levels, starting with the state superintendent's office, school districts, schools, parents, and students. Together they can define and set rules, policies, and procedures for implementing anti-bullying programs. Laws should require anti-bullying training, anti-bullying education for students and staff, and guidelines for prevention

6. mandates for anti-bullying, not suggestions or guidelines

7. clearly stated dates for policy framing, passage, implementation, and assessment of mandates

8. policies for protection of individuals and groups from reprisal, retaliation, or false accusation when they report bullying or intervene according to policy

9. protocols for legal protection against lawsuits for those who comply with anti-bullying policies

10. emphasis on the rights of victims of bullying, such as free counseling for victims who suffer abuse

11. procedures and formats for accountability reports that are made either to lawmakers or state education superintendents, including details of consequences for schools/districts that don't comply with the law. There should be mandatory posting and/or notification of policies and reporting—procedures for students, professionals, and parents.

12. a Cyberbullying or "Electronic Harassment" law that addresses evolving technological platforms through which bullying practices can be perpetrated in relation to but beyond the physical school environment.

The Bully Police also suggest that policies should avoid zero-tolerance approaches, group therapy models, and conflict resolution-based practices, because they either have no demonstrable effect on the school climate or do not sufficiently confront or prevent bullying behaviors.

Anti-Bullying Presence in Schools

Another method for reducing bullying in schools is to have an active on-site organization that is committed to anti-bullying. "Project 10" is a bullying reduction program for LGBT students at Fairfax High in Los Angeles, California, and it has helped significantly to decrease bullying in that school. Studies from GLSEN similarly report that

> having a Gay-Straight Alliance in school was related to more positive experiences for LGBT students, including: hearing fewer homophobic remarks, less victimization because of sexual orientation and gender expression, less absenteeism because of safety concerns and a greater sense of belonging to the school community. (Kosciw, Greytak, Diaz, & Bartkiewicz, 2009, p. 64)

This study also found that the presence of staff who were allies contributed to a range of positive trends, including fewer reports of absenteeism, fewer reports of feeling unsafe, greater academic achievement, higher educational aspirations, and a greater sense of belonging to the school community. Overall, the researchers found that students attending schools with anti-bullying policies that included protections based on sexual orientation and/or gender identity/expression

> heard fewer homophobic remarks, experienced lower levels of victimization related to their sexual orientation, were more likely to report that staff intervened when hearing homophobic remarks and were more likely to report incidents of harassment and assault to school staff than students at schools with a general policy or no policy. (p. 64)

When all school personnel have a warm and inviting attitude not only toward LGBTQGV students but toward *all* students, the potential exists to shift the tone of the entire school. This model, by design, could be used by other organizations that wish to have a presence within schools.

Payne and Smith (2012) offer an extensive critique of anti-bullying programs. They suggest that anti-bullying discourses typically reduce the assessment of school climates to either positive or negative, which means that "anti-bullying programs are pushing violent behavior underground rather than calling systemic privileging and marginalization into question...." They also charge that "programs are designed to recognize and address overt, non-normative aggression, but they cannot address how social stigma and marginalization work 'in the most mundane moments everyday inside schools' (Youdell, 2006, p. 13), or 'how school processes act unwittingly to exclude particular students from the educational endeavour' (Youdell, 2006, p. 1)" (p. 7). In other words, these programs are not sustainable because they fail to live up to the real-time, authentic needs of the students who most need support. And because the system fails to change and adapt, those who suffer the most continue to suffer (and may even suffer more because of adaptations in bullying behavior).

We suggest that schools and professionals go beyond the flat rhetoric of more traditional anti-bullying programs and instead employ an organizational model that includes the following:

1. systems-level interventions

2. preventive and interventionist education for teachers, school staff, parents, and community members

3. K–16 educational and preventive approaches with students through curriculum and instruction

4. student involvement (prevention and intervention)

5. interventions with bullies and victims by school authorities

6. school- and district-level accountability to state and national overseers responsible for bullying reduction

7. state and national follow-up protocols that include ongoing assessment, reflection, reward, and funding through federal and state education agencies

Preventive Health Care

Another possible approach to mitigating the effects of bullying in schools is to link anti-bullying efforts with preventive mental health and health care screenings that become a standard component of the school citizenry's annual checkups. Most schools require students to undergo physical examinations before the school year starts, so part of the medical exam could entail a series of questions that help to identify an individual's past or present experience as a victim or perpetrator of bullying, or even that individual's potential for playing those roles in the future. Were it possible to also have mental health screenings that could do the same work, bullies and victims might be able to receive much-needed support prior to or even during the school year. Perhaps bullying can be bundled into insurance policies and then to adult wellness and health care programs so that educators, parents, guardians, and even relatives may become more alert to the signs of bullying and thus be better prepared to intervene and interrupt this activity at local sites.

Social Justice Work

Stopping bullying is the custodial work and responsibility of all people—not just schoolteachers and public officials. While there is no panacea for eliminating prejudices from manifesting in the form of bullying or microaggressions, we have offered proactive and interventionist strategies that can make a difference for the common good. Cruel assaults and insults that stem from prejudiced thoughts, and prejudiced thoughts that stem from cruel assaults and insults, might decrease over time if we provided a 360-degree model of anti-bullying work in our nation at large. While we suggest that stopping bullying is the custodial work of all people, we also see it as a central part of the work of social justice advocates in public education, wherein we are confident there exists a deep pool of allies and advocates who can make a tremendous difference if they are encouraged and supported by structured programs and legislative mandates. Anti-bullying theory can be seamlessly woven into rich scientific narratives by those conducting social justice research so that professionals and members of the public can better understand that support for anti-bullying is both morally and materially in the best interests of our entire society, regardless of an individual's position and status within that society. In other words, since social justice work in schools tends to include teaching about situations in which injustice and discrimination occur with regard to differences in race, ethnicity, gender, gender expression, age, appearance, ability, disability, national origin, language, spiritual belief, size (height and/or weight), sexual orientation, social class, economic circumstances, environment, ecology, culture, and the treatment of animals (Conference on English Education Commission on Social Justice, 2009), the continued efforts of various commissions, committees, nonprofit organizations, and universities with social justice degree programs[10] can incorporate anti-bullying work into their missions.

If it were possible to shift all of the myriad political and educational values that our society uses to inform policymaking, we would do so. If it were possible to disseminate all of the information necessary to inform the countless identity groups and individuals with diverse value systems about why putting an end to bullying matters, we would do so. We believe that this book, the research consulted in writing it, and the organizations we've referred to who work to eliminate bullying all prove that such things are possible. In a country where people's values and ideals tend to be defined by the binaries of inclusion/exclusion, normal/abnormal, superiority/inferiority, and desirability/undesirability, we believe this book and the strategies we highlight can help bring about real social change. We believe it is possible to transcend prejudice and oppression based on social, cultural, gendered, ableist, sexist, heteronormative, and religious/spiritual inequities. We believe these are *not* American values. We believe there are better ways. We believe it is the responsibility of professional educators, lawmakers, and adults everywhere to work toward ending such prejudices, and we have learned from scientific research that doing so would help support not just the success of more individuals, but the collective success of our entire nation. We believe that bullying can be stopped, should be stopped, and must be stopped. We believe. We invite you to believe with us, and to act now.

Notes

1 Genderism is "an ideology that reinforces the negative evaluation of gender non-conformity or an incongruence between sex and gender" (Hill & Willoughby, 2005, p. 534).

2 Ableism refers to a form of discrimination that favors people without disabilities and maintains that disability in and of itself is a negative concept, state, and experience (Sue, 2010).

3 Religist refers to bullying that assumes (a) all people identify and practice a particular and dominant religion (in the United States, Christianity), and (b) that holidays in U.S. schools revolve around Christian values (76.5% of Americans are Christian, 1.3% are Jewish, 0.5% are Islamic, 0.5% are Buddhist, 0.4% are Hindu, and 14% do not identify with a religion (Sue, 2010).

4 For more information on Olweus's foundational work, which has been implemented in more than a dozen countries and in thousands of schools in the United States, see http://www.olweus.org/public/index.page. His Bullying Prevention Program is the only model program of non-U.S. origin that the U.S. Department of Justice has used in a national violence prevention initiative in the United States.

5 See Department for Education, http://www.education.gov.uk/search/results?q=bullying for additional resources on anti-bullying.

6 Quoted in http://www.cnsnews.com/news/article/obama-warns-about-dangers-bullying-school-and-internet, retrieved on July 5, 2011.

7 Bullying can be integrated into the Common Core and Health and Wellness Standards. For ideas, consult these sites: http://www.dc.gov/DCPS/In+the+Classroom/Health+and+Wellness (D.C. public schools) and http://www.portal.state.pa.us/portal/server.pt/community/current_initiatives/19720/student_health_and_wellness/792455 (Pennsylvania).

8 See http://www.bullypolice.org/program.html

9 See http://www.bullypolice.org/program.html

10 Arizona State University offers a master's degree in Social Justice and Human Rights (MAS-JHR); Loyola University of Chicago offers a master's in Social Justice and Community Development; Boalt Law School has the Center for Social Justice; the University of Massachusetts, Amherst, offers master's and doctoral degrees in Social Justice Education. In addition, many colleges and universities have programs focused on teaching for social justice, including the University of Massachusetts, Amherst, the University of Regina, Evergreen State College, the State University of New York at Oswego, Pennsylvania State University, Swarthmore College, the University of California, Los Angeles, and the University of Washington. A number of nonprofit organizations also support the practice in schools, including Mosaic, the Institute for Community Leadership, and the Freechild Project.

References

Bansel, P., Davies, B., Laws, C., & Linnell, S. (2009). Bullies, bullying and power in the contexts of schooling. *British Journal of Sociology of Education, 30*(1), 59–69.

Conference on English Education Commission on Social Justice. (2009). CEE position statement: Beliefs about social justice in English education. *First Biennial CEE Conference.* Chicago: CEE.

Crick, N.R., & Bigbee, M.A. (1998). Relational and overt forms of peer victimization: A multiinformant approach. *Journal of Consulting and Clinical Psychology, 66*(2), 710–722.

Department for Education. Retrieved January 28, 2013, from http://www.education.gov.uk/schools/pupilsupport/behaviour/bullying

Ministry of Education and Research (Norway). (2007). *Brochure about Ministry of Education and Research*. Retrieved January 28, 2013, from http://www.regjeringen.no/en/dep/kd/documents/brochures-and-handbooks/2007/broshure-about-ministry-of-education-and.html?id=482407

Hill, D.B., & Willoughby, B.L.B. (2005). The development and validation of the genderism and transphobia scale. *Sex Roles, 53*(7/8), 531–544.

Kosciw, J., Greytak, E., Diaz, E., & Bartkiewicz, M. (2009). *The 2009 National School Climate Survey: The experiences of lesbian, gay, bisexual and transgender youth in our nation's schools*. New York: GLSEN.

Olweus, D. (1984). Aggressors and their victims: Bullying at school. In N. Frude & H. Gault (Eds.), *Disruptive behaviour in schools* (pp. 57–76). Chichester, UK: John Wiley & Sons.

Olweus, D. (1993). *Bullying at school: What we know and what we can do*. Mahwah, NJ: Blackwell Publishing.

Payne, E., & Smith, M. (2012). Rethinking safe schools approaches for LGBTQ students. *Multicultural Perspectives, 14*(4), 187–193.

Rigby, K. (2000). Effects of peer victimization in schools and perceived social support on adolescent well-being. *Journal of Adolescence, 23*, 57–68.

Roland, E., & Vaaland, G.S. (2006). *Teachers' guide to the Zero anti-bullying programme*. Stavanger, Norway: University of Stavanger, Center for Behavioral Research.

Sherer, Y.P., & Nickerson, A.B. (2010). Anti-bullying practices in American schools: Perspectives of school psychologists. *Psychology in the Schools, 47*(3), 217–229.

Smith, P.K., Smith, C., Osborn, R., & Samara, M. (2008). A content analysis of school anti-bullying policies: Progress and limitations. *Educational Psychology in Practice, 24*(1), 1–12.

Sue, D.W. (Ed.). (2010). *Microaggressions and marginality: Manifestation, dynamics, and impact*. Hoboken, NJ: Wiley.

Tikkanen, T.I., & Junge, A. (2004). *Evaluation of the national manifesto against bullying 2002–2004 in Norway*. Paper presented at the Taking Fear Out of Schools: International Policy and Research Conference on School Bullying and Violence, September 5–8, Stavanger, Norway.

CHAPTER TEN

Shifting the Tide of Bullying Through Teacher Education

Tools for the Classroom

sj Miller

We believe in the possibility of deep and sustained change that will serve to stop bullying in classrooms and in our school communities by shifting the prevailing attitudes in the environment. While policy matters related to bullying are still being debated in Washington, D.C., we recognize that this is unacceptable and that we cannot afford to wait any longer. Kids are suffering each and every day they come to school. So what can we do in the meantime? We can take action now, be foot soldiers, and include these issues in our teacher education courses. For each of the most vulnerable populations discussed in the book, this chapter provides concrete strategies for the secondary classroom that can be used to repair the vital and long-ago-broken trust between students and their schools, while building the communities necessary to enact profound social change.

According to the National Council of Teachers of English's *Standards for Initial Preparation of Teachers of Secondary English Language Arts, Grades 7–12* (National Council of Teachers of English, 2012), in recent years the National Council for the Accreditation of Teacher Education has begun to more consistently back policies related to supporting diversity in public schools, and particularly to ensuring that teacher education programs produce teachers who believe that all students can learn at high levels. Further, it has historically supported the ethical disposition that professional educators are responsible for making sure all students receive the support, resources, curriculum, and instruction they need to succeed in school. However, supporting diversity and teaching for social justice, though related concepts, are distinct, with the latter supporting the former. Many consider supporting diversity in classrooms to be a matter of simple recognition, tolerance, and inclusion. Teaching for social justice, however, involves assertions that professionals (and therefore teacher education programs) are responsible not only for developing but also for demonstrating dispositions and methods that systematically reduce and even eliminate social inequities, including unequal access, unequal opportunity to learn, and social or institutional practices that are (intentionally or otherwise) unfairly biased with regard to race, ethnicity, gender, gender expression, age, appearance, ability, disability, national/geographic origin, language/dialect use, spiritual belief, appearance (including, but not limited, to variance in height and/or weight), sexual orientation, social class, economic circumstance, environment, ecology, and culture.

While NCATE itself has raised concerns about the use of "social justice" pedagogies to potentially indoctrinate and thereby discriminate against people whose ideologies lead them to hold certain beliefs that are counter to a non-specific but particularly "liberal" approach to teaching, considerable research has been done that demonstrates how teaching for social justice is not merely a particular or partisan moral argument about education (National Council for Accreditation of Teacher Education, 2006). Teaching for social justice can be based on a significant body of both qualitative and quantitative scientific research. Its approaches may be collectively referred to as "responsive" methods for teaching in contemporary society, and that research stems from well-developed and widely accepted theories related to Culturally Responsive Pedagogy, linguistics, Funds of Knowledge research, Third Space pedagogies, and studies focused on educational access, opportunity, race, social class, and other factors we have discussed.

Designing teacher education programs that ensure candidates graduate with a deep understanding of social justice issues and the knowledge they need to teach in ways that are socially just is emphatically necessary in order to reduce student achievement gaps and disparities in U.S. public schools. When teachers do *not* respond to diverse students, or when they respond to diverse students in ways that are negative, undifferentiated, or otherwise discriminatory, those students are found to consistently and significantly underperform compared to their peers, whose identities, linguistic backgrounds, funds of knowledge, and out-of-school literacies are affirmed, reflected in curricula, and actively used to contextualize core academic content and assessments.

As we stated in Chapter 8, teaching for social justice is not simply a moral act that reflects certain activist or partisan movements in public education (though it *is* emphatically a moral act). Rather, teaching for social justice is based on scientific research demonstrating that when teachers understand the nature of social diversity and how to support it, their students are more likely to engage, persevere, and achieve at higher levels than those in classrooms where teachers are averse to using responsive curriculum and instructional methods. In this concluding chapter, we offer strategies, tools, resources, and activities that any teacher can use to support diversity and teach in socially just ways for the good of all students. We have organized the chapter according to the social groups discussed earlier in this book so that readers can refer to specific items for consideration and use.

Stopping Bullying Against LGBTQGV Students: Tools for the Classroom

sj Miller and James R. Gilligan

We begin by offering suggestions for normalizing approaches to teaching beyond the gender binary that can empower teachers to incorporate LGBTQGV themes into middle and secondary English curricula, integrating them with other social justice themes, in order to help schools become centers for envisioning a more just society. At the root of LGBTQGV bullying is conscious or unconscious ignorance of how gender and sexuality operate in our lives. By introducing a different way of talking about gender, we can challenge some of the forms of gender and sexuality oppression that do exist. Exposing students to non-normative approaches to understanding gender will better prepare them for handling sexism, sexual harassment, bullying, self-injury, or even hate crimes.[1] It is vital that we develop a social consciousness with our students regarding gender bias issues so as not to perpetuate oppressive gender-based hierarchies that are already deeply entrenched in society. As we heighten awareness about gender oppression with our students, we ultimately shift gender dynamics in the dominant culture and thereby, it is hoped, thwart attacks on individuals who fall outside of the gender or sexuality binary.

Lesson Plans and Classrooms

Gender Fluidity/Normalizing Classroom Discourse

From Day One, teachers can be taught to show their support for all students by using inclusive language. Typically, students don't realize that a teacher is an ally unless s/he/per[2] makes a point by modeling inclusivity. Below are some examples of how to normalize issues relating to gender in the classroom for secondary teachers.

- Only put up posters, announcements, or pictures that include all representations of gender and gender identity/expression.

- Create a classroom library that values non-normative gender expressions, gender roles, and mannerisms. (See suggested titles in Appendix A at end of this chapter.)

- Introduce non-binary perspectives on gender and gender identity through dialogue, role-plays, research, observation, discrimination, and policy.

- Discuss how the school has addressed issues relating to non-normative representations of gender and works with students to consider ways to engender social change.

- Adopt a pedagogy for change that values social justice, agency, and social action (see Chapters 3 and 7 in Miller & Norris [2007]).

- When discussing gender, ask students to consider how the texts that were used valued or disqualified representations of gender. Ask questions such as: How is language used to describe gender? Who is given power while speaking? Who is excluded? How is gender portrayed in the text? Describe any variations of gender. Is the text current or dated, and how might that affect representations of gender? Are the voices of the disenfranchised present? What resources were used in writing the book? What is the gender of the author? What are the politics of the press, and who published the text?

- Use gender-inclusive language in all communications with students, parents, school administrators, and peers. Talk about the broader issues of gender bias, sex-role stereotyping, and discrimination, and work to promote equitable representations of gender identity.

- Always design lessons that provide students with ongoing opportunities to challenge and disrupt dominant ideologies of gender, gender expression, gender roles, and behaviors, for example:

- Research which states have school policies protecting students' gender identity and gender expression. Contrast that to your school's policy and review what protections are in place for LGBTQ students.

- Do a critical discourse analysis of a TV show on gendered language use and how gender is represented.

- Do a discourse analysis of one's personal use of gendered language.

- Rewrite a scene or passage from a film, play, poem, or other text and shift the use of gendered language to make the characters' representations of gender more inclusive. (See Appendix B for sources that challenge the gender binary.)

- Conduct an analysis of how gendered language is used in a passage or scene. Review the number of positive or negative stereotypes that affirm/disaffirm gender differences.

- Ask students to observe how the gender binary is reinforced in their school.

- Ask students to conduct observations of where they see the gender binary challenged in popular culture or in society at large.

- Ask students to reflect on what their biological sex forces them to do in a given day. Ask them to contrast that to how their gender role is performed over a 24-hour period.

- Ask students to share which books, TV, and films challenge or subvert traditional gender norms.

- Ask students to explore how a text reinforces heteronormativity.

- Teach about microaggressions and invite students to reflect on the microaggressions they've enacted. Ask them to reflect on what they can change about their behaviors and attitudes toward LGBTQGV students.

- Discuss complex post-traumatic stress disorder (C-PTSD) and the possible long-term consequences of bullying on an individual.

- Ask students what different representations of gender they have observed outside of school in other peer groups.

- Discuss the African runner Caster Semenya, who is intersexed but who experienced scrutiny for being perceived as male.

- Discuss the controversy of transgender people who want to compete in sports or in the Olympics.

- Do a unit on sexism and explain/show that it stems from a history of institutional policies and social values defined by men, and operates to the advantage of men—most often White men—and to the disadvantage of women.

- Teach texts from all cultures that challenge gender norms and gender identity/expression.

- Discuss evolving vocabulary about gender and invite discussion and debate.

- Invite discussion and debate about gender norms, gender roles, and mannerisms.

- Ask students to describe where and how they first developed their concept of their own gender identities. What evidence did they have that reinforced those perceptions? Who told them? How were those beliefs socialized?

- Ask students to describe how they express their gender and enact gender norms and roles, and explore how that aligns with the gender binary/nonbinary.

- Ask students at what age they began to challenge what they learned about themselves, and what made them reconsider those beliefs.

- Discuss gender as performance.

- Invite students to consider gender and sexuality as continuums or spectrums (or both) that are either socially constructed (fluid) or biologically determined (fixed)

- Reflect on whether there was ever a time when the students thought their answers did not fit the images society had ingrained in them. How did they respond?

- Research former laws related to gender and have students look for bias. Reflect on current change. Do a critical discourse analysis of current hate crimes legislation and reflect on which groups are still marginalized.

- Review antidiscrimination laws.

- Research Title IX, its past and its future.

- Research which states have nondiscrimination laws and understand how nondiscrimination policies work by state.

- Research which states have laws that privilege homosexuals and transgender people.

- Research which states discriminate against homosexuals and transgender people.

- Research which states have laws excluding homosexuals and transgender people.

- Interview people in the local community who challenge the gender binary.

- Invite guest speakers who challenge the gender binary.

- Deconstruct how mainstream ads reinforce the gender binary.

- Examine what kinds of TV commercials and TV shows are on at particular times and how their scheduling sustains and reinforces the gender binary.

- Examine different genres of musical lyrics and how they affirm or challenge the gender binary.

- Review clips in the media about how female politicians are compared to male politicians.

- Examine random pay scales in various professions and look for gender equity.

- Review the history of all human rights and all of the major social movements (civil rights, gay/lesbian/bisexual/transgender/two-spirited,[3] intersexed, women, second-language speakers, bilinguals, immigrants, Asian Americans, Native Americans, Latina/o Americans, veterans, war dissenters, the disabled, students with disabilities or special needs, and any other non-dominant groups).

- Talk about what it means to be an ally and how students can become allies for others.

- Explore derogatory terminology for transgender and non-normative representations of gender and the consequences it can have.

- Conduct a unit on exploring the medical model approaches to homosexuality and transgender in the DSM over time. Help students observe how homosexuality has been depathologized but transgender is still under scrutiny.[4]

- Share statistics from the Gay, Lesbian & Straight Educational Network (GLSEN) and talk about bullying and harassment in the students' school.

The following activities may be more risky, so first consider discussions with the principal, other teachers, and parents/guardians.

- Challenge students to dress outside of the gender norm (gender expression) for a class period and then, if it is safe, for an entire school day.

- Invite your students to design a non-binary gender day for the school with speakers, panelists, and poetry.

- Invite students to attend lectures or community presentations at local universities or colleges to expose them to different perspectives about gender.

Preferred Gender Pronouns

Frequently, transgender and gender non-conforming students are not addressed by appropriate pronouns or names. Having one's gender recognized and validated is important for one's emotional and psychological health. As anyone can imagine, it is extremely disrespectful to be called by a pronoun or name one does not choose for oneself. It invalidates one's identity and self-concept. This lack of validation and recognition can and often does lead to depression and suicide (Kosciw, Greytak, Diaz, & Bartkiewicz, 2009).

Some transgender and gender non-conforming students may use pronouns in their lived experiences with peer groups but be afraid to do so in school. Although students may be reluctant to come out as transgender for fear of harassment, there are possible ways to speak with the student about how s/he might want pronouns or even non-pronouns used. There is a cadre of non-standardized, emerging pronouns for those who express gender non-normatively (Chase & Ressler, 2009). The teacher-student relationship has much to do with how comfortable the student feels in disclosing how s/he might want to be referred to. A strategy that can address this is to hand out a slip of paper on the first day of class (or have students write a letter) that is based on the idea of *assigned* versus *chosen* name, gender, and pronoun. The slip of paper reads:

What is your assigned name?
What is your chosen name?

What is your assigned gender?
What is your chosen gender?

What are your assigned pronouns?
What are your chosen pronouns?

Public vs. Private
Do you have any particular pronouns that you want me to use when I refer to you in the classroom?

Do you have any particular pronouns that you want me to use when I refer to you on your writing assignments?

Anything else you want to share?

Students who hesitate to come out publicly have the option of having their privacy respected on paper. In fact, what the teacher might learn is that the vocabulary students use becomes an educational tool for everyone. Approaching students on the first day with these questions sets an immediate tone that the teacher is an ally for transgender students and those who express their gender non-normatively.

Tools for the School Community: School-Wide Awareness

One strategy for combating bullying is to form a *gay-straight alliance* (GSA). The GLSEN website has comprehensive details about starting a GSA as well as working with administrators and district personnel. The "Day of Silence" is also an effective strategy for bringing awareness to the number of LGBTQGV students and even teachers who are out in a given school. The day provides an opportunity for those who are LGBTQGV and their allies to hand out slips of paper that explain the day of silence as a way to draw attention to those people who have at one time felt oppressed or marginalized at school because they are LGBTQGV (see www. glsen.org). Another strategy is to have an "Anti-Bullying" or "Ally Week" that occurs frequently throughout the school year. Schools can describe what bullying is and inform students about different types of bullying. Some students may not be aware that they are bullying, so bringing attention to what bullying is can help them recognize their own behaviors (Miller, 2012). This could take the form of roundtable discussions, guest presentations, peer-to-peer or classroom-to-classroom teaching, and watching and discussing bullying documentaries. Schools might also consider placing various posters and fliers throughout the school that share positive statements about LGBTQGV students. High schools can also partner with neighboring middle and elementary schools to discuss and explore the effects of bullying across contexts. They might work together to create a club or an alliance that can provide a buttress for students against bullying or create a partner or buddy system for students making the change from middle to high school.

Classrooms and public spaces in school buildings can be adorned with pro-LGBTQGV images (for example, rainbow flags, pink triangles, the HRC yellow "=" on a blue background, safe zone signs, and so on), which can send a subtle but powerful message that LGBTQGV students are welcome and supported. More important, teachers of all sexual orientations can model—through their behavior, their speech, and their pedagogy—not just tolerance but inclusion of diverse sexualities.

A final strategy is to have a rich selection of LGBTQGV books shelved in the school library or in classrooms. Such books should be advertised or displayed facing out on bookshelves alongside other texts. Librarians and media specialists should have lists of recommended books for students and teachers, and they should regularly invite dialogue around LGBTQGV-related texts with students during visits to the library.

Bathrooms
Every person at school has the right to safe and appropriate restroom facilities. However, many transgender and gender non-conforming students fear using bathrooms in schools because of potential harassment. Often transgender and gender non-conforming students do not feel safe in either the men's or women's restroom. Many students are harassed in these restrooms because they are perceived to be insufficiently feminine or masculine. In fact, some students are told to use bathrooms that do not correspond to their gender identity and in some extreme cases, expelled from school because the school does not know where the person should use the bathrooms.

School districts should provide an easily accessible unisex, single-stall bathroom for use by any student who desires more privacy, regardless of the underlying reason. However, use of a unisex single-stall restroom should always be a matter of choice for a student. No student should be compelled to use one either as a matter of policy or because of continuing harassment in a gender-appropriate facility (Transgender Law and Policy Institute).

Locker Room Accessibility
The Transgender Law and Policy Institute, which suggests that transgender and gender non-conforming students also face difficulties in locker room facilities, has suggestions that address such difficulties. The institute writes:

In locker rooms that involve undressing in front of others, transgender students who want to use the locker room corresponding to their gender identity must be provided an accommodation that best meets the student's needs. Such accommodations can include: (A) use of a private area within the public area (a bathroom stall with a door, an area separated by a curtain, a PE instructor's office in the locker room), (B) a separate changing schedule in the private area (either utilizing the locker room before or after the other students), (C) use of a nearby private area (a nearby restroom, a nurse's office), (D) access to the locker room corresponding to the student's sex assigned at birth, or (E) satisfaction of PE requirement by independent study outside of gym class (either before or after school or at a local recreational facility).

Sports and Gym Class

Transgender and gender non-conforming students are often forced to join a sports team that does not fit their gender identity. The message students receive is that their gender identity is not taken seriously and is indeed not valid. When people are told repeatedly that their self-perception is invalid, it can be extremely harmful psychologically. Students should therefore be permitted to participate in gender-segregated sports and gym class activities in accordance with their gender identity. In some situations, legitimate questions about fairness in athletic competitions will need to be resolved on a case-by-case basis.

Waiting for passage of the Safe Schools Improvement Act, H.R. 2262, should not stop us from doing advocacy work in our classrooms, schools, and districts. It is important that we work to influence people at all levels so they are aware of bias against transgender students and those who express themselves outside of the binary. The study *From Teasing to Torment* (Markow & Fein, 2005) showed that schools with a comprehensive policy with enumerated categories that included sexual orientation and gender identity/expression were less likely to report a serious harassment problem than those that did not have such a policy (33% vs. 44%, respectively). LGBTQGV students in the 2007 *National School Climate Survey* (Kosciw, Greytak, & Diaz, 2008) who reported having a comprehensive anti-bullying policy experienced lower levels of harassment and were more likely to report incidents of harassment to school staff. Without question, clearly stated policies and anti-bullying programs make a difference in schools.

Resources

- GLSEN: Anti-Bullying Resources for LGBTQGV Youth. The Gay, Lesbian & Straight Educators Network has dozens of resources for fighting back against LGBTGV bullying.
- http://www.glsen.org/cgi-bin/iowa/all/antibullying/index.html
- It Gets Better Project. Individuals speaking out against LGBTQGV bullying with the message that it does get better!
- http://www.itgetsbetter.org/

- Stopbullying.gov. Lesbian, gay, bisexual, or transgender (LGBT) youth and those perceived as LGBT are at increased risk of being bullied. There are important and unique considerations for strategies to prevent and address bullying of LGBT youth.

- http://www.stopbullying.gov/at-risk/groups/lgbt/index.html

- The themed issued of the *English Journal*, *98*(4) (2009), edited by Rebecca and Paula Ressler, was dedicated to exploring sexual identity and gender variance of secondary school students.

Stopping Body-Type Bullying: Tools for the Classroom

Tara Star Johnson and Elana Cutter

Although students who are perceived as LGBTQGV are the number one victims of bullying, people of size—girls more so than boys—are also frequently targeted. And, unlike the other groups represented in this book, overweight people are often blamed for their body type, as if their weight were caused by a moral failing on their part. This, in the minds of bullies, can justify such behavior. Consciously or not, teachers may share this perception or attitude, so sizism is rarely included in classroom conversations or lessons about social justice. Similarly, body type isn't typically recognized as a legitimate part of one's identity, as Elana Cutter, the co-author of Chapter 3, noted in a reflection about an activity in her multiculturalism class.

> During the spring 2011 semester, I took a section of Multiculturalism in the Classroom, as it is required by our major. One instructional activity in which we participated was the creation of an "Identity Circle." The concept is fairly easy to follow, and I find that I use it often because I end up learning a lot about how my students view themselves as well as the priorities they have when it comes to their identity. So we were asked to fill out a pie chart with specific characteristics that we used to identify ourselves, and we would assign a percentage to each of these characteristics. For example, because I am aware of my gender identity, I assigned 40% of the pie chart to being female. Then, as I started to think about what other characteristics defined me, I came to one with which I was somewhat uncomfortable: my body size and shape. Even though it was (and is) a significant part of how I identified myself, I talked myself out of adding it to the pie chart for two reasons. First of all, I was ashamed and did not want my teacher to judge me for having "body image" as a way in which I defined myself. Secondly, I didn't consider my size or my weight to contribute to who I was as a person. I'd had countless experiences that were based around my weight, but I rationalized these thoughts away by saying, "Surely it couldn't be a significant characteristic, especially one that would be considered positive or normal. We've never talked about this as an issue in class before."

Thus a relatively easy first step for teachers and teacher educators to take in order to raise awareness of weight-based bullying is to acknowledge sizism as a social justice issue and body type as a facet of identity. An instructor using an activity such as the one Cutter describes could ask students to brainstorm possible identity characteristics before creating their own circles, and if body type is not mentioned, say something along the lines of, "I see nobody suggested body type as a characteristic. Why is that, do you suppose?" and facilitate the conversation from there.

For teachers desiring more in-depth dialogue on the issue of sizism, we recommend the following in-class and school-wide activities, along with a few additional resources.

Lesson Plans

- Discuss and define terms that relate to weight-based bullying, for example, sizism, fatism, anti-fat stigma, weight discrimination, and anti-fat prejudice. Discussion could include appropriate terms to replace pejorative language, such as "people of size" or "people of substance."

- Analyze the media's representations of people who are overweight or obese: What trends do the characters' behaviors follow? What stereotypes are repeated most often? Then, deliberately interject samples from the media that challenge these stereotypes.

- Integrate sizism into larger units of study on any of the following: social justice (people of size are routinely discriminated against; fair and equitable treatment is a human rights issue); bullying (bullying based on physical appearance such as weight is second only to LGBTQGV bullying); gender and/or media literacy (sizism is salient to the disproportionate emphasis placed on physical appearance for women); current events/social issues (for example, health care, the obesity epidemic, and the relationship between obesity and SES).

- Incorporate texts that portray people of size so that discussion of the issue can be "othered" to characters—real or fictional—rather than addressed on a personal level. The following is a short list of texts we have used.

  1. Bass, M. (2001). On being a fat Black girl in a fat-hating culture. In M. Bennett & V. Dickerson (Eds.), *Recovering the Black female body: Self-representations by African American women* (pp. 220–230). New Brunswick, NJ: Rutgers University Press. Personal essay about the author's traumatic experiences with weight-based bullying; she reflects that her parents prepared her for racism in the Jim Crow South but not for living life as a fat person.

  2. Maynard, R. (n.d.) The fan club. Retrieved January 7, 2011, from http://www.ronamaynard.com/index.php?the-fan-club. Short story written by a teenager about a girl who succumbs to popular classmates' peer pressure to mock an overweight student who thinks she

is the narrator's friend. An example of how people rarely occupy exclusively "bully" or "bullied" subject positions but are typically a blend of both.

3. Howe, J. (1992). *The misfits*. New York: Simon & Schuster. A coming-of-age young adult novel narrated by an overweight seventh grader about his friends' campaign to end name-calling at their school.

4. Peck, C. (2005). *Revenge of the paste eaters: Memoirs of a misfit*. New York: Warner Books. An autobiographical piece that includes an essay titled "Fatso," a wry and powerful description of the author's experiences with sizism.

5. Newsom, J.S. (2012). *Miss Representation*. New York: Vergil Films. A documentary on the media and advertising industries' pervasive and pernicious effect on women's body images containing versions and support materials appropriate for elementary, secondary, and adult audiences. Viewing this film pairs nicely with an activity in which students look through magazines (or other form of media) for examples that reinforce or refute the documentary's claims.

6. Rothblum, E., & Solovay, S. (Eds.). (2009). *The fat studies reader*. New York: New York University Press. An excellent resource for instructors to use to increase their understanding of sizism so that they're better equipped to facilitate conversations about the issue.

7. *The Fat Boy Chronicles*, a book and film based on a true story about an obese eighth grader subjected to bullying, vividly and sensitively demonstrates that the humiliation and self-loathing the main character experiences as a result of his peers' cruelty is not the sole domain of girls.

School-Wide Ideas

In order to raise awareness of sizism in schools, school leaders can facilitate professional development activities by inviting school personnel to reflect on their personal beliefs about students who are fat and analyze their interactions with them. They can explore how their implicit beliefs affect their treatment of fat students, asking such questions as what their verbal and nonverbal communications convey to these students and whether and how they intercede when a person of size is being bullied.

Teachers can also address the logistics of classroom space by arranging classrooms to accommodate students of substance. Desks with chairs that are separated are preferable, as they allow students to fit comfortably into their seats. Health curricula should emphasize body type acceptance and emotional well-being along with nutrition and exercise. Most important, perhaps, a systemic school culture that models respect and human dignity for all people at all levels will reinforce what individual teachers may be doing in their classrooms. When the entire school honors behavioral standards according to which bullying of any kind is unwelcome and good citizenship is rewarded, it's not only easier for teachers to do their jobs but also more likely that positive behaviors will extend beyond the school walls.

Resources

The field of fat studies is an emerging discipline, so scholarly resources are scant. *The Fat Reader*, mentioned above, is a cornerstone text, and there are a growing number of books and blogs about fat acceptance aimed at popular audiences. This website describes many of them: http://feministcupcake.wordpress. com/2011/11/05/fat-studies-blogs-and-sites-that-bring-a-tear-of-joy-to-my-eye/. Another seminal work that informs fat studies is Susan Bordo's (2004) *Unbearable Weight: Feminism, Western Culture, and the Body*, which is now in its second (10th-anniversary) edition. Bordo uses feminist theory—but writes accessibly— to explore weight and weight loss, exercise, media images, the entertainment and advertising industries, and eating disorders. Selections from this book would pair well with Jean Kilbourne's (2010) *Killing Us Softly 4*, the fourth edition of her lecture on advertising's image of women, for college or mature high school audiences. Examining sizism within the broader context of the standard of beauty imposed upon women vis-à-vis popular culture might be one way to draw attention to the issue without singling out students of size.

Stopping Bullying Against Students with Disabilities: Tools for the Classroom

Joseph John Morgan and Deanna Adams

Knowing that students with disabilities are often at high risk for being both the victims and the perpetrators of bullying within the school environment, it is important that preservice and inservice educators identify strategies and techniques that can be used within the school environment to reduce this risk. The twin foci of these interventions should be: (a) increasing awareness of disability within the school community in order to lower the instances of bullying against students with disabilities, and (b) ensuring that the educational programming of students with disabilities focuses on social and emotional communication skills so that this population is aware of bullying when it occurs. We offer some ideas that educators can use to help prevent the bullying of, and bullying by, students with disabilities.

Lesson Plans

Educators can implement targeted lessons within the classroom that discuss disability with students, thereby demystifying this category and making students more aware of the impact of disability within society. Topics of these lessons could include:

- the definition of disability and the impact of disability within the school environment

- the social construct of disability and the variables that impact a disability (for example, being in a wheelchair and not having an accessible ramp, having a learning disability in reading but having strengths in reading or writing)

- individuals who have disabilities who have overcome obstacles (for example, teaching about actors with learning disabilities or athletes with physical disabilities)

- the need for adaptation to environments in order to provide access for individuals with disabilities (such as focusing on the fact that fair is not always equal, talking about accommodations and supports)

- specific lessons on social and emotional skills used within the school environment. The skills targeted can be identified through a functional analysis of typical student interactions (Rose, Espelage, Aragon, & Elliott, 2011).

- inclusion of social and emotional communication goals and benchmarks within a student's individualized education program (IEP)

School-Wide Ideas

School-wide strategies can also be implemented to create learning environments that are supportive of students with disabilities. Ideas for school-wide strategies are:

- modifying anti-bullying programs to ensure that they discuss students with disabilities (Raskauskas & Modell, 2011)

- making instructional adaptations to anti-bullying programs to ensure accessibility by students with disabilities (for example, reading assessment questions aloud, allowing students to listen to materials in audio format instead of reading) (Raskauskas & Modell, 2011)

- provision of professional development training to the teaching staff to ensure understanding of disability

- policies and procedures for identifying bullying involving students with disabilities, and training on how to notice and report bullying activities

- implementation of school-wide positive behavioral support systems

- school-wide instruction on appropriate social and emotional communication skills

Texts

The following texts and resources provide additional information and support for preventing the bullying of students with disabilities.

- Cooper, B., & Widdows, N. (2008). *The social success workbook for teens: Skill-building activities for teens with nonverbal learning disorder, Asperger's disorder & other social-skill problems.* Oakland, CA: New Harbinger Publications.

- Gray, C., Bvm, F., & Gray, C. (2012). *The new social story book.* Arlington, TX: Future Horizons Inc.

- Jackson, L. (2002). *Freaks, geeks & Asperger syndrome: A user guide to adolescence.* London: Jessica Kingsley Publishers.

- Mannix, D. (2009). *Social skills activities for secondary students with special needs* (2nd ed.). San Francisco: Jossey-Bass.

Resources

- PACER, Facts about Bullying of Students with Disabilities and Strategies for Peer Advocacy http://www.pacer.org/bullying/resources/students-with-disabilities/

- Stopbullying.gov, Bullying and Youth with Disabilities and Special Health Needs http://www.stopbullying.gov/at-risk/groups/special-needs/index.html

- The National Dissemination Center for Children with Disabilities http://nichcy.org/schoolage/behavior/bullying

- Autism Speaks, Combating Bullying and Students with Autism Spectrum Disorders http://www.autismspeaks.org/family-services/bullying

- The Council for Exceptional Children, Bullying of Childrern With Exceptionalities http://www.cec.sped.org/AM/Template.cfm?Section=Home&TEMPLATE=/CM/ContentDisplay.cfm&CONTENTID=12979

- Center on Human Policy at Syracuse University has resources for teachers wanting to teach about disability. Disability Studies for Teachers at http://www.disabilitystudiesforteachers.org/

- The Disability History Museum provides lesson plans and essays and can be used as a site for research projects in class. http://www.disabilitymuseum.org/dhm/index.html

- Disability Social History Projects has links to bibliographies, exhibits, and resources on history, arts and culture, disability-specific topics, GLBTQ disability, gender, and race http://www.disabilityhistory.org/

- *Infusing disability studies into the general curriculum* by P. Ferguson and National Institute for Urban School Improvement. A PDF that provides information on how to include disability into curriculum, dos and don'ts, and many resources for educators can be found at http://www.urban-schools.org/pdf/OPdisability.pdf

Interrupting Roastin' Among Students of Color: Lesson Plans and School-Wide Ideas

Tyrone Rivers and Dorothy Espelage

Given the value placed on high verbal ability in the Black community, a challenge to educators, researchers, and policymakers is how to maximize the benefits gained from roasting while also eliminating its costs. Some suggestions are these:

1. Apply culturally responsive teaching (Brayboy & Castagno, 2009; Santamaria, 2009; Villegas & Lucas, 2007) allowing for more student verbal creativity in assignments (for instance, verbal presentations).

2. Because boredom fuels roasting perpetration, decrease down time in classrooms where roasting is an issue, and then implement a zero-tolerance policy for roasting in classrooms. There is usually zero tolerance for saying "gay" and "homo" to describe things and/or people, but there is nothing to prevent a student from tearing down a classmate's self-esteem through roasting. This should not be the case.

3. Teachers should have candid discussions with students about roasting (that is, how it started, why it started, its place in society) and its power to hurt others. (For a deeper understanding of roasting see Labov, 1972; Percelay, Dweck, & Ivey, 1995; Smitherman, 2000.) Just because the activity is largely portrayed as harmless in the media does not make it so. Teachers can have students discuss their experiences with roasting (Do they like it or not? Does it bother them? Would they rather not do it?).

4. Adults in the school need to set the example. If the adults are roasting each other and also the students, they cannot expect the students to refrain from roasting others, either.

Resources

Building empathy on the part of students can help them understand how hurtful roasting can be. The Character Education Partnership (CEP; www.character. org) provides free lesson plans for educators of all grade levels on relevant topics such as empathy, caring, conflict resolution, tolerance, bullying, relationship building, and respect. CEP also provides a high-quality annual conference and powerful training opportunities for educators. The evidence-based Roots of Empathy (www.rootsofempathy.org) is a proven classroom program for decreasing levels of bullying and aggression among K–8 children by building empathy and social/emotional skills. In the United States, Roots of Empathy has programs in California, New York, and Washington State. Second Step (www.cfchildren.org/second-step.aspx) is a cost-effective, evidence-based program that also builds empathy and social/emotional skills in K–8 students. Further, Second Step focuses on emotion management, problem solving, self-regulation, and executive function skills. The lesson plans are easy to follow and media-rich.

Teacher Education Resources

- *Bullying prevention and intervention: Realistic strategies for schools* (2009) by Susan Swearer, Dorothy Espelage and Scott Napolitano; and, *Dignity for all: Safeguarding LGBT students* (2012) by Peter Dewitt
  These two books provide lesson plans, teacher approaches, and practical strategies to stop bullying and foster a safe, caring environment for learning.

- *Bullying, suicide, and homicide: Understanding, assessing, and preventing threats to self and others for victims of bullying* (2011)
  Butch Losey humanizes victims and survivors of bullying with details about how it affects their sense of purpose and self. This book can (a) help teachers understand the pervasive culture of bullying and (b) safeguard students through schooling and counseling.

- *Crossing boundaries: Teaching and learning with urban youth* (2012)
  Valerie Kinloch emphasizes the role of storytelling in the lives of young adults and describes how teachers can foster venues for universal and responsive literacies in and out of the classroom. This book is helpful for the teacher-researcher who wants to advance students' exposure across disciplinary literacies.

Stopping the Bullying Against Latina and Latino Students: Tools for the Classroom

Rodrigo Joseph Rodríguez

As educators, our awareness about the experiences of Latino[5] students can help us to be caring about and responsive to their realities, struggles, and needs in our classrooms and schools. To become aware, we can begin with a self-reflection of our practice and then proceed to an assessment of tools and readings that we can introduce to our students. This requires planning and discussions with our teaching colleagues in order to share ideas and gain support for our anti-bullying methods in the classroom.

In the essay "Teaching, Caring, and Transformation," Nieto (2012) explained: "A look, a gesture, a word: All of these can speak volumes about a teacher's perceptions concerning students, their identities, abilities, families, and the community in which they live" (p. 29). Nieto provided three lessons learned about teaching and student learning and how we can be caring and responsive to our students.

1. One must know oneself. Learning about oneself, one's shortcomings and flaws, and one's biases and values, one's vices and virtues, is a difficult but also empowering process. (p. 29)

2. Educators need to learn about their students…. [E]ducators also need to learn about the sociocultural realities of their students, and about the sociopolitical conditions in which they live. (p. 30)

3. To survive and grow, educators need to develop allies. (p. 31)

These three lessons provide the tools for teachers to launch strategies and techniques to stop bullying in their classrooms and schools. Resources such as novels and professional development books not only provide lasting learning, care, and empathy, but can also change our school experience as well as that of our students. We can begin by selecting fiction and nonfiction titles that reflect both the lives of our students and lives that are different from theirs. We can also select books that help students question their belief structures as they shape their own identities and affiliations. In our teaching life, whether through intentional or subliminal messaging, we communicate what is normal and acceptable. As a result, we can move from norms to demonstrating responsible ways of teaching and learning with our students.

As we examine books and images, we can use tools to assist us in designing and planning activities that help us question what we consume, including a questioning-based model that empowers students to seek deeper learning about media literacy and how power influences decision-making and the accessibility of resources. The purpose of the following list of recommended tools is to: (a) increase awareness of Latina and Latino student diversity to foster a caring, learning environment and prevent bullying and peer harassment; (b) provide channels for students to become knowledgeable about the prevalence and consequences of bullying and peer harassment; (c) openly communicate instances of bullying and harassment in our classrooms and schools; and (d) gain familiarity with adolescent vernacular language and expressions.

Lesson Plans

Teachers can embed anti-bullying themes through lesson plan implementation with tools that model culturally relevant and responsive instruction. For instance, lesson plans can challenge stereotypes about Latinos and provide opportunities for emphasizing their positive contributions to American society. Topics for lessons can focus on the following:

- the definition of Latino and its influence on American society

- the human diversity within the Latino ethnic group
- the need to work collaboratively with diverse populations to succeed in schools and the workplace
- the literary and interdisciplinary contributions of Latinos

In an article about teaching and performing *The Laramie Project*, Pincus (2008) identified the impact that literature and drama education can have on ethical development for students across various issues, including the prevention of bullying and peer harassment. Among the questions and issues Pincus identified, the following emphasize engagement among students by building relationships with culturally responsive lessons.

- the ways in which students connected this text [essay, play, poem, short story] to their own lives
- the ways in which students' ethnic, racial, sexual, and religious identities played into their responses to the [essay, play, poem, short story]
- the ways in which students moved along a continuum of engagement and detachment
- the ways in which individual students expressed their emotional and intellectual responses
- the ways in which students reacted to one another's responses

Texts

The following texts and resources provide additional information and support for preventing the bullying of Latina and Latino Students.

- *Bullies: Monologues on bullying for teens and adults* (2011)
  This book features various thematic monologues with a wide range of voices for staging in class or in a school theater production to combat bullying and harassment in schools and workplaces. Some of the monologues help to define bullying, especially in the lives of students for whom differing interpretations persist (Waasdorp & Bradshaw, 2009).

- *Bullying: Replies, rebuttals, confessions, and catharsis, an intergenerational and multicultural anthology* (2012)
  This book provides original essays, poems, plays, and commentaries on how bullying affects children, adolescents, and parents. As community leaders and activists Gómez and Arroyo explain in the foreword: "Anti-bullying legislation will not stop bullying, until individuals as well as institutions, become *intentionally* [emphasis in original] pro-active in anti-bullying efforts. This includes what we model in our daily interac-

tions.... Even the smallest actions speak volumes about consciousness and character" (p. xii).

- *The letter Q: Queer writers' notes to their younger selves* (2012)
  Various writers of diverse backgrounds look back on their young adulthood with a stronger adult voice. The approach would be useful to consider in the teaching of memoir/autobiographical writing in the English language arts classroom.

- *Stop bullying now!* (2012)
  This series from Rosen Publishing Group/PowerKids Press features volumes on various groups that have made significant contributions to life in the United States but faced discrimination, bullying, and violence. Although this is an emergent reader series, it is a good way to introduce the following groups: Latino Americans, African Americans, Asian Americans, Disabled Americans, LGBT Americans, and Muslim Americans. These books can launch discussions on human diversity through specific backgrounds, histories, and timelines.

Young Adult Literature

The resources listed below are recommended for culturally relevant teaching and contain bullying prevention and self-affirmation themes. Any resource under consideration should be reviewed before use in the classroom to determine if it is age-appropriate. Also, it is suggested that teachers consult their peers to determine if any of the materials listed have been previously taught and to encourage team teaching.

- *Aristotle and Dante discover the secrets of the universe* (2012)
  This novel, by Benjamin Alire Sáenz, follows diverse male characters trying to find their identities and sexualities in their own time and space in the world.

- *Yaqui Delgado wants to kick your ass* (2013)
  The author Meg Medina chronicles the life of a young girl who, to become a heroine, must thrive and survive in the face of relational bullying in school.

Additional young adult literature titles are listed below with a few children's titles that are adaptable for instructional use with adolescents.

- Alvarez, J. (2004). *Before we were free.* New York: Dell Laurel-Leaf.
- González, R. (2009). *The Mariposa Club.* Maple Shade, NJ: Tincture, Lethe Press, Inc.
- Hijuelos, O. (2008). *Dark dude: A novel.* New York: Atheneum Books, Simon & Schuster.

- Jiménez, F. (2009). *Reaching out.* New York: Graphia, Houghton Mifflin Harcourt.

- McCall, G.G. (2011). *Under the mesquite.* New York: Lee & Low Books.

- Mohr, N. (2011). *Nilda.* Houston: Arte Público Press.

- Mora, P. (2000). *My own true name: New and selected poems for young adults, 1984–1999.* Houston: Arte Público Press.

- Olivas, D.A. (2011). *Benjamin and the word/Benjamin y la palabra.* Houston: Arte Público Press.

- Ortiz Cofer, J. (2004). *Call me María: A novel in letters, poems, and prose.* New York: Scholastic.

- Peña, M. de la. (2010). *I will save you.* New York: Ember, Random House.

- Saldaña, R., Jr. (2001). *The jumping tree: A novel.* New York: Dell Laurel-Leaf.

- Sanchez, A. (2006). *Getting it.* New York: Simon Pulse, Simon & Schuster.

- Soto, G. (2006). *Petty crimes: Stories.* New York: Sandpiper, Houghton Mifflin Harcourt.

Teacher Education Resources

- *Borderlands: La frontera, The new mestiza* (1987, 2012)
  Gloria Anzaldúa discusses what she calls "linguistic terrorism" and acts of English-language dominance posited against Spanish-language speakers in public spaces—including schools and universities—to the detriment of students and their shared, familiar cultures. Various excerpts from the book can launch classroom discussions on becoming a writer and accepting one's own ethnic, cultural, and sexual identity in the face of violence and indifference.

- The themed issue "Characters and Character" of *English Journal, 102*(1) (2012), edited by Ken Lindblom, is inclusive of classic and modern characters "whose literary lives grip our attention and become part of how we think about the world" (p. 11). The articles present literary characters who endured bullying and harassment, eventually gaining their own sense of self and belonging. The issue is recommended for teachers thinking about diverse, young adult titles and ways of engaging students across genres that help them to question their beliefs and attitudes about norms.

- *How to teach students who don't look like you: Culturally responsive teaching strategies* (2012)
  Bonnie Davis's book provides resources about diverse learners and includes new and expanded coverage about Latino students. A variety of

strategies offer examples, vignettes, case studies, and stories for working with diverse student populations, such as English language learners and students who are identified as homeless and immigrant.

- *The new bullying: How social media, social exclusion, laws and suicide have changed our definition of bullying—And what to do about it* (2012)
  Undergraduate students from the Michigan State University School of Journalism collected interviews and resources on bullying that offer new definitions of bullying and approaches and ideas for prevention. Teachers might consider using some of the text (edited by Joe Grimm) for discussion in class about human diversity and possible projects launched by the undergraduate students themselves. The interviewing and research approaches found in the book are useful in the English language arts classroom.

- *Zing! Seven creativity practices for educators and students* (2010)
  The children's book author, poet, and essayist Pat Mora provides a series of seven letters addressed to teachers and librarians about the creative process and ways to value students and their family backgrounds.

Online and Media

- *An honest conversation*, Cuéntame
  http://www.mycuentame.org/honestconversation
  In Spanish, "cuéntame" means tell me your story or count me in regard. This site features stories about Latinos designed to connect with general audiences. This particular series features stories from our LGBTQ Latino adolescents and their friends, families, and civic communities. The narratives include struggles with bullying, abuse, and violence. The featured stories challenge taboos within the Latino community.

- *Harvest of empire* (2012)
  This documentary examines the role that U.S. economic and military interests play in migration patterns across the continental Americas and the Caribbean. Based on the book by Juan González, the documentary uses personal recollections to record violent U.S. interventions, including the bully-style international policies of the United States. The diversity of the U.S. Latino population and its many contributions to American life and thought are addressed.

- *It Gets Better Project*, Latino Voices (2012)
  http://www.itgetsbetter.org/video/c/latino
  This project has brought together many adolescents and adults of various backgrounds to speak out against hate, intolerance, and anti-LGBTQ bias in various private and public spaces, including schools, workplaces,

and family dinner tables. The Latinos featured address the public about bullying and peer harassment and let them know that "it gets better."

- *Not in our town: Class actions* (2012), Center for Public Broadcasting
http://www.niot.org/classactions
This 30-minute documentary, which profiles students and community members who respond to acts of violence that include racism, anti-Semitism, and bullying, premiered in February 2012 on PBS stations nationwide.

- *Not in our town: Light in the darkness* (2012), Center for Public Broadcasting
http://www.niot.org/blog/hispanic-heritage-month-screen-light-darkness
In response to anti-immigrant hate crimes directed at new Americans of Latino descent, this documentary follows the actions of a group of individuals who ensure the safety, inclusion, and respect of newly arrived immigrants in Patchogue, New York.

School-Wide Suggestions

Media Literacy
Boske and McCormack (2012) conducted a study on the role of media literacy in the lives of Latino students through the animated children's film *Happy Feet*. The students identified negative cultural images about Latinos and LGBTQ populations. Overall, the need for more media literacy with a critical lens focused on schools is necessary to help students recognize normative bias and opposition to cultural diversity.

Diverse Literature
Every effort must be made to select culturally responsive, age-appropriate literature that reflects Latino families as well as families that are not identified as traditional, nuclear families.

Performing Arts
Students benefit from performing arts that portray characters making decisions and confronting bias in their lives. As a result, instructional theater can influence students' ways of thinking and knowing to make informed decisions about their own lives and interests.

Guest Speakers and Enactments
Invite guest speakers who are committed to stopping bullying and promoting healthy school culture environments that are not based on difference and punishment, but learning and growing in a pluralistic society. These speakers can address students' challenges and provide a firsthand, engaging experience.

Section Resources

- Anzaldúa, G. (1999). *Borderlands: La frontera, The new mestiza* (4th ed.). San Francisco: Aunt Lute Press.

- Chevallier, J. (2011). *Bullies: Monologues on bullying for teens and adults.* Los Angeles: Chez Jim Press.

- Davis, B.M. (2012). *How to teach students who don't look like you: Culturally responsive teaching strategies* (2nd ed.). Thousand Oaks, CA: Corwin Press.

- Medina, M. (2013). *Yaqui Delgado wants to kick your ass.* Somerville, MA: Candlewick Press.

- Mora, P. (2010). *Zing! Seven creativity practices for educators and students.* Thousand Oaks, CA: Corwin Press.

- Sáenz, B.A. (2012). *Aristotle and Dante discover the secrets of the universe.* New York: Simon & Schuster Books for Young Readers.

- Santamaria, L.J. (2009). Culturally responsive differentiated instruction: Narrowing gaps between the best pedagogical practices benefiting all learners. *Teachers College Record, 111*(1), 214–247.

New Jersey: A Model for Change

We end this chapter by recognizing and applauding recent anti-bullying legislation in New Jersey that was enacted almost immediately after the tragic events that culminated in the suicide of Tyler Clemente. These laws are the toughest and most rigorous in the nation, and we hope they can mobilize us all to make a stand against bullying.

On September 22, 2010, at 8:42 p.m., Tyler Clemente, a Rutgers University freshman, committed suicide by jumping off the George Washington Bridge. His suicide was provoked by the unforgivable crime of his college roommate, Dharun Ravi, who sent out 100 Twitter announcements that he'd set up an iChat to catch Tyler in their dorm room being intimate with another male. Because of public and media reaction to the suicide, on January 5, 2011, after it received nearly unanimous support in both houses of the New Jersey legislature, Governor Chris Christie signed into law the Anti-Bullying Bill of Rights Act, P.L. 2010, Chapter 122. To date, New Jersey has become the most aggressive reformer with the toughest anti-bullying laws in the country. In fact, Bullypolice.org has given New Jersey an A++ for its current laws. On September 1, 2011, The Anti-Bullying Bill of Rights Act became effective. The law requires that all public K–12 schools and higher education institutions in New Jersey adopt comprehensive anti-bullying policies for incidents both on and off campus. There are 18 pages of requirements that must be adopted.[6] Public institutions of higher education are required to include policies in their student codes of conduct that prohibit harassment, intimidation, or bullying (HIB). These policies must specify penalties for violation and be distributed to students by email within 7 days of the start of each semester. Schools are required to post the anti-bullying policy on their websites (New Jersey Education Association, 2011).

All public schools must adopt comprehensive anti-bullying policies that include clear punishments for perpetrators and penalties for false reporting, provision of staff training, and adherence to rigid deadlines for reporting episodes. Each school is also required to designate an anti-bullying specialist to investigate complaints. Each district must have an anti-bullying coordinator, and the State Education Department will evaluate schools' every effort, posting grades twice a year on its website. The law also requires districts to appoint a safety team at each school made up of teachers, staff members, and parents to review complaints. It mandates that principals begin an investigation within one school day of a bullying episode, and superintendents must provide reports to Trenton twice a year detailing all episodes. The law also designates the first Monday in October as the beginning of a "Week of Respect" in New Jersey. School districts must observe the week by providing age-appropriate instruction focusing on preventing HIB. Throughout the school year, districts are expected to provide similar instruction in accordance with the New Jersey Core Curriculum Content Standards. Public school teachers are required to discuss the district's HIB policy with their students, report any incidents of HIB that come to their attention, teach bullying prevention in their classes, complete at least 2 hours of instruction on HIB prevention in each professional development period, listen to students who say they're being bullied or see someone being bullied, and take seriously and report incidences of bullying that take place off school grounds (New Jersey Education Association, 2011). Superintendents are authorized to revoke the licenses of teachers who fail to comply.

There is much to be learned from the anti-bullying work being done in New Jersey. Districts around the country might spend time studying this model with the goal of incorporating items in the legislative documents into their own district policies. New Jersey has set a precedent for the rest of the country, and it is our hope that, in time, enough other states will develop systems approaches that will further the creation of federal anti-bullying legislation.

Next Steps in the Stance Against Bullying

Throughout this chapter, we have offered a variety of resources and pedagogical tools for use in schools. We recognize the diversity and range reflected in our suggestions and understand that they vary along with our individual expertise and teaching experiences. Though this chapter was written as a pushback against bullying of specific populations, it is possible to tailor our proposals for use with different populations that may be bullied in your school. We invite you, our readers, to use these recommendations and to let us know how they work with your students, and then to send us your own strategies for pushing back and taking a stand against bullying. We want to keep this dialogue alive, because we believe that it will take a nationwide, collective effort to bring an end to bullying once and for all.

As we come to a close in this last chapter before the afterword, we wish to note that the media constantly remind us of the high level of bullying that has now become normalized in American culture. We wonder how many students are experiencing C-PTSD and how many are suffering quietly. We wonder how we can reach those students and provide them with the loving and emotional guidance they need to be able to live a life filled with the human decency deserved by all people. Where do we go from here? Tomorrow is too late to begin. We and the readers of this book know that we can each play an active and immediate role in disrupting bullying when we see it. We can help to shift the tide from a culture of bullying in schools to one that reflects the social model described by Siebers (2008), which strives to help students understand and then embody a belief holding that all students should be treated fairly and equitably. As we stay active and attuned to the fact that bullying is taking place in our country, we can grow stronger by disrupting and eliminating the social environments that sustain bullying. We can share stories, write letters, protest, and become agents of change today. We can integrate suggestions and solutions from Norway and the United Kingdom and learn from recent reforms enacted in New Jersey. We can read the July 2012 issue of the *English Journal*, which is dedicated to teaching about, interrupting, and intervening in bullying behavior, and share, post, and disseminate the recent National Council of Teachers of English's "Resolution on Confronting Bullying and Harassment" (see http://www.ncte.org/positions/statements/confrontingbullying). As we know, deciding to stop bullying in its tracks is a small piece of the larger pandemic, but every effort helps and can possibly redirect bullying behavior. We hope that you and your colleagues, friends, and students will start to make a dent in this growing trend. We don't think it is too much to ask that all students learn and thrive in schooling environments that are bully-free. Our collective moral consciousness cannot be eased or placated until each of our children is able to walk up to a school and look forward to opening the doors—not just for themselves, but for everyone else. We hope that we have all grown wiser as a result of Columbine. For all those who have died since, let their deaths not be in vain.

We can put an end to bullying.

Rise up! Now—right now—is the time! Together let's put an end to bullying.

Additional Resources on Bullying in the United States

Agatston, P., Kowalski, R., & Limber, S. (2007). Students' perspectives on cyberbullying. *Journal of Adolescent Health, 41*(6), S59–S60.

Boske, C., & McCormack, S. (2012). Building an understanding of the role of media literacy for Latino/a high school students. *The High School Journal, 94*(3), 167–186.

Brayboy, B.M.J., & Castagno, A. (2009). Self-determination through self-education: Culturally responsive schooling for indigenous students in the USA. *Teaching Education, 20*(1), 31–53.

Chase, B., & Ressler, P. (2009). An LGBT/queer glossary. *English Journal, 98*(4), 23–24.

Cohen, A. (2011, September 6). Why New Jersey's antibullying law should be a model for other states. Retrieved November 8, 2012, from http://ideas.time.com/2011/09/06/why-new-jerseys-antibullying-law-should-be-a-model-for-other-states/

DeWitt, P. (2012). *Dignity for all: Safeguarding LGBT students.* Thousand Oaks, CA: Corwin and National Association of School Psychologists.

Douglas, S. (2012). High school football player starts kindness campaign on Twitter. Retrieved January 28, 2013, from http://www.thebiglead.com/index.php/2012/08/18/high-school-football-player-starts-kindness-campaign-on-twitter/

Gómez, M., & Arroyo, M.L. (2012). *Bullying: Replies, rebuttals, confessions, and catharsis, an intergenerational and multicultural anthology.* New York: Skyhorse Publishing.

Kinloch, V. (2012). *Crossing boundaries: Teaching and learning with urban youth.* New York: Teachers College Press.

Kosciw, J., Greytak, E., & Diaz, E. (2008). *The 2007 National School Climate Survey: The experiences of lesbian, gay, bisexual and transgender youth in our nation's schools.* New York: GLSEN.

Kosciw, J., Greytak, E., Diaz, E., & Bartkiewicz, M. (2009). *The 2009 National School Climate Survey: The experiences of lesbian, gay, bisexual and transgender youth in our nation's schools.* New York: GLSEN.

Labov, W. (1972). Rules for ritual insult. In T. Kochman (Ed.), *Rappin' and stylin' out* (pp. 265–314). Urbana: University of Illinois Press.

Lindblom, K. (2012). From the editor: Character and characters. *English Journal, 102*(2), 11–12.

Losey, B. (2011). *Bullying, suicide, and homicide: Understanding, assessing, and preventing threats to self and others for victims of bullying.* New York: Routledge.

Markow, D., & Fein, J. (2005). *From teasing to torment: School climate in America—A survey of students and teachers.* Gay, Lesbian & Straight Educational Network. New York: Harris Interactive.

Michigan State University School of Journalism. (2012). *The new bullying: How social media, social exclusion, laws and suicide have changed our definition of bullying—And what to do about it* (J. Grimm, Ed.). East Lansing: Michigan State University School of Journalism.

Miller, s. (2012). Mythology of the norm: Disrupting the culture of bullying in schools. *English Journal, 101*(6), 107–109.

Miller, s., & Norris, L. (2007). *Unpacking the loaded teacher matrix: Negotiating space and time between university and secondary English classrooms.* New York: Peter Lang.

Moon, S., & Lecense, J. (Eds.). (2012). *The letter Q: Queer writers' notes to their younger selves.* New York: Scholastic.

National Council for Accreditation of Teacher Education (NCATE). (2006). *Standards, procedures, and policies for the accreditation of professional educational units.* Washington, DC: Author.

National Council of Teachers of English. (2012). *Standards for initial preparation of teachers of secondary English language arts, grades 7–12.* Retrieved February 7, 2013, from http://www.ncte.org/library/NCTEFiles/Groups/CEE/NCATE/ApprovedStandards_111212.pdf

Nieto, S. (2012). Teaching, caring, and transformation. *Knowledge Quest, 40*(5), 28–30.

New Jersey Education Association. (2011). *Anti-bullying.* Retrieved November 8, 2012, from http://www.njea.org/issues-and-political-action/anti-bullying

Percelay, J.L., Dweck, S., & Ivey, M. (1995). *Double snaps.* New York: Quill.

Pincus, M.R. (2005). Learning from Laramie: Urban high school students read, research, and reenact *The Laramie Project.* In T. Hatch, D. Ahmed, A. Lieberman, D. Faigenbaum, M.E. White, & D.H.P. Mace (Eds.), *Going public with our teaching: An anthology of practice* (pp. 147–165). New York: Teachers College Press.

Raskauskas, J., & Modell, S. (2011). Modifying anti-bullying programs to include students with disabilities. *Teaching Exceptional Children, 44*, 60–67.

Rose, C.A., Espelage, D.L., Aragon, S.R., & Elliott, J. (2011). Bullying and victimization among students in special education and general education curricula. *Exceptionality Education International, 21*(3), 2–14.

Santamaria, L.J. (2009). Culturally responsive differentiated instruction: Narrowing gaps between the best pedagogical practices benefiting all learners. *Teachers College Record, 111*(1), 214–247.

Savage, D., & Miller, T. (Eds.). (2012). *It gets better: Coming out, overcoming bullying, and creating a life worth living.* New York: Plume.

Siebers, T. (2008). *Disability theory.* Ann Arbor: University of Michigan Press.

Smitherman, G. (2000). *Talkin that talk: Language, culture and education in African America.* New York: Routledge.

Transgender Law & Policy Institute. Retrieved February 14, 2013, from http://www.transgenderlaw.org/

Villegas, A. M., & Lucas, T. (2007). The culturally responsive teacher. *Educational Leadership, 64*(6), 28–33.

Waasdorp, T. E., & Bradshaw, C. P. (2009). Child and parent perceptions of relational aggression within urban predominantly African American children's friendships: Examining patterns of concordance. *Journal of Child and Family Studies, 18*(6), 731–745.

Webley, K. (2012). *Using Twitter to crack down on bullying*. Retrieved January 28, 2013, from http://newsfeed.time.com/2012/08/17/using-twitter-to-crack-down-on-bullying

Additional Websites

Colorado Center for the Prevention of Violence
http://www.Colorado.EDU/cspv
Provides extensive violence prevention information produced by the Center for the Study and Prevention of Violence (CSPV).

Department of Justice
http://www.ojp.usdoj.gov/bjs/
Provides data from the Bureau of Justice Statistics such as crime and victims, criminal offenders, special topics, law enforcement, prosecution, federal justice system, courts and sentencing, corrections, expenditures and employment, and criminal record systems.

National Center for Educational Statistics (NCES)
http://nces.ed.gov
The National Center for Education Statistics is the primary federal entity for collecting and analyzing data related to education. National K–12 bullying statistics and indicators can be found here.

National Resource Center for Safe Schools
http://www.safetyzone.org
Provides information for schools, communities, and state and local education agencies to help establish safe learning environments and prevent school violence.

National School Safety Center
http://www.NSSC1.org/
Provides information (such as books, papers, films, and workshops on school safety-related topics) that helps combat school safety problems.

New Jersey Education Association
http://www.njea.org/issues-and-political-action/anti-bullying
Provides an overview of New Jersey's comprehensive plan to report and stop bullying. The site has resources for teachers, parents, and policymakers.

Appendix A

Texts and films have been taken from pp. 43–44 of Miller & Norris (2007). Many new titles have been added.

Middle School Texts
(including gay/lesbian/bisexual/transgender themes)
After Tupac and D Foster, Jacqueline Woodson
Alice Alone, Phyllis Reynolds Naylor
Alice on the Outside, Phyllis Reynolds Naylor
Between Mom and Jo, Julie Ann Peters
The Eagle Kite, Paula Fox
From the Notebooks of Melanin Sun, Jacqueline Woodson
The House You Pass on the Way, Jacqueline Woodson
I Feel a Little Jumpy Around You: A Book of Her Poems & His Poems Collected in Pairs, Naomi Shihab Nye and Paul B. Janeczko
The Misfits, James Howe
Risky Friends, Julie A. Peters
7 Days at the Hot Corner, Terry Trueman
The Skull of Truth, Bruce Coville and Gary A. Lippincott
Totally Joe, James Howe
Touching Stone, M. Sindy Felin

High School Texts with Fluid Expressions of Gender
(*adapted to film)

Heterosexual:
Absolute True Diary of a Part-Time Indian, Sherman Alexie
Boys Lie, John Neufeld
The Butterfly and the Flame, Dana De Young
Liar, Justine Larbalestier
Lucky, Alice Sebold
Misfits, James Howe
My Most Excellent Year: A Novel of Love, Mary Poppins, and Fenway Park, Steve Kluger
Out of Control, Shannon McKenna
Persepolis, Marjane Satrapi
Shattering Glass, Gail Giles

Speak, Laurie Halse Anderson
To Kill a Mockingbird, Harper Lee
Totally Joe, James Howe
Unexpected Development, Marlene Perez

Gay/bisexual themes
Absolutely Positively Not, David LaRochelle
Alt Ed, Catherine Atkins
Am I Blue? Marion Dane Bauer and Beck Underwood
Angels in America, Tony Kushner
Boy Meets Boy, David Levithan
The Drowning of Stephan Jones, Bette Greene
Freak Show, James St. James
Geography Club, Brent Hartinger
Getting It, Alex Sanchez
The God Box, Alex Sanchez
Hero, Perry Moore
Nothing Pink, Mark Hardy
The Order of the Poison Oak, Brent Hartinger
The Perks of Being a Wallflower, Stephen Chbosky
Rainbow Boys, Alex Sanchez
Rainbow High, Alex Sanchez
Rainbow Road, Alex Sanchez
The Rules for Hearts, Sara Ryan
Saints of Augustine, P.E. Ryan
Shattering Glass, Gail Giles
Simon Says, Elaine Marie Alphin
So Hard to Say, Alex Sanchez
Someday This Pain Will Be Useful to You, Peter Cameron
Split Screen: Attack of the Soul-Sucking Brain Zombies/Bride of the Soul-Sucking Brain Zombies, Brent Hartinger
Tough Love: High School Confidential, Abby Denson
What Happened to Lani Garver? Carol Plum-Ucci

Lesbian/bisexual themes
Am I Blue? Marion Dane Bauer and Beck Underwood
Annie on My Mind, Nancy Garden
Breathing Underwater, Lu Vickers
The Color Purple, Alice Walker
Down to the Bone, Mayra Lazara Dole
Empress of the World, Sara Ryan
grl2grl, Julie Ann Peters

Hard Love, Ellen Wittlinger
Keeping You a Secret, Julie Anne Peters
Kissing Kate, Lauren Myracle
Love and Lies: Marisol's Story, Ellen Wittlinger
Name Me Nobody, Lois-Ann Yamanaka
Out of the Shadows, Sue Hines
Skim, Mariko Tamaki

Transgender themes
Almost Perfect, Brian Katcher
Define "Normal," Julie Anne Peters
Far from Xanadu, Julie Ann Peters
The Flip Side, Andrew Matthews
I am J, Cris Beam
Luna, Julie Anne Peters
Middlesex, Jeffrey Eugenides
My Heartbeat, Garret Freymann-Weyr
Parrotfish, Ellen Wittlinger
Shine, Lauren Myracle
Standing Naked on the Roof, Francess Lantz
Written on the Body, Jeanette Winterson

Appendix B

Films
A Girl Like Me
Anatomy of a Hate Crime
Antonia's Line
Beautiful Thing
Becoming Chaz
Better than Chocolate
Billy Elliot
Boys Don't Cry
Breaking the Surface
But I'm a Cheerleader
Camp
Confronting Date Rape: The Girl's Room
Date Violence: A Young Woman's Guide
Diagnosing Difference
The Family Journey: Raising Gender Nonconforming Children
Gender Matters
Get Ready

I'm Just Anneke
It Gets Messy in Here
Just Call Me Kade
It's Elementary
Milk
Ma Vie en Rose
Normal
Out of the Past
Saved
School Ties
Screaming Queens
Speak
That's a Family
This Boy's Life
Times of Harvey Milk
Tongues Untied
Torch Song Trilogy
Trans
Transgender Basics
Treading Water
Wedding Banquet
XXY
You Ought to Know: Teens Talk About Dating and Abuse

Appendix C: Resources with Cyber-Digital Themes

Fiction

Many current Young Adult (YA) novels are written with the tech-savvy generation in mind. Use any of the following novels in your classroom to express how important it is for students to avoid cyber-digital bullying.

Feed, by M.T. Anderson
1984, by George Orwell
How I Live Now, by Meg Rosoff
The Fault in Our Stars, by John Green
Thirteen Reasons Why, by Jay Asher
Ender's Game, by Orson Scott Card
Please Stop Laughing at Me, by Jodee Blanco
Rootless, by Chris Howard
It's Kind of a Funny Story, by Ned Vizzini
Teen Angst…Naaah, by Ned Vizzini
Okay for Now, by Gary D. Schmidt

Perfect, by Ellen Hopkins

Books on Cyber-Digital Bullying

Hinduja, S., & Patchin, J. (2008). *Bullying beyond the schoolyard: Preventing and responding to cyberbullying.* Thousand Oaks, CA: Corwin Press.

Ivester, M. (2011). *lol...OMG! What every student needs to know about online reputation management, digital citizenship and cyberbullying.* CreateSpace Independent Publishing Platform.

Jacobs, T. (2010). *Teen cyberbullying investigated: Where do your rights end and consequences begin?* Minneapolis, MN: Free Spirit Publishing.

Kowalski, R., Limber, S., & Agatson, P. (2012). *Cyber bullying: Bullying in the digital age.* Hoboken, NJ: John Wiley & Sons.

Limber, S., Kowalski, R., & Agatson, P. (2008). *Cyber bullying: A prevention curriculum for grades 3–5.* Center City, MN: Hazelden.

Limber, S., Kowalski, R., & Agatson, P. (2008). *Cyber bullying: A prevention curriculum for grades 6–12.* Center City, MN: Hazelden.

Shariff, S. (2008). *Cyber-bullying: Issues and solutions for the school, the classroom and the home.* New York: Routledge.

Websites

CyberBullyHelp
http://www.cyberbullyhelp.com/about/
Provides information for teachers to help scope and sequence lessons into grades 3–12.

Cyberbullying Research Center
http://www.cyberbullying.us/
Provides up-to-date information about the nature, extent, causes, and consequences of cyber-bullying among adolescents.

Embrace Civility in the Digital Age
http://www.embracecivility.org/
Promotes approaches that ensure that all young people become "Cyber-Savvy" and addresses youth risk in a positive and restorative manner.

Ikeepsafe
http://www.ikeepsafe.org
Provides teachers, parents, students, policymakers, media psychologists, law enforcement officers and health care professionals tools to develop habits that prepare youth to be ethical, responsible, and resilient digital citizens.

Stop Cyber Bullying
http://www.stopcyberbullying.org/index2.php
Provides tools for schools, students, and their parents to create their own grassroots campaign and address cyber-bullying and hate online.

Film
ABC News Primetime Cyber-Bullying
Cyberbully
Odd Girl Out

Notes

1   In some cases teachers, when working with students, may have to solicit parental or principal approval.

2   We use the invented pronoun *per* to honor students whose identities are gender non-conforming, gender variant, or transgender. We alternate it with s/he at various times throughout the book. While there are other pronouns such as "hir," "ze," and "they" that also refer to gender non-conforming, gender variant, or transgender people, using *per* is an intentional stylistic decision.

3   Two-spirited is a term used by many First Nation peoples and refers to someone who embodies both genders.

4   In 1973, homosexuality was deleted from DSM II and replaced with "Sexual Orientation Disturbance," and is no longer considered a mental illness. In 1994, the DSM IV entry was changed from "Transsexual" to "Gender Identity Disorder" as a mental illness. Since 2006 debates have raged over depathologizing gender identity disorder (GID) as a mental identity. A new manual is due out in 2013 (for more information see http://gidreform.org/).

5   The term *Latino* is used to describe male and female individuals who are either U.S. or non-U.S. born with ancestral heritage from any Latin American or Caribbean country and are identified as an ethnic group by the U.S. Census Bureau. The U.S. Latino population is diverse and by no means monolithic.

6   To see the complete text of the law, visit: "from the state legislature: http://www.njleg.state.nj.us/2010/Bills/A3500/3466_S1.HTM

Afterword

Dennis Carlson

This is a timely volume both because bullying has been pushed to the forefront of concerns in education and because it is time for bullying to be recognized as a social justice concern (that is, in terms of human rights, equity, and battles against diverse forms of oppression and internalized oppression). But it is also a timely and important volume because its authors insist that we must do more than critique bullying and theorize about social justice. We are called to an ethical response, to do something about bullying now, to live our commitments to social justice in ways that are pragmatic but also visionary. The contributors to this volume hold our public educational institutions to high standards of inclusiveness and equity, but they also provide specific ideas about how educators can effect change in their own practice, starting here and now. This reengagement with a democratic, pragmatic project is welcome in an age when it is all too easy to be cynical, all too easy not to respond. Of course, as the authors make clear, this response must begin by critiquing the many efforts already under way to establish anti-bullying programs in schools and universities, since these programs all too often inadequately address the underlying culture of bullying in American public education and its broader cultural politics.

In the past several years there was been much talk in the media and among politicians and public educators about an "epidemic" of bullying affecting millions of young people on a daily basis in schools and on college campuses. We should be suspicious when we hear talk of "epidemics" of the non-medical type in our culture, for sometimes it is just a matter of finally noticing and paying attention to something that's been there all the while, right before our eyes, invisible because bullying has been a taken-for-granted ritual of everyday life in educational institutions. But there is also good reason to believe that we are witnessing an increase in bullying for a number of interrelated reasons, and that to effectively respond to a culture in which bullying in public education is pervasive, we will need to do more than reform the system by adopting policies of "zero tolerance" or instituting a few staff-development workshops for teachers. These reforms are worth supporting, and certainly part of a democratic response. But we will need to understand bullying as a cultural phenomenon if we are serious about moving beyond reform to the reconstruction of everyday life in schools. This must involve questioning what has been taken for granted in what Bourdieu (1977) has called the "habitus," the ritualistic, commonsense, taken-for-granted character of everyday life in institutions such as schools, for bullying has been a ritual of power and "Othering" within the habitus of schooling rather than something alien or foreign to that habitus. Framed as a ritualized performance, bullying may be recognized or made visible as a hegemonic practice that polices the borders between "normal" and "abnormal," normative and non-normative, performances of gender and sexual identity—particularly among boys. In this sense, bullying is part of a "hidden curriculum" of gender and sexuality that young people learn in schools and classrooms and through exposure to images in popular culture. It is indeed hypocritical to announce that there is to be a zero-tolerance policy for bullying in schools if the habitus and hidden curriculum of schooling that produces bullying is not questioned in the process. By implication, a truly democratic education must challenge "schooling" in its current hegemonic forms and reassert the primacy of the democratic vision and promise of what public education should and could be (Carlson, 2003, 2012).

In this type of reconstructive praxis, theory is always situated in the specificity of practice and in the historical moment. It becomes a tool for addressing pragmatic questions: How does the problem of bullying emerge out of a particular school culture that needs to be reconstructed? How can we respond in ways that move beyond simplistic, tacked-on, anti-bullying workshops to help teachers and students challenge the culture of pervasive bullying in the school? In addressing these democratic, pragmatic questions, several critical theoretical discourses have proved particularly useful. I want to name several of those discourses here, ones that the contributors to this volume make use of in one way or another.

One of these is a discourse on *hegemonic masculinities* that has emerged over the past two decades out of masculinity studies. Hegemonic masculinity can be defined as any performance of masculinity that "Others" women and all males represented or perceived as "weak," "feminine," or in other ways not "real" males. Bullying and sexual harassment might be thought of as "tools" in the "toolbox" of hegemonic masculinities. Of course, girls can engage in bullying and sexual harassment, too, and the press has highlighted incidents of girls bullying other girls to suggest that bullying is a general social and educational problem, and not just a "boy problem." The truth, however, is that bullying is primarily a problem of the performance of masculine identity. When girls bully other girls (or boys), it may be a case of "acting masculine" in order to gain some of the power that boys who bully possess. At the same time, I want to be careful not to imply that bullying is naturally a boy thing. In fact, bullying is often legitimated and excused through a gendered ideology that asserts "boys will be boys" and a developmental ideology that asserts "they'll outgrow it." Hegemonic masculinities is a performance theory of gender that views bullying as something young males learn to perform because it gets rewarded within its context of performance. It is also something they see performed in commercialized popular culture, where aggressive, hypermasculinity is celebrated. Any given act of bullying is consequently a performance of hegemonic masculinity that is a copy of a copy of a copy, for which there is no "original"—what the theorist of the postmodern Jean Baudrillard (1995) called a *simulacrum*. Nevertheless, as Judith Butler (2000) has observed, once a performance of gender has been repeated or reiterated many times, it may begin to feel natural, so the educational challenge is to "un-do" the naturalness of gender. In calling for a response that "un-does" gender by deconstructing its naturalness, Butler (2004) has observed that gender has long been "un-doing" women and queer youth in a different sense: "Sometimes a normative conception of gender can undo one's personhood, undermining the capacity to persevere in a livable life" (p. 1). How else do we account for the fact that so many queer youth still, in this "tolerant" and enlightened age, attempt suicide—the ultimate erasure and un-doing of the self? And how, in a similar way, do we account for the fact that so many young Black men still end their lives on the mean streets of the inner city, or in prison? This is a coming un-done that is the result of internalized oppression. For Butler the flip side of this form of coming un-done that is a result of internalized oppression is the "un-doing," disassembling, and deconstructing of normative performances of gender and sexuality. This deconstructive "un-doing" is a necessary step in the reconstructive project of re-doing gender. We have to come un-done by calling into question normative constructions and performances of identity before we can re-think and re-perform gender and sexual identity along more equitable, free, and livable lines.

To un-do hegemonic masculinities we will also have to move beyond gender and sexuality analysis to consider how class and race intersects with gender and sexuality. For example, when R.W. Connell (1995) coined the term "hegemonic masculinities," he linked it to a neo-Marxist theory, suggesting that the masculinist culture of capitalism is implicated in bullying culture. Aggressive, competitive, "top-dog" masculinity operates in the world of Wall Street, and bullying—both verbal and physical intimidation—is used to establish a pecking order of masculinity with "Alpha Males" on top. This business culture of hegemonic masculinity is represented in popular films like *Wall Street* (1987), in which males who succeed do so by literally bullying themselves to the top. We see a real-life example of such a culture of masculinity in media coverage of accusations that Mitt Romney, the 2012 Republican presidential candidate, bullied a fellow classmate when he was a young man attending an elite preparatory academy—an academy that prepared elite White males for leadership positions in the world of business and government. *The Washington Post* broke the story that Romney had been a bully when in high school (Horowitz, 2012). Witnesses reported that he had taunted a young man (who later came out as gay) in class and, along with others in his "posse," had followed the young man outside where they pinned him to the ground and cut off his long hair as he screamed for help. Interestingly, most of the mainstream media was quick to give Romney a "pass" on the incident. He said he didn't remember it and that everybody does "dumb" things when they are young. It was just a case of "boys being boys," as they say, of Romney the future business leader asserting his Alpha Male status and thus (no doubt for some males) proving he would not be bullied by China or Russia as president, as Romney implied Barack Obama was.

Over the past decade or so, this complex analysis of hegemonic masculinities has been infused with new perspectives from queer studies. In queer studies a distinction is often made between the language of *homophobia* and *heteronormativity.* The former is part of a discourse that tends to blame individual young people for having a psychological "phobia"—a bias that is "abnormal" by definition and that requires either counseling and/or a zero-tolerance policy for acting on that phobia. The latter term, heteronormativity, implies a taken-for-granted culture in which being heterosexual is presumed to be "normal," and anything else "abnormal," a "problem." This means that hegemonic masculinity is also performed as "straight" masculinity, in relation to its Other, queer masculinity, and as a way of keeping this Other in its place at the margins. When queer and gender-variant youth experience bullying, they face a culture of silence and shame and the assumption that there is something wrong with them—an assumption reinforced by media representations, teacher and administrator silence, and community and family judgment. In other words, they have to cope with living in a *heteronormative* world where bullying of "deviants" is still normal and normalized. As Loutzenheiser and Moore (2009) argue, by focusing on heteronormativity rather than homophobia, educators open up "critical discussions of gender norms, the rights of those who are sexual minorities, [and] the systemic reinforcement of heteronormativity" (p. 158). These are discussions that will engender discomfort but that will be needed in responding to the call to do something about bullying.

Democratic responses, this volume suggests, require an understanding of both the specificity of bullying in each educational site and the broader cultural context of education in a rapidly changing world. For example, the current rise in the incidence of bullying in schools may represent the assertion of a *reactive* form of hegemonic masculinity, in reaction to gains made by women and LGBTQ groups over the past several decades, and to an "out and proud" movement among queer youth who refuse to be silenced or conform to hegemonic gender norms. Bullying in such a cultural context is about restabilizing gender norms being destabilized in a postmodern age. Ironically, one of the effects of being "out" is that these youth have become more visible targets for bullying. For those who are not "out" (except perhaps to a few close friends), the fear of being "outed" and bullied may lead them to drop out of school, become withdrawn, and even contemplate or commit suicide. It is these youth who are un-done by forms of internalized oppression, who have learned in the habitus of schooling, and in popular youth culture, that it really is not okay to be queer, in spite of efforts by queer advocacy groups to convince them that "things get better." This calls for a critical pedagogy that recognizes queer youth as continuing victims of internalized oppression whose very survival depends on being able to "name" and deconstruct the "bully within" and assert a positive sense of self in relation to others. Certainly this has been, and must continue to be, a primary concern of the LGBTQ movements, as it was for the early "gay pride" movement.

This volume gives us reason to be hopeful that the current questioning of bullying will lead to changes in the school habitus that go far beyond mere reformism in the direction of a democratic reconstruction. But it is a hopefulness tempered with caution and with an awareness of the difficulty of the task. Over the past few years, educational institutions at all levels, from elementary to higher education, have rushed to implement anti-bullying staff-development programs and curriculum materials and to adopt tough zero-tolerance policies for bullying. One of the reasons educational institutions took these proactive steps is that students and their parents, along with social networks and advocacy groups like GLSEN (the Gay, Lesbian & Straight Education Network) had begun to hold schools accountable for protecting the right of all young people to a "safe" school environment. While these initiatives are encouraging, the contributors to this volume demonstrate that they are limited in fundamental ways that need to be addressed if schools and college campuses are to be "bully-free zones."

These limitations are complex but are related in one way or another to an *individualization* and *naturalization* of bullying and bullies. Individualization reduces complex social and institutional problems to psychological or social problems "owned" by individuals, thereby deflecting attention from the cultural roots of the problem. Bullies are represented as socially maladjusted and delinquent, and also as individually responsible for their "deviant" behavior. By shifting the blame to individual bullies and appearing to be taking effective action to stop bullying, institutional leaders get themselves off the hook from having to adopt the more far-reaching changes needed. Anti-bullying initiatives also may reinforce rather than challenge commonsense beliefs that naturalize gender, that is, treat it as having an authentic, essential character. Bullies are to be punished, and efforts are to be made to reduce incidents of bullying. But these efforts are represented as relating to a need for educators to counter the "natural" impulse in males to fight and establish pecking-order hierarchies. The belief that bullying is a "guy thing," a natural aspect of male behavior, is related as well to a taken-for-granted developmental theory of masculinity that presumes most boys will "grow out of" bullying as they mature. This volume affirms that the problem of bullying cannot be effectively resolved through a response that individualizes and naturalizes bullying, but it also demonstrates that meaningful change, consistent with a teaching for social justice ethic, can take place in public school spaces. This collection goes a long way toward opening the democratic possibilities of such spaces, limited as they now are.

References

Baudrillard, J. (1995). *Simulacra and simulation* (S. Glaser, Trans.). Ann Arbor: University of Michigan Press.

Bourdieu, P. (1977). *Outline of a theory of practice* (R. Nice, Trans.). Cambridge, UK: Cambridge University Press.

Butler, J. (2000). *Gender trouble*. New York: Routledge.

Butler, J. (2004). *Undoing gender*. New York: Routledge.

Carlson, D. (2003). *Leaving safe harbors: Toward a new progressivism in American education and public life*. New York: Routledge.

Carlson, D. (2012). *The education of eros: A history of education and the problem of adolescent sexuality*. New York: Routledge.

Connell, R.W. (1995). *Masculinities*. Berkeley: University of California Press.

Horowitz, J. (2012, May 10). Mitt Romney's prep school classmates recall pranks, but also troubling incidents. *Washington Post*. http://articles.washingtonpost.com/2012-05-10/news/35456919_1_school-with-bleached-blond-hair-mitt-romney-george-romney

Loutzenheiser, L., & Moore, S. (2009). Safe schools, sexualities, and critical education. In M. Apple, W. Au, & L. Gandin (eds.), *The Routledge international handbook of critical education* (pp. 150–162)New York: Routledge.

Contributors

Deanna Adams is a Ph.D. candidate in Special Education, Disability Studies, and Women and Gender Studies at Syracuse University, New York. Her interests are in the critical study of special education, the school-to-prison pipeline, the over-representation of kids of color in special education, strategies for supporting LGBTQ students in schools, and school-wide behavior management. Deanna has been a teacher in special education in public schools and correctional facilities for boys in New York State. She is currently an Instructor in Special Education at National Louis University in Chicago and at Syracuse University.

Stephanie Beyer is a graduate student at Indiana University of Pennsylvania. She is currently pursuing a Master of Arts degree in Teaching English. During the course of her studies, she has focused on bullying in secondary schools and hopes to utilize her studies in the classroom. She also hopes to continue publishing on this topic. In her spare time, Stephanie enjoys reading, singing in her band, and performing in her local community theater.

Leslie David Burns is Associate Professor of Literacy and Program Chair of English Education at the University of Kentucky. He is a teacher educator, curriculum theorist, and policy expert specializing in English education, adolescent literacy, sociocultural theories, responsive pedagogies, identity theories, and the ways these phenomena interact in educational systems. Dr. Burns served as lead author for the Social Justice and Professional Knowledge standards used by the National Council of Teachers of English and the National Council for Accreditation of Teacher Education for the review and assessment of all English teacher preparation programs in the United States. In 2007, he was honored with the Janet Emig Award for best article in *English Education* and the Edwin Hopkins Award for best article in *English Journal*. He is a 2012 recipient of the Literacy Research Association's Edward B. Fry Award for the advancement of knowledge, inquiry, and intellectual risk-taking for his work in the book *Empowering Struggling Readers: Practices for the Middle Grades*, with co-authors Leigh Hall and Elizabeth Carr Edwards.

Elana Cutter is a recent graduate of the English Secondary Teaching program at Purdue University. Her aspirations include taking on her own English classroom and attending graduate school with a focus on socially just education.

Dorothy L. Espelage, Ph.D. (Professor in the Department of Educational Psychology at the University of Illinois, Urbana-Champaign), has conducted research on bullying, homophobic teasing, sexual harassment, and dating violence for the last 20 years. She has authored over 100 research publications and 4 books. She is Associate Editor of the *Journal of Counseling Psychology*, Vice-President of Division E of the American Educational Research Association, and Co-Chair of the National Partnership to End Interpersonal Violence. She is principal investigator on a CDC-funded randomized clinical trial of a prevention program in 36 middle schools to reduce bullying and sexual violence. The National Science Foundation has funded her work to develop better observational methods for assessing bullying among adolescents. She attended the White House Conference in 2011. Dr. Espelage has appeared on many television news and talk shows, including *The Today Show, CNN, CBS Evening News, The Oprah Winfrey Show*, and *Anderson Cooper 360º*.

James R. Gilligan currently serves as the assistant director of the Office of Field Experiences in the College of Education at Purdue University in West Lafayette, Indiana. In addition to his full-time duties arranging placements for preservice teachers at Purdue, Jim—a former high school English teacher—is also pursuing a Ph.D. in Literacy and Language Education. His research interests include queer literacy, queer theory, and LGBTQ issues in education. His dissertation will examine the factors that affect both LGBTQ and straight educators' decisions to be "out" in their professional lives and the personal and professional impact of those decisions.

Tara Star Johnson is Associate Professor of English Education at Purdue University in West Lafayette, Indiana. Her primary research interest is teacher–student relationships, with an emphasis on how intersecting identity categories such as race, class, gender, and sexual orientation affect classroom dynamics. She blends a critical and poststructural epistemological stance to theorize and address issues of embodiment in her work with preservice teachers and teacher educators. Blending and embodiment are also integral to her personal identities as mother and partner.

sj Miller is Associate Professor of Urban Teacher Education/Secondary English and Language Arts at the University of Missouri, Kansas City. sj has published widely in journals and presented at national conferences on a variety of topics related to teaching young adult literature, anti-bullying pedagogy, challenging the gender binary, multimodal applications of popular culture in secondary classrooms, and cultivating socio-spatial justice dispositions with secondary preservice English teachers. Most notably, sj won the 2005 Article of the Year Award from the *English Journal* for "Shattering Images of Violence in Young Adult Literature: Strategies for the Classroom"; co-authored *Unpacking the Loaded Teacher Matrix: Negotiating Space and Time Between University and Secondary English Classrooms*, which received the Richard A. Meade award from NCTE; co-authored *Narratives of Social Justice Teaching: How English Teachers Negotiate Theory and Practice Between Preservice and Inservice Spaces*; and co-authored *Change Matters: Critical Essays on Moving Social Justice Research from Theory to Policy*. sj helped draft the Beliefs Statement Related to Social Justice in English Education and helped pass the NCTE Resolution on Social Justice in Literacy Education.

Joseph John Morgan is Assistant Professor of Special Education at the University of Nevada, Las Vegas. His areas of research include using data to make instructional decisions in general education classrooms, making general education classrooms and curricula accessible for students with high-incidence disabilities, appropriate social skills instruction for students with emotional and behavioral disorders, and culturally responsive teaching practices in school environments. In his spare time Joseph enjoys reading, attending shows, and spending time with family and friends.

Tyrone Rivers, Jr., is an Educational Psychology doctoral student at the University of Illinois at Urbana-Champaign, where he works under Dr. Dorothy Espelage. His research interests include social interaction, bullying, bullying in the Black community, American culture, and mindsets. His career plan is to conduct research in a university setting that addresses innovative intervention programs for K–12 students, making for safer schools and improved lives. Tyrone was raised in

Marietta, Georgia, and his other interests include Jesus Christ, playing basketball, and learning how the world works.

Rodrigo Joseph Rodríguez teaches in the College of Education at the University of Texas at Austin and is a research associate in the Center for Teaching and Learning. His research interests include assessment and evaluation and the teaching and learning of disciplinary literacies, multilingual studies, and academic writing. He is active in the National Council of Teachers of English, College Section and Conference on English Leadership. He is a peer reviewer for *English Education* and *English Journal* and has published articles on English- and Spanish-language arts education and research. He volunteers in local Austin public schools and libraries to promote family literacy and health and wellness initiatives.

Dianne Smith is Professor in the Division of Educational Leadership, Policy, and Foundations, School of Education, at the University of Missouri-Kansas City. Her research interests include urban education and social justice issues, womanist/feminist theory and practice, and qualitative research. Dianne has been honored for her work on diversity and social justice. The American Educational Research Association (AERA), SIG: Critical Examination of Race, Ethnicity, Class, and Gender in Education presented her an "Award for Senior Scholar" during its 2010 annual meeting. She is a former president of the American Educational Studies Association (AESA). Dianne saw the original *Star Trek* television series and always wanted to be "beamed up" by Scottie.

Index

AB-States (anti-bullying states), 139
Adams, Deanna, 11, 61, 160, 189
Adolescent Experience, 8
African Americans
 bullying of, 20
 females, xiii–xv, 55–58
 men and boys, 185
 poverty and, 90
 roasting and. *see* Black ritual insults
 sizism and, 158
 stereotype threat and, 116
 verbal harassment of, 22
 women and girls, 158
"Ally Week," 154–155
Alpha Males, 186
Alvarez, J., 167
American Academy of Pediatrics, 100
American Federation of Teachers, 135
anorexia, 52
anti-bullying
 history of, 12–13
 internationally, 12, 132–135
 legislation on. *see* legislation
 presence in schools for, 141–142
 prevention as. *see* preventive policies

reasons for, 9–10
resources on, 174
right-wing groups for, 17–18
Anti-Bullying and Harassment Act of 2011. *see*
 U.S. House of Representatives
Anti-Bullying Bill of Rights Act, 171–172
anti-bullying states (AB-States), 139
"Anti-Bullying Week," 154–155
Anti-Defamation League, 86
Anzaldúa, Gloria, 92, 168, 171
*Aristotle and Dante Discover the Secrets of the
 Universe*, 167, 171
arousal, 27
Arroyo, M.L., 166
Ashland, Wisconsin, 33
assigned identity attributes, 154
athletic programs, 89
Aukerman, M.S., 126
Austria, 39
*Autism Speaks, Combating Bullying and Students
 with Autism Spectrum Disorders*, 162
avoidance, 27

Bansel, P., 139
Bass, Margaret Kent, 55–57, 158

bathrooms, 155
Baudrillard, Jean, 185
Bauman, S., 87–88
Before We Were Free, 167
behavioral intervention plans (BIPs), 72
belief structures, 90–93
Beliefs Statement Related to Social Justice in
   English Education, 191
Benjamin and the Word/Benjamin y la Palabra,
   168
Berdie, R.F., 81
Beyer, Stephanie, 99, 189
Big Bullies (MassResistance), 17
binaries, 132, 143
biomedical model, 63, 65–66, 70
BIPs (behavioral intervention plans), 72
Birkett, M., 37
bisexuality. *see also* LGBTQGV (Lesbian/Gay/
   Bisexual/Transgender/ Questioning/Gender
   Variant) students
   Freud on, 35
   texts with themes on, 178–179
Black experience. *see* African Americans
Black ritual insults
   bullying and victimization in, 75–76
   conclusions about, 81–83
   definition of, 76–78
   harmfulness vs. harmlessness of, 78–81
   introduction to, 11, 75
   references on, 83–84
   roasting in, generally, 76
   teacher education on prevention of,
      163–164
   vulnerability to, 5
Blackburn, M.V., 92
Bloom, L., 26
Bomer, R., 90
Borderlands: La Frontera, The New Mestiza,
   168, 171
Bordo, Susan, 160
boredom, 163
Boske, C., 170
Bourdieu, P., 184
boys. *see* males
Brown, Governor Jerry, 21
Brown, Hubert "Rap," 77
Brown v. Board of Education, xiii
browning of America, 86–87
bulimia, 52–53

bullies. *see also* bullying
   females as, xiv–xv
   psychology of, 6, 17–18, 22–23
   students with disabilities as, 68–70, 72
*Bullies: Monologues on Bullying for Teens and
   Adults*, 166, 171
Bully Police, 19, 139–140, 171
bullycide. *see also* suicide
   cases of, 16, 29
   of David Ray Ritcheson, 85–86
   definition of, 18
   of Megan Meier, 11–12, 99–100
   of Phoebe Prince, 1–2
   psychological violence and, x
   social conditions and, 120
   of Tyler Clemente, 29, 171
bullying. *see also specific vulnerable populations*
   of children with exceptionalities, 162
   consequences of. *see* consequences of
      bullying
   current state of. *see* current state of bullying
   definitions of, 6–8, 12–13, 100–101
   via Internet. *see* cyber-digital bullying
   origins of, 34–36
   prevention of. *see* anti-bullying
*Bullying Prevention and Intervention: Realistic
   Strategies for Schools*, 94, 164
*Bullying: Replies, Rebuttals, Confessions,
   and Catharsis, an Intergenerational and
   Multicultural Anthology*, 166
*Bullying, Suicide, and Homicide: Understanding,
   Assessing, and Preventing Threats to Self and
   Others for Victims of Bullying*, 164
Burns, Leslie David, xix, 12, 113, 189–190
Butch, 49–51, 59
Butler, Judith, 185

California
   anti-bullying programs in, 141, 164
   education on sexual minorities in, 21
   prevalence of bullying in, 19
*Call Me María: A Novel in Letters, Poems, and
   Prose*, 168
Carlson, Dennis, 12, 183
Carter, B.B., 67
cell phones, 102
Center for Public Broadcasting, 170
Center on Human Policy, 162
Centers for Disease Control and Prevention, 52

Centre for Behavioral Research, 133
CEP (Character Education Partnership), 163
Change Matters: Critical Essays on Moving Social Justice Research from Theory to Policy, 191
Character Education Partnership (CEP), 163
"Characters and Character," 168
chat rooms, 102
Chesir-Teran, D., 39
Chevallier, J., 171
chosen identity attributes, 154
Christie, Governor Chris, 171
cisgender, 46
civil rights
    Anti-Bullying Bill of Rights Act and, 171–172
    bullycide and, 2
    First Amendment rights, 105
    of LGBTQ students, 21, 24
    of students with disabilities, 71–72
    in teacher education, 153
classroom safety. *see* safety in schools
Clemente, Tyler, 29, 171
cognition, 117–119
collaboration, 124–125
Colorado, 13–16, 176
Colorado Center for the Prevention of Violence, 176
Columbine Massacre, 13–16
Columbine Tapes, 16
Commissioner for Education Statistics, 136
Common Core State Standards, 137
complex post-traumatic stress disorder (C-PTSD)
    education about, 151
    hate-motivated bullying and, 86
    introduction to, xi, 26–27
    in LGBTQGV students, 45
    teacher education on, 173
Concerned Women for America, 17
Conchas, G.Q., 90
Connecticut, 17, 19
Connell, R. W., 185
Conoley, J.C., 45
consequences of bullying
    bullycide and, 3
    classrooms safe from, 122–126
    cognition and, 117–119
    conclusions about, 126–128
    current, 18

engagement and, 121–122
GPAs and, 41
introduction to, 12, 113–115
in LGBTQGV students, 44–45
microaggressions and, 9
motivation and, 121–122
references on, 128–129
stereotype threat and, 115–117
teacher expectation and, 119–121
Cooper, B., 162
Core Curriculum Content Standards, 172
Council for Exceptional Children, 162
counseling, 106–107
C-PTSD (complex post-traumatic stress disorder). *see* complex post-traumatic stress disorder (C-PTSD)
Crossing Boundaries: Teaching and Learning with Urban Youth, 88, 164
Cuéntame (An Honest Conversation), 169
Culturally Responsive Pedagogy, 148
culture, defined, 96
current state of bullying
    beginning of, 18–19
    Columbine Massacre, 15–16
    cycle of, 23–26
    failure to act in, 26–27
    introduction to, 10
    notes on, 28–29
    perpetuation of hate in, 26–27
    reasons for, 22–23
    references on, 30–32
    reform in, 27–28
    student safety in, 24
    students who bully in, 17–18
    vulnerable populations in, 20–22
Cutter, Elena, 10–11, 49, 157–158, 190
cyber-digital bullying
    cyber-literacy vs., 104–109
    definition of, 8, 100–101
    H.R. 975 on, 6–7
    introduction to, 11–12
    known incidence of, 102–103
    legislation on, 104, 140
    of Megan Meier, 99–100
    notes on, 110–111
    prevalence of, 5–6
    realities of, 102–104
    reasons for, 23
    references on, 111–112

school climate and, 109–110
signs of, 103–104
statistics on, 17
of Tyler Clemente, 29, 171
cyber-harassment, 104, 111
cyber-literacy, 104–109
cyber-stalking, 104, 111
cyber-support, 106–109
cycle of bullying, 23–26

Dardenne Prairie, Missouri, 99–100
Dark Dude: A Novel, 167
Davis, Bonnie, 168–169, 171
Davis vs. Monroe County Board of Education,
12–13, 18
"Day of Silence," 154
defenders, 23–24
Deferred Action for Childhood Arrivals
Process, 87
definitions of bullying, 6–8, 12–13, 100–101
demographics, 86–89, 119
Department for Education in Skills (DfES),
135
Department of Justice, 17, 20, 176
deviations from norm, 66–68
DfES (Department for Education in Skills),
135
*Diagnostic and Statistical Manual of Mental
Disorders* (DSM I-III), 35, 182
*Diagnostic and Statistical Manual of Mental
Disorders IV* (DSM IV), 6, 26, 35–36, 182
dichotomous definitions of disability, 64–66
Die Nigger Die!, 77
dignity, 94–96, 164
Dignity for All: Safeguarding LGBT Students,
164
direct bullying, 6–8, 101
Disability History Museum, 162
Disability Social History Projects, 162
Disability Studies (DS), 65
disabled students. *see* students with disabilities
discourse on preventive policies, 139–141
discrimination, 126
disengaged onlookers, 23–24
"Don't Ask, Don't Tell," 45
Don't Suffer in Silence, 135
Doom, 16, 28
Drew, Lori, 100
DS (Disability Studies), 65

DSM I-III (*Diagnostic and Statistical Manual of
Mental Disorders*), 35, 182
DSM IV (*Diagnostic and Statistical Manual of
Mental Disorders IV*), 6, 26, 35–36, 182

Education and Inspections Act (EIA), 135
educational disabilities, 70
EIA (Education and Inspections Act), 135
"Electronic Harassment" law, 140
Elementary and Secondary Education Act
(ESEA), 70–71
elementary schools
anti-bullying programs in, 136, 187
bullying starting in, 18
Latina/Latino students in, 86, 91
students with disabilities in, 64
teacher education for, 155
Ellis, Havelock, 35
Elsa, 61–62, 69, 72–73
emails, 102
engagement, 121–122
English Journal, 157, 168, 173
ESEA (Elementary and Secondary Education
Act), 70–71
Espelage, Dorothy L.
about, 190
on Latina/Latino students, 11
on queer-related bullying, 37
on ritual insults, 75
on students with disabilities, 64, 68, 94
on teacher education, 163, 164
Estell, D.B., 64, 67
Evans, Josh, 99–100

Facebook
bullying of Phoebe Prince on, 2
fear of posts on, 108
permanence of posts on, 106
fags, 36
failure to act, 26–27
Fairfax High, 141
false normalcy, 114–115
familiarity, 126
Family Research Council, 17
The Fan Club, 54–55, 158–159
FAPE (free and appropriate public education),
71
Fartacek, R., 39
The Fat Boy Chronicles, 52, 159

"Fat Studies," 54
The Fat Studies Reader, 159–160
fatism. *see* weight-based bullying
"Fatso," 58
FBA (functional behavioral analysis), 72
FCC (Federal Communications Commission), 106
Federal Hate Crimes Bill, 28, 45
federal legislation, 28, 45, 71–72. *see also* legislation
federal policies, 132–133
Fein, J., 20–21
females
  access to sports by, 89
  bullying by, 20
  cyber-digital bullying of, 103
  gender policing of, 36
  relational aggression by, 101
  sexual harassment by/of, 185
  stereotype threat and, 116
Ferguson, P., 163
Ferreira, D., 93
films, 114, 179–180
financial incentives, 138–139
First Amendment rights, 105
Florida, 19
fluid expressions of gender, 177–178
Flynt, S.W., 67, 69
Focus on the Family, 17
followers, 23–24
Fránquiz, María E., 94–95
Freaks, Geeks & Asperger Syndrome: A User Guide to Adolescence, 162
free and appropriate public education (FAPE), 71
Freedman, Estelle, 35
Freud, Sigmund, 35
Frost, Robert, 106
"fun," 121
functional behavioral analysis (FBA), 72
funds of knowledge, 121, 148

Gaga, Lady, 108
gatekeeping functions of language, 90
Gay and Lesbian Independent School Teachers' Network (GLISTN), ix
Gay, Lesbian & Straight Education Network (GLSEN)
  Anti-Bullying Resources for LGBTQGV Youth by, 156
  on bullycide, 29
  education about, 153
  on gay-straight alliances, 141, 154
  on queer-related bullying, 19–22
  on safe school environments, 187
  statistics on LGBTQGV students by, 39–41
gay-straight alliances (GSAs), 141, 154
Gender Identity Disorder (GID), 35, 182
gender issues. *see also* LGBTQGV (Lesbian/ Gay/Bisexual/Transgender/ Questioning/ Gender Variant) students
  bisexuality, 35, 178–179
  bullying and. *see* queer-related bullying
  GLSEN on. *see* Gay, Lesbian & Straight Education Network (GLSEN)
  homosexuality and. *see* homosexuality
  microaggressions and, 43–44
  "norms" in, 36–38
  pronouns and, 4
  texts on, 177–178
  types of bullying and, 8
gender policing, 36–37
genderism, 132, 144
Georgia, 12–13
Getting It, 168
GID (Gender Identity Disorder), 35, 182
Gilligan, James R., 10, 33, 149, 190
girls. *see* females
Glee, 114
GLSEN (Gay, Lesbian & Straight Education Network). *see* Gay, Lesbian & Straight Education Network (GLSEN)
goals, 124
Gómez, M., 166
González, Juan, 169
González, R., 167
goth, 15, 28
grade point averages (GPAs), 41
Graham, S., 37, 76
Gray, Carol, 162
Greenleaf, C., 51
GSAs (gay-straight alliances), 141, 154
Guffy, Ossie, 81
Guillory, R.M., 88

habitus, 184
Happy Feet, 170

harassment
  cyber, 23, 102–104, 111
  definition of, 25
  sexual, 13, 18–23, 102, 149, 184–185
  verbal, 22, 40–41, 76
harassment, intimidation, or bullying (HIB), 172
Harris, Eric, 15–16
Harris Interactive, 103
Harsh Realities: The Experiences of Transgender Youth in Our Schools, 39
Harvest of Empire, 169
Hate Crimes Prevention Act, 10
hate-motivated bullying, 6–8, 85–86
Hatzenbuehler, M.L., 39
Health and Wellness Standards, 137
heatin,' 77. *see also* Black ritual insults
hegemonic masculinities, 184–188
henchmen, 23–24
Hermann-Wilmarth, Jill, 59
Herrera, Jaheem, 29
heteronormativity, 186
HIB (harassment, intimidation, or bullying), 172
Higdon, M.J., 26
high schools
  African American students in, 75
  bully prevention in, 155
  bullying acceptance in, 45
  bullying starting in, 18
  gender norms in, 36
  Latino students in, 87–88
  LGBTQ students in, 21, 108
  Obama on bullying in, 135
  students with disabilities in, 64, 68–69
  texts for, 177–178
Hijuelos, O., 167
Hinduja, S., 103
HIPAA guidelines, 107
history of legislation, 12–13
Hitler, Adolf, 16
homophobia
  at Columbine, 16
  heteronormativity vs., 186
  preventing, 93, 132–134, 141
  sources of, 34–37
  in student remarks, 22
  in teacher remarks, 41
homosexuality
  in *Diagnostic and Statistical Manual of Mental Disorders*, 182

history of society on, 34–35
of Jamie Nabozny, 33–34
legislation on portrayal of, 21
An Honest Conversation (Cuéntame), 169
Hooker, Evelyn, 35
Hoover-Walker, Carl, x
House of Representatives. *see* U.S. House of Representatives
How to Teach Students Who Don't Look Like You: Culturally Responsive Teaching Strategies, 168–169, 171
Howe, James, 159
H.R. *see* U.S. House of Representatives
Hughes, D., 39
Human Rights Campaign symbol "=" (HRC), 155
hyper-networking, 103

I Will Save You, 168
Iannotti, R.J., 75
iChat, 171
IDEA (Individuals with Disabilities Education Act), 70–72
idealism, 133
IEP (Individualized Education Program), 72
Illinois, 19
immigration, 87
implied stereotypes, 116
indirect bullying, 6–8, 101
individualization, 187
Individualized Education Program (IEP), 72
Individuals with Disabilities Education Act (IDEA), 70–72
Infusing Disability Studies into the General Curriculum, 163
international anti-bullying reforms
  introduction to, 12
  in Norway, 132–135
  in United Kingdom, 134–135
Internet. *see* cyber-digital bullying
intersexed students, 46
interventionist policies. *see* preventive policies
Irish Americans, 1–2
It Gets Better Project
  introduction of, 95
  media literacy and, 169–170
  psychological safety and, 126
  as resource, 156
  website of, 108

Jackson, L., 67, 162
Jiménez, F., 168
Johnson, C.S., 81
Johnson, Tara Star
    about, 191
    on body-type bullying prevention, 157
    inviting readers' participation, xix
    on weight discrimination, 10–11, 49
Journal of Counseling Psychology, 190
The Jumping Tree: A Novel, 168
junior high schools, 22
Juvonen, J., 76

K-12 schools
    Anti-Bullying Bill of Rights Act and, 171
    in California, 21
    mandatory anti-bullying education in,
        136–138
Kaffar, B.J., 93
Keith, S., 101
Kilbourne, Jean, 160
Killing Us Softly 4, 160
King, Martin Luther, vi
Kinloch, Valerie, 88, 164
Kinsey, Alfred, 35
Klebold, Dylan, 15–16
Klein, J., 92
Klein Collins High School, 85–86
Kochman, T., 77–78
Koresh, David, 16, 29
Kosciw, J., 40
Krehbiel, M., 51

Labov, W., 77
Lambda Legal, 33
The Laramie Project, 166
Latina/Latino students
    belief structures and, 90–93
    bullying of, generally, 85–86
    definition of, 96
    demographic trends and bullying of, 86–89
    dignity of, 94–96
    introduction to, 11
    norms and, 90–93
    notes on, 96
    references on, 96–98
    statistics on, 20
    teacher education on, 164
    vulnerability of, 5

Leach, J.B., 71
learning strategies, 125–126
Leary, J.D., 82
legal accountability, 51–52, 71–72
legislation
    Anti-Bullying Bill of Rights Act, 171–172
    Anti-Bullying and Harassment Act, 25, 136
    on cyber-digital bullying, 104, 140
    Education and Inspections Act, 135
    Elementary and Secondary Education Act,
        70–71
    federal, 28, 45, 71–72
    Hate Crimes Prevention Act, 10
    history of, 12–13, 24–26
    H.R. 975, 6–7, 13, 25, 101, 136
    H.R. 1648, 26, 136
    H.R. 2262, 156
    Individuals with Disabilities Education Act,
        70–72
    Local Law Enforcement Hate Crimes
        Prevention Act, 86
    in Massachusetts, 2
    Matthew Shepard and James Byrd, Jr. Hate
        Crimes Prevention Act, 86
    Megan Meier Cyberbullying Prevention
        Act, 102, 105–106
    No Child Left Behind Act, 9–10, 71
    on portrayal of homosexuality, 21
    recommended elements of, 140
    Rehabilitation Act, 71–72
    Safe and Drug-Free Schools and
        Communities Act, 9–10, 25
    Safe Schools Improvement Act, 26, 136, 156
    School and Standards Framework Act, 135
    by states, 19
lesbian students
    research findings about, 35
    suicide risk and, 39
    texts with themes on, 178
Lesbian/Gay/Bisexual/Transgender/
    Questioning/Gender Variant (LGBTQGV)
    students. *see* LGBTQGV (Lesbian/Gay/
    Bisexual/Transgender/ Questioning/Gender
    Variant) students
lesson plans
    on disabilities, 160–161
    on gender fluidity, 149–155
    on Latina/Latino students, 165–166
    on Netiquette, 105–106

on ritual insults, 163–164
on weight-based bullying, 158–159
"Let's Move" campaign, 52
The Letter Q: Queer Writers' Notes to Their Younger Selves, 167
LGB (Lesbian/Gay/Bisexual) microaggressions, 42–43
LGBTQGV (Lesbian/Gay/Bisexual/ Transgender/ Questioning/Gender Variant) students
  anti-bullying policies and, 141
  bullying of. *see* queer-related bullying
  introduction to, 10
  It Gets Better website for, 108
  right-wing anti-bullying groups vs., 17–18
  vulnerability of, 5, 20–21
Liberty Institute, 17
Lindblom, Ken, 168
Local Law Enforcement Hate Crimes Prevention Act of 2007, 86
locker rooms, 155–156
Loeber, R., 68–69
Lord of the Flies, 105
Lortie, D., 119
Los Angeles, 141
Losey, Butch, 164
Loutzenheiser, L., 186

Maine, 19
"Making Schools Safe for Gay and Lesbian Youth," ix
males
  African American, 185
  bullying by, 20
  gender policing of, 36
  hegemonic masculinities and, 92, 184–188
  reporting cyber-digital bullying, 103
  roasting and. *see* Black ritual insults
  stereotype threat and, 116
  weight discrimination and, 52, 159
Mancl, D.B., 93
mandatory anti-bullying education, 136–138
Mannix, D, 162
The Mariposa Club, 167
Markham, C.M., 75
Markow, D., 20–21
marriage equality, 37
Martin, M., 101
masculinity, 36, 92, 184–188. *see also* males

Massachusetts, 1–2
Massachusetts Governor's Commission on Gay and Lesbian Youth, ix
MassResistance (Big Bullies), 17
material bullying, 6–7
Matthew Shepard and James Byrd, Jr. Hate Crimes Prevention Act, 86
Maynard, R., 158
McCall, G.G., 168
McCormack, S., 170
McEvoy, A., 64
McVeigh, Timothy, 28–29
media
  literacy in, 169–170
  queer-related bullying and, 37–38
  social. *see* cyber-digital bullying
  social cliques in, 114
Medina, Meg, 167, 171
Megan Meier Cyberbullying Prevention Act, 102, 105–106
Meier, Megan, 11–12, 99–100
men. *see* males
Mendez, J.J., 85, 88
Metaverse+, 108
Mexican-origin students, 88. *see also* Latina/ Latino students
Meyer, Elizabeth J., ix–xi, 10, 91
Michigan State University, 169
microaggressions, 9, 42–44
middle schools
  bullying starting in, 18
  Obama on bullying in, 135
  students of color in, 76–78, 80
  students with disabilities in, 61–64, 68
  texts for, 177
  weight discrimination in, 51–52
Miller, sj
  on aggression, 66
  on bullying, generally, 1
  chapters by, 10–12
  on complex post-traumatic stress disorder, 86
  on current state of bullying, 15
  on cyber-digital bullying, 99
  inviting readers' participation, xix
  on LGBTQGV bullying, 51
  on mythology of the norm, 90
  on preventive policies, 131
  on queer-related bullying, 33
  on social norms, 117

on stories, 5–6
on teacher education, 147, 149
on tools for classrooms, 177
on why bullies bully, 23
Ministry for Anti-Bullying, 136
Ministry of Education, 134
Minnesota, 109
The Misfits, 54–55, 159
Miss Representation, 159
Missouri, 99–100, 110
Mohr, N., 168
Monda-Amaya, L.E., 64, 68
Montana, 19
Moore, S., 186
Mora, P., 168, 171
Morgan, Joseph John
    on LGBT students with disabilities, 93
    on students with disabilities, 11, 61, 160
Morton, R.C., 67, 69
motivation, 121–122
Multiculturalism in the Classroom, 157
music, 16
My Own True Name: New and Selected Poems for Young Adults, 1984–1999, 168
MySpace, 99–100
"Mythology of the Norm: Disrupting the Culture of Bullying in Schools," 90

Nabozny, Jamie, 33
Nabozny v. Podlesny, 10, 33–34, 45
Nansel, T.R., 75
Napolitano, Scott, 94, 164
Narratives of Social Justice Teaching: How English Teachers Negotiate Theory and Practice Between Preservice and Inservice Spaces, 191
Nastoh, Hamed, 29
National Association of Student Councils, 135
National Bullying Summit, 136
National Center for Education Statistics (NCES), 17, 20, 176
National Center for Educational Statistics, 103
National Conference of State Legislatures, 104
National Council for the Accreditation of Teacher Education (NCATE), 147–148
National Council of Teachers of English, 147, 173
National Crime Prevention Council, 103
National Dissemination Center for Children with Disabilities, 162

National Education Association, 135
National Health and Nutrition Survey, 52
National Institute for Urban School Improvement, 163
"National Manifesto Against Bullying in Schools," 133
National Parent Teacher Association, 135
National Resource Center for Safe Schools, 176
National Safe Schools Partnership (NSSP), 24–25
National School Boards Association, 135
National School Climate Survey, 2007, 20–21, 156
National School Climate Survey, 2009, 21, 39
National School Safety Center, 6, 176–177
naturalization, 187
naturalness of gender, 185
NCATE (National Council for the Accreditation of Teacher Education), 147–148
NCES (National Center for Education Statistics), 17, 20, 176
NCLB (No Child Left Behind) Act, 9–10, 71
Netiquette, 105–106
New Bullying: How Social Media, Social Exclusion, Laws and Suicide Have Changed Our Definition of Bullying—And What To Do About It, 169
New Hampshire, 13, 19
New Jersey, 21, 171–173
New Jersey Education Association, 177
The New Social Story Book, 162
New York, 19
Newsom, J.S., 159
Nieto, S., 164–165
Nilda, 168
No Child Left Behind (NCLB) Act, 9–10, 71
normalization
    of bullying, 2–5, 45, 94–95, 114
    Latina/Latino students and, 90–93
    of linguicism, 11
    normal/abnormal dichotomies in, 6
    of roasting, 11, 78, 163
normative concepts
    Latina/Latino students and, 89–92
    microaggressions and, 42–43
    normal/abnormal dichotomies in, 23
    policing of, 115–117
    queer-related bullying and, 36–39

students with disabilities and, 62–68, 72
vulnerable populations vs., 20–23
weight discrimination and, 52–53
Norris, L., 177
Northampton, Massachusetts, 1
Norway, 132–135
Not in Our Town: Class Actions, 170
Not in Our Town: Light in the Darkness, 170
"Nothing Gold Can Stay," 106
NSSP (National Safe Schools Partnership),
    24–25

Obama, First Lady Michelle, 52
Obama, President Barack
    on bully prevention, 37, 135
    on "Don't Ask, Don't Tell," 46
    on Federal Hate Crimes Bill, 45
    on hate crime prevention, 86
    hegemonic masculinities vs., 186
    on It Gets Better Program, 95–96, 108
obesity. *see* weight-based bullying
Office of Civil Rights (OCR), 71
Office of Safe and Drug-Free Schools
    (OSDFS), 25
Oklahoma City bombing, 16, 28–29
Olivas, D.A., 168
Olweus, Dan, 134
Olweus Bullying Prevention Program, 23–24, 139
Olweus Cycle of Bullying, 6, 13
"On Being a Fat Black Girl in a Fat-Hating
    Culture," 55–57, 158
organizational models, 142
origins of bullying, 34–36
Ortiz Cofer, J., 168
OSDFS (Office of Safe and Drug-Free
    Schools), 25
Osseo High School, 109
Otherness, 184–186

PACER, 162
Pascoe, C.J., 36
passive bullies, 23–24
Patchin, J., 103
Payne, C.M., 141
PBS, 170
Peck, C., 58, 159
Pediatrics and Adolescent Medicine, 17
peer physical assault, 76
Peguero, A.A., 87

Peña, M. de la., 168
perceived perpetrators, 68–70
perpetuation of hate, 26–27
Peskin, M.F., 75
Petty Crimes: Stories, 168
Phoebe's Law, 2
physical bullying, 6–7, 76
Pincus, M.R., 166
playing the dozens, 77
Plöderl, M., 39
political correctness, 127
polyvictimization, 76
possible bullies, 23–24
preventive health care, 142
preventive policies
    anti-bullying presence in schools, 141–142
    discourse in, 139–141
    federal, 132–133
    financial incentives in, 138–139
    introduction of, 131–132
    mandatory anti-bullying education in,
        136–138
    Miller on, 131
    Ministry for Anti-Bullying in, 136
    Norwegian, 133–134, 135
    notes on, 144
    preventive health care in, 142
    references on, 144–145
    school climate and, 139
    social justice work in, 142–143
    systems approaches in, 132–133, 138
    in United Kingdom, 134–135
    in United States, 135–142
primary knowers, 126
Prince, Phoebe, x
private schools, 41–42
"Project 10," 141
pronouns, 4, 110, 154
Protect Kids Foundation, 17
psychological safety, 122–124
public schools
    academic accountability of, 71
    elementary level. *see* elementary schools
    high schools. *see* middle schools
    K-12 education in. *see* K-12 schools
    middle schools. *see* middle schools
    statistics on bullying in, 29, 41, 113–114
    students with disabilities in, 62

queer-related bullying. *see also* LGBTQGV (Lesbian/Gay/Bisexual/Transgender/ Questioning/Gender Variant) students
classroom tools for prevention of, 149–157
distressing realities about, 33–34, 38–42
gender norms and bullying of, 36–38
introduction to, 20
media and, 37–38
microaggressions in, 42–44
notes on, 46
origins of bullying of, 34–36
references on, 46–47
school environments and, 44–45
vulnerable populations in, 20–22

Ravi, Dharun, 171
Reaching Out, 168
Recovering the Black female body: Self-representations by African American women, 158
Rehabilitation Act of 1973, 71–72
relational bullying, 6–7
religist, 132, 144
reliving bullying events, 27. *see also* complex post-traumatic stress disorder (C-PTSD)
Renfrew Center, 52
"Resolution on Confronting Bullying and Harassment," 173
Resolution on Social Justice in Literacy Education, 191
resources
on anti-bullying, generally, 174–176
with bisexual themes, 178–179
on cyber-digital bullying, 180–182
films, 179–180, 182
on gender issues, 177–178
high school texts, 177–179
with lesbian themes, 178–179
middle school texts, 177
with transgender themes, 179
websites, 176–177, 181
Ressler, Paula, 157
Ressler, Rebecca, 157
restrooms, 155
Revenge of the Paste Eaters: Memoirs of a Misfit, 159
Rigby, K., 95
right-wing anti-bullying groups, 17–18
Ritcheson, David Ray, 85, 88–89, 93–96

rites of passage, 131
ritual of power, 184
Rivers, Tyrone, Jr., 11, 75, 163, 191–192
roasting
conclusions about, 81–83
definition of, 76–78
harmfulness vs. harmlessness of, 78–81
introduction to, 76
Rodríguez, Rodrigo Joseph, 11, 85, 164, 192
Romney, Mitt, 186
Roots of Empathy, 163–164
Rose, C.A., 64, 68, 69
Rothblum, E., 159
Russell, S.T., 39
Rutgers University, 171

Sáenz, Benjamin Alire, 167, 171
Safe and Drug-Free Schools and Communities Act, 9–10, 25
Safe Schools Improvement Act (H.R. 1648), 26, 136
Safe Schools Improvement Act (H.R. 2262), 156
safety in schools
current state of, 24
in current state of bullying, 24
GLSEN on, 187
"Making Schools Safe for Gay and Lesbian Youth" on, ix
National Resource Center for Safe Schools for, 176
National Safe Schools Partnership for, 24–25
National School Safety Center for, 6, 176–177
Office of Safe and Drug-Free Schools for, 25
psychological, 122–124
Safe and Drug-Free Schools and Communities Act for, 9–10, 25
Safe Schools Improvement Act for, 26, 136, 156
school success and, 122–126
of students with disabilities, 93
Saguy, A.C., 54
Salamanca Statement, 134
Saldaña, R., Jr., 168
Sanchez, A., 168
Sánchez, Juan, 85
Sanchez, Representative Linda, 105
Santamaria, L.J., 171
Saylor, C.F., 71

School and Standards Framework Act (SSFA), 135

school success. *see also* schools
  bullying and cognition in, 117–119
  classroom safety in, 122–126
  conclusions about, 126–128
  engagement in, 121–122
  false normalcy in, 114–115
  motivation in, 121–122
  reference on, 128–129
  statistics on bullying vs., 113–114
  stereotype threat vs., 115–117
  teacher expectation in, 119–121

schools
  anti-bullying education in, 154–156, 159–163, 170–171
  cyber-literacy and, 109–110
  elementary. *see* elementary schools
  K-12, 21, 136–138, 171
  middle. *see* middle schools
  preventive policies and, 139
  queer-related bullying and, 44–45
  safety in. *see* safety in schools
  secondary. *see* high schools
  success of. *see* school success
  systems approaches to, 138
  teacher education and, 90–91

Second Step, 164
Semenya, Caster, 151
sexting, 7
sexual assault, 85
sexual harassment
  current state of, 18–23
  cyber-digital bullying as, 102
  hegemonic masculinities and, 184–185
  prevention of, 149
  Title IX on, 13
"Sexual Orientation Disturbance," 182
Shaeff, Aiden Rivera, 29
Shared Differences: The Experiences of Lesbian, Gay, Bisexual, and Transgender Students of Color in Our Nation's Schools, 39
Sheffield Anti-Bullying Project, 135
siblings, 9
Sieben, Nicole, 8
signifyin', 77. *see also* Black ritual insults
simulacrum, 185
sizism. *see* weight-based bullying
slavery, 81–82

Smith, Dianne, xiii–xv, 10, 141, 192
SNCC (Student Nonviolent Coordinating Committee), 77
social justice
  advanced degrees in, 144
  in preventive policies, 142–143
  teaching for, 147–149
social model, 65–66
social skills, 66–67
Social Skills Activities for Secondary Students with Special Needs, 162
Social Success Workbook for Teens: Skill-Building Activities for Teens with Nonverbal Learning Disorder, Asperger's Disorder & Other Social-Skill Problems, 162
Solovay, S., 159
Soto, G., 168
South Dakota, 139
Spencer, V.G., 67
sports programs, 89
SSFA (School and Standards Framework Act), 135
stalking, 2
Standards for Initial Preparation of Teachers of Secondary English Language Arts, Grades 7–12, 147
Stanford University, 116
statutory rape, 2
Steele, C.M., 115–116
stereotype threat, 115–117
Stone, J., 116
Stop Bullying Now! 167
stopbullying. gov, 136, 157, 162
stopping bullies. *see* anti-bullying
Student Nonviolent Coordinating Committee (SNCC), 77
students with disabilities
  dichotomous definitions of disability and, 64–66
  introduction to bullying of, 11, 61–63
  legal aspects of bullying and, 71–72
  normative concepts and, 66–68
  as perpetrators of bullying, 68–70
  references on, 73–74
  safety of, 93
  social environment and, 70–71
  support for, 72–73
  teacher education on, 160–163
  as victims of bullying, 63–64

vulnerability of, 5
Subtractive Schooling: U.S.-Mexican Youth and the Politics of Caring, 88
"Successful, Safe, and Healthy Students," 136
suicide. *see also* bullycide
  at Columbine, 15
  of David Ray Ritcheson, 86
  by LGBTQGV students, 21, 39
  of Megan Meier, 99–100
  of Phoebe Prince, 2
  school-related, 134
  of Tyler Clemente, 29, 171
Summers, J.J., 87–88
support networks, 68, 72–73
supporters of bullies, 23–24
Survey of Internet Mental Health Issues, 102–103
Swearer, Susan, 36, 94, 164
Sweeting, H., 36
Syracuse University, 162
systems approaches, 132–133, 138

Taylor, N., 52
teacher education
  bathrooms in, 155
  on Black ritual insult prevention, 163–164
  on body-type bullying prevention, 157–160
  diverse literature in, 170
  enactments in, 170
  on gender fluidity, 149–153
  on gender pronouns, 153–154
  guest speakers in, 170
  gym class in, 156
  introduction to, 147–149
  lesson plans in, 149–157, 160–161, 165–166
  locker rooms in, 155–156
  media literacy in, 169–170
  in New Jersey, 171–172
  next steps in, 172–173
  normalizing classroom discourse in, 149–153
  online resources on, 169–170
  performing arts in, 170
  on psychological safety, 122–124
  on queer-related bullying prevention, 149–157
  resources on, 156–157, 160, 162–163, 168–170

school-wide participation and, 154–155, 159, 161, 170
  section resources for, 171
  sports in, 156
  on students with disabilities, 160–163
  teacher expectation and, 119–121
  texts for, 162, 166–167
  on weight discrimination, 52–58, 157–160
  young adult literature in, 167–168
teacher expectation, 119–121
Teachers College Record, 171
"Teaching, Caring, and Transformation," 164–165
From Teasing to Torment: School Climate in America, 20–21, 156
television, 114
Terms of Service, 100
Texas, 19
text messages, 102
Tharinger, D.J., 37
therapy, 106–107
Third Space pedagogies, 148
Title 18, 105
Title IX
  access to sports by girls in, 89
  education about, 152
  queer-related bullying and, 33
  on sexual harassment, 13, 18
Todd, Amanda, x
Todd, Evan, 16
Tortolero, S.R., 75
Transgender Law and Policy Institute, 155–156
transgender students
  Diagnostic and Statistical Manual of Mental Disorders on, 182
  harassment of, 40–41
  introduction to, 35
  microaggressions toward, 43–44
  texts on, 179
transphobism, 132, 144
"The Trenchcoat Mafia," 15
Tuck, David Henry, 85
Turner, Keith Robert, 76, 85
Twitter, 108–109, 171
two-spirited, 182

Unbearable Weight: Feminism, Western Culture, and the Body, 160
Under the Mesquite, 168

un-doing of gender, 185
unifying definition of bullying, 12–13
unisex single-stall restrooms, 155
United Kingdom, 134–135
United States (U.S.)
    anti-bullying resources in, 174
    bullying in, generally, 18–19
    bullying reform in, 27–28
    Census Bureau, 87, 96
    Columbine Massacre in, 15–16
    cycle of bullying in, 23–26
    Department of Education, 71, 135–136
    Department of Justice, 17, 20, 176
    failure to act in, 26–27
    House of Representatives. see U.S. House of
        Representatives
    notes on, 28–29
    perpetuation of hate in, 26–27
    preventive policies in, 135–142
    reasons for bullying in, 22–23
    references on, 30–32
    Secretary of Education, 136
    student safety in, 24
    students who bully in, 17–18
    Supreme Court, 12–13, 18
    U.S. Supreme Court, 12–13
    vulnerable populations in, 20–22
University of Stavanger, 133
Unpacking the Loaded Teacher Matrix:
    Negotiating Space and Time Between University
    and Secondary English Classrooms, 191
U.S. (United States). see United States (U.S.)
U.S. House of Representatives
    Anti-Bullying and Harassment Act (H.R.
        975) by, 6–7, 13, 25, 101, 136
    on cyber-digital bullying, 100–101
    Judiciary Committee of, 85–86
    Safe Schools Improvement Act by (H.R.
        2262) by, 156
    Safe Schools Improvement Act (H.R. 1648)
        by, 26, 136
USDOE (U.S. Department of Education), 71

Valenzuela, Angela, 88
verbal ability, 82
verbal aggressiveness model, 78
verbal bullying, 6–7
victimization types, 76
video games, 16

Vidovic, Sladjana, 29
Vigil, J.D., 90
Virtual Iraq, 108
virtual therapy, 107
Virtually Better, Inc., 107–108
vulnerable populations, 20–22

Waco, Texas, 16
Wall Street, 186
Walsh, Seth, x
Wang, J., 75
Ward, A., 54
Washington, 19
Washington Post, 186
websites, 176–177
"Week of Respect," 172
weight-based bullying
    addressing, 54–58
    challenges in talking about, 53–54
    classroom tools for overcoming, 157–160
    conclusions about, 58–59
    introduction to, 10–11, 20, 49
    notes on, 59
    overview of, 50–52
    personal story of, 49–50
    references on, 59–60
    teacher education and, 52–58, 157–160
Weinstock, J., 51
White, N.A., 68–69
Widdows, N., 162
Wikis, 110
Williams, L.M., 87
Wisconsin, 33
*Wolfenstein 3D*2, 16
women. see females
WorldStar Hip Hop, 77

Yaqui Delgado Wants to Kick Your Ass, 167, 171
Young, R., 36

Zero Program, 133–134
zero tolerance, 34, 133, 163, 184
Zing! Seven Creativity Practices for Educators and
    Students, 169, 171